Sam's Story

Sam's Story

~

Amanda Murray

ISBN: 1540589528
ISBN 13: 9781540589521

Introduction

WRITING SAM'S STORY GAVE ME something to do in the long, quiet months following his death, and helped to focus my mind. It gave me a reason to get up in the morning and a structure to my day. It also kept our son at the centre of my life, even though we no longer had him with us.

Embarking on parenthood in our mid-thirties, and seventeen years into our relationship, changed our lives dramatically. It took a long time for my mind to catch up with this new reality. Sadly, it had only just become "normal" to us when Samuel was diagnosed with leukaemia and we had to get used to another, more frightening, way of life. Writing his story helped ground the events. It helped to slow down the rush of time as I relived the twenty months that we had our amazing son. After some time, it also helped me to come to terms with, and eventually accept, his death.

When Samuel died, two questions, and the search for their answers, became fundamental to my grieving: Why him? And where, if anywhere, had he gone? He was such a special person; so unique and full of character that it seemed unbelievable he should no longer be here. I know every mother thinks her child is exceptional but, even so, these questions persisted.

In my search for answers, I read many books about death, the spiritual dimension, religion, and other people's personal accounts of losing family members, including children. This was all I could relate to for a long time, and I could hardly comprehend watching television or doing other activities. When my husband, Stuart, and I took a break in the Peak District three weeks after losing Samuel – to be alone and to grieve in private – it seemed completely natural to take *The Tibetan Book of Living and Dying* with me.

The questions persisted, but as I wrote, read and reflected, I gradually felt I found answers that made sense to me. Up until Samuel died, I thought death was the end and that the personality, or soul, dies with the body. When he was ill, I received cards and messages from people saying that they were praying for him, but whilst I appreciated the sentiment, I felt a prayer was no more effective than wishing on a star. My rational brain still believed this when he died and perhaps, I told myself, it was just my reluctance to accept Samuel's death which kept me feeling that he'd not completely gone.

However, there had been many strange occurrences whilst Samuel was alive which I'd labelled as coincidences, but now I wonder if there was more to them. I can't say for certain whether they were just a string of coincidences or if they added up to there being a plan for Samuel, but it does now feel to me that his life was meant to be short. I have included these accounts in his life story, although I'm sure that they'll sound strange or delusional to many.

More coincidences occurred after Samuel died, which gradually persuaded me there is more to our existence than I'd previously permitted myself to believe. I wanted to include the first of these – which happened shortly after his death – in this introduction, in the hope it may provide some comfort for anyone who is grieving and suffering and looking for answers, just as I was.

After Samuel died, Stuart and I were left with such a mix of emotions it was hard to know what to say or do. Words and thoughts tumbled out as we struggled to come to terms with our loss – a loss that was horrendously hard to bear, even though we had been anticipating it.

Samuel was our first and only child, and the three of us were incredibly close. The last six months of his short life had brought us even closer, as we lived together in one small room in Addenbrooke's Hospital whilst supporting him through his chemotherapy. It was going to be very difficult to live without this very special person in our lives.

Samuel was taken to the chapel of rest wrapped in the shawl his nanny had knitted him, cuddled up with his beloved toys, BB and Woof Woof. I remember Stuart and me trying to talk about the practicalities and arrangements for his funeral, all the while shaking with the realisation that he wouldn't be waking up.

The enormity of our loss was too much to bear, and perhaps that's why I continued to focus on caring for him. This must have been why, sometime later, I realised he didn't have his dummy and felt the need to take it to him. We'd always joked that Samuel's dummy throwing was a trademark, as he so frequently tossed it aside as one might do a hat after a long day. Over the course of his treatment, Samuel's dummy had become increasingly important to him, and even though the rational part of my brain knew it was futile to take it to him now, I still felt he should have it with him.

Samuel had a vast collection of dummies and he was content with any of them. However, if he saw his pale-yellow one he would quickly take out the one in his mouth and make an exchange. And so it was this particular pale-yellow dummy we took to him.

On that day our families accompanied us to the chapel of rest. It was important for them to see him one last time to say their goodbyes. It was difficult to see them upset, and I wished they hadn't had to go through something so horrendously painful. I wanted very much to make it better and it felt alien to me that I couldn't, for once, find anything positive to say.

After we had spent some time with Samuel, we left the building and crossed the road towards the car park. Stuart was walking in front with my brother-in-law, Richie, and my sister and I were walking behind. Suddenly we heard something drop to the ground between the four of us.

"What was that?" I asked as Stuart bent down to pick up... a pale-yellow dummy.

There was nobody else around who could have thrown it, and we could not think where it had appeared from. We naturally began to question if we had actually left the dummy with Samuel earlier. A visit later confirmed that we had left it and this was a different dummy, albeit exactly the same in style and colour. We both strongly began to feel that this was a sign for us Samuel had gone on and that everything was meant to be.

When someone you love dies, you have to find a new reason to live. For a long time, Samuel remained our reason, but in a different way. Someone said he left a very deep footprint. Not a big one, but deep all the same. He touched many people's hearts and everyone who came into contact with him found him remarkable. Some months after his death, I ran into a nurse who'd cared for him for just one night in our local hospital. She said he was talked about often, as he seemed like such a special little boy.

As she walked away, she called over her shoulder, "You were lucky to have him."

We think so. He is our inspiration, and many other people's, too.

After Samuel died, we received many kind letters and cards from family, friends and even friends of friends; all of them wanting to offer some words of comfort. One letter, in particular, struck me. It was from a lady I did not know but who wrote to tell me she had lost a baby at birth. She said that although what we'd been through in many ways must be more difficult, if she'd been offered a year or two with her child she would have grabbed it with both hands. She would have been happy to have known her child and to give her love. When I read this I instantly felt grateful for the time we had with Samuel. Now I can genuinely say we feel fortunate to have been the parents of such a wonderful child and to have known him and loved him.

In the brief time we shared, he lit up our world. He left us different people; wiser in all respects. He was brave, bright and kind, and we will always love him. And that's the legacy he leaves behind. I realised when he died that although his body had gone, our love for him remained. Our love for him will never die. Although two emotions prevail within me – love and pain – love is by far the stronger.

CHAPTER 1

The Birth

~⁀

HE CAME OUT FROWNING. THE midwife held him up for us to see, and before I'd even taken in whether it was a boy or girl I'd noticed the frown. Knowing him as I do now, I can just imagine his indignation at being clamped around the head with forceps and yanked out. He was long and thin, with a look of resigned displeasure on his face. I remember thinking he didn't look at all like the image I'd had in my mind of a shrivelled-up, screaming baby.

"It's a boy," the midwife said.

"A boy," I repeated, followed by, "Hello, darling," and then, "I feel sick."

Samuel (we'd already chosen his name) was handed to Stuart and a sick bowl was produced for me. The last thing I remember before passing out was an oxygen mask being placed over my mouth and nose.

As I came round, I noticed Samuel being walked along a table by the midwife, who was holding him under the arms, checking his stepping reflex. He was still naked, and it was strange to see this little baby picking its feet up and looking like a miniature adult. In fact, that was always how we saw Samuel: like a miniature adult and not like a baby at all.

Stuart was at my side and the room was full of people: two midwives, two surgeons, an anaesthetist and several others, all wearing theatre blues. After a long and complicated labour, they had expected a caesarean, but one last try with forceps had produced him – along with a litre and a half of blood. Samuel James Murray was born at 7.27 p.m. on Thursday 2nd August 2007.

I'd come into hospital at ten o'clock the night before – three centimetres dilated with contractions every five minutes – but I'd actually been in labour much longer. Midwives don't count this time, however, as it's not considered to be "established labour". The first contraction had come on Sunday evening and it was no more painful than a period pain.

Stuart and I had gone for a walk around town. We live in Bury St Edmunds, close to the town centre, and although my stomach was large I felt fit and agile. It was a lovely evening. The sun was out and, to me, everyone looked as happy as I felt. Every now and then I experienced a mild pulling feeling, at which point we would pause for a moment before carrying on. I remember thinking it was all about to begin and that in the next day or two (at the most) we would have our baby.

We strolled around the town centre then walked back to our house through the Abbey Gardens and the old cemetery. I don't remember our conversation, but I expect it was about our imminent arrival and my hopes and fears about the birth.

The walk took us down a lane lined with old trees. Although the path was in shade, the sun shone through the leaves, illuminating them the most brilliant green. I turned and smiled at Stuart, then noticed a football heading towards me, followed by a boy of about three. A woman behind him called out and, at the last minute, I dodged the ball. As I did so, I felt a sharp pain in my lower back.

I stopped and let the boy collect his ball, but on taking a step realised I'd done some damage. Stuart has suffered on and off with a bad back for years, and for the past few weeks he'd really been in pain with it, so we must have looked a strange pair hobbling back to our house.

The bad back coupled with contractions was a painful combination, but until the birth I was still able to get about quite well. I was so filled with excitement about our baby arriving that I didn't rest as I should have done. Instead, I decided to be even more active, as I'd read this would bring about the birth more quickly. (I was already a few days past my due date.) Years before, my friend Angela had been induced and I'd heard how painful this could make labour. Anxious to avoid this, I spent the next three days walking as fast as I could manage around the house and garden and up and down the stairs. Stuart, who worked from home at the time, sat at his computer and looked up initially with indulgence, then irritation, as I distracted him with my pacing.

I phoned the midwife every day until our admission. They must have heard my story a million times before, but I couldn't believe they didn't consider me to be properly in labour. My contractions stayed a steady ten minutes apart and, although bearable, kept me awake at night and were wearing me out. By Wednesday I was beginning to think I was never going to give birth and that my stomach would stay the size of a beach ball forever. I remember sitting by our living-room window as our neighbour Nancy walked past.

"Anything happening?" she mouthed.

I shook my head sadly, as if I was the only woman ever to have experienced such a wait.

Stuart and I ate dinner in the garden that evening. Stuart, now convinced I wasn't giving birth anytime soon, poured himself a beer and settled in his chair. I was just berating him for drinking alcohol when I could go into established labour any minute when we noticed the smell of Indian food wafting over the fence from next door.

"That's what we should have had for dinner," Stuart said. "Hot, spicy foods are supposed to start off labour."

Well, it seemed that just the smell of all that hot, spicy food had the desired effect, because suddenly the pain of the contractions went up a notch. We started timing them again and found that they were now coming every five minutes.

"I knew that would happen if I had a beer," Stuart said.

The drive to hospital was more problematic than it should have been. Stuart carried my bag and the baby car seat out to the car. It seemed so strange to be taking clothes and a car seat for a person who was not yet in the world. Even though I'd seen the scans and felt kicks, I could not imagine really having a baby in our lives.

Stuart and I had been together for seventeen years, during which all we'd had to think about was ourselves. Our Victorian terraced house was pretty, but small and impractical, with steep stairs and a downstairs bathroom. At weekends we went out, stayed up late and had long lie-ins. The baby would change our lives dramatically, but it was very much wanted.

The journey to the hospital should have been quick, as we live just a few minutes' drive away. The roads were quiet and Stuart, not known for his calm demeanour, was holding up well. However, we'd almost got to the entrance when we saw the road was closed due to roadworks ahead of us. A diversion sign led us into a nearby housing estate. We followed the road round, eventually appearing back on the road we'd originally been on, only at the other side of the hospital. I was just reassuring Stuart that I was fine when we saw the road was also closed from this direction and there was another diversion sign pointing us back the way we'd just come! At this point, Stuart could keep up his calm façade no longer.

"I've got to get my wife to hospital!" he called out to the workmen – his stress clearly audible.

A workman came over but shrugged his shoulders and shook his head.

"How do we get into the hospital?" Stuart asked.

"Hospital?" the man repeated in a foreign accent.

"Oh, Christ! My wife – she's pregnant!" He pointed to my tummy. "Baby!" He was almost shouting now. "She's having a baby!"

And then, suddenly, the workman understood.

"Baby!' he exclaimed happily. "Baby!" he shouted to the other workmen.

The diversion sign was moved, a digger was driven to the side, and Stuart manoeuvred our car around piles of sand and cement, over the bumpy road and into the hospital grounds. To this day he is utterly incredulous that the council allowed the access road into the hospital to be blocked from both ends.

We arrived at Central Delivery at ten o'clock. Labour initially went better than I'd expected. Jenny (the midwife) was friendly, confident and reassuring. On examination, it was determined that I was three centimetres dilated. I was pleased to have got this far on my own, as I'd heard of many people arriving at hospital and being sent straight back home again as things had barely begun. We discussed a plan for labour and delivery. I'd originally wanted a home birth, but this was ruled out when one of my scans revealed I had too much amniotic fluid, which posed a potential risk.

Jenny thought a lavender bath might be a good start to proceedings, so whilst I soaked in bubbles Stuart settled in front of the telly in one of the delivery rooms. My bath was followed by a cup of hot chocolate and a bowl of Rice Krispies to keep my strength up. I must admit I felt thoroughly indulged and, despite the contractions, was feeling rather pleased with how things were progressing.

After a while, I was given a mild sedative to help me get a bit of sleep before the big event. I lay on the bed, but because of the contractions I wasn't able to drop off. However, I was fairly comfortable and relaxed. When Jenny examined me again I was six centimetres dilated. I was proud that I'd got this far with no pain relief. Despite having had little sleep the past few days, I suddenly felt full of energy and ready to meet our new baby.

"That baby will be here by the end of my shift," Jenny said at one point, and I remember thinking, *I wonder when the pain will get really bad.*

She told us we still had a little way to go, so at about four in the morning Stuart was instructed to take a break. Jenny assured him she would call if things really got going, so he disappeared to another delivery room to rest his bad back and get some sleep. Jenny asked if I wanted to try a bit of gas and air. My pain hadn't increased but, thinking it would pre-empt any further pain, I decided to give it a go. I'd not written a birth plan and had decided instead to just go with the flow. I'd heard too many stories of people determined to do it all naturally only to be disappointed when they needed an epidural and emergency caesarean. And so for a few hours I sucked on gas and air, watched TV and chatted to Jenny. When Stuart returned a little later, I was bouncing on a big rubber ball and eating chocolate.

At one point, we heard a woman across the corridor screaming out in pain and I looked at Jenny in alarm.

"That baby's almost here," she said, before returning to her paperwork.

"Thank Christ for that," Stuart said. "I thought she was being branded!"

The noise scared me, but at the same time I was feeling quietly confident with my handling of the situation. The thought occurred to me that I must be quite good at this and it wasn't anything like as bad as I'd been led to believe.

"We'll have to film you as an example of a natural birth!" Jenny said.

The room was lighter by now. I'd been up all night, and with morning came an increase in activity. Jenny's shift was nearing its end but there was still no sign of the baby. Although my waters hadn't broken, I still believed I couldn't be far off. Before she left, Jenny checked how dilated I was. Much to my dismay, she told me I was still only six centimetres dilated! So much for being good at labour – the reason I had coped so well with the pain was because nothing was happening! I was still having contractions but they weren't doing anything. Something would have to happen to speed things along, but Jenny's time was now up and she needed to hand me over to the next shift. She left, promising to telephone in a few hours to find out whether I'd had a boy or girl.

Two new midwives arrived on the scene. These ladies were much younger than Jenny. In fact, they both looked considerably younger than me. We learnt that one was a student and the other had been a midwife for just a few years. I couldn't help feeling worried by this. I'd put my trust in Jenny and felt confident with her. I think any woman giving birth for the first time would prefer to have a more senior and experienced midwife by her side. My anxiety increased further when it was decided my waters would need to be broken and a gynaecologist would be required to perform the procedure.

A doctor entered the room. He examined me and then, with the aid of a medical instrument, broke the waters. Amniotic fluid gushed everywhere. The midwives had put pads on the floor to soak everything up, as my notes had warned them about the increased amount of fluid. It looked an awful lot to me, but they assured me they'd seen worse.

"One woman had so much amniotic fluid that it ran right out the door!" the older midwife said.

I don't know if that was true or not but it made me laugh and relaxed me. Now there was nothing for me to do but wait and see if having my waters broken would speed up the contractions. *Friends* was found on the television and some tea and toast for my breakfast. The midwife even wrote in her notes that I was watching *Friends*; she seemed genuinely impressed that I was able to concentrate on it whilst in labour with only gas and air for pain relief. However, I had learnt from my earlier, misplaced confidence and worried that, again, I wasn't actually dilating.

Indeed, this turned out to be true when a couple of hours later I was checked and I hadn't budged at all from six centimetres. By now it was ten o'clock – twelve hours since our arrival the night before – and I was starting to get tired. The excitement that had got me this far was fast turning into anxiety. I hadn't even dilated fully, let alone given birth. Although I'd been told that was the quick bit, I was se-cretly worried about the baby getting stuck and not coming out.

A strap was placed over my stomach and I was wired up to a monitor to check the baby's heartbeat. There were concerns. They couldn't catch the heartbeat for long enough to be sure of the read-ing. They would have to perform a procedure called a foetal head swab. I'd never heard of this before, but was assured it was a quick procedure and completely harmless to the baby. It involved going into my cervix and scraping the surface of the baby's head for some blood. That blood would then be analysed, from which it could be deduced whether the baby was in distress and if an emergency caesarean needed to be performed.

Stuart stood on one side of me and held my hand, and the midwives sat on the other side. The gynaecologist started the procedure and I can honestly say I have never felt anything so painful in all my life. For the first time since labour began, I screamed out. Everyone looked at me.

"Where's the pain?" the surgeon asked.

"Down there!"

"This won't take long," he reassured me before continuing.

I screamed again.

"I'm sorry, but I have to do this. You will have to stay calm for just a few minutes longer."

I closed my eyes and breathed deeply. I was totally locked in my own head. I could hear Stuart's voice but I couldn't make out what he was saying.

He shook my hand, leaned close to me and said, "… Don't you, babe?"

I had no idea what he was talking about, but I nodded. It seemed he was asking for pethidine to be administered as pain relief and was checking that I wanted it. This was given to me, but I noticed no effect from it, apart from it starting to send me to sleep.

I later learnt that Stuart had been so concerned about the length of my labour – and how little pain relief I'd had – that he'd asked to see the most senior consultant for a second opinion. A female gynaecologist came in to see him and said she was happy with how things were progressing. However, she added that the foetal head swab is usually done with more pain relief (such as an epidural), but there hadn't been time to administer it because they needed to assess quickly if the baby was in distress. Shortly afterwards, the original gynaecologist returned with the results.

"The baby's fine. However, we need to speed things up. The baby's positioned back to back, which has slowed down the contractions. We'll attach you to a drip, which should make things happen a bit quicker." As he left the room he added, "We may need to repeat that procedure in another four hours."

Our hearts sank at the prospect of another four hours' labour, followed by a foetal head swab and then, of course, giving birth.

"She wants an epidural," Stuart said suddenly.

"Do you?" the surgeon asked.

I hadn't thought of it before, but it seemed like a very good idea considering how much longer I still had to go, and the possibility of another procedure. I nodded.

An anaesthetist was brought in to see me. By now the pethidine, together with the lack of sleep, had made me so drowsy I was having trouble staying awake. The anaesthetist was a brusque woman who seemed irritated with life in general. She became even more irritated when I could hardly keep my eyes open whilst she talked to me. When I asked her to repeat what she'd just said, she tutted and rolled her eyes. I can only conclude she had never experienced labour herself, as she had so little compassion. When she administered the epidural she tugged on my back and pulled me so hard I felt like a rag doll in her uncaring hands.

The effect of the epidural was immediate and seemed to bring calmness about the room. It also coincided with another shift change for the midwives. Out went the two young ladies and in came another two midwives. By this time, I was so tired I barely took any notice of them.

It was now mid-afternoon and it seemed a very long time since I'd been chatting happily to Jenny about lavender baths and back rubs. I'd never had delusions about birth and had been pleasantly surprised by my early experience. What had transpired after Jenny's departure was closer to what I was expecting from the word go. The drip was attached to speed up contractions and I finally got some sleep. Stuart took the opportunity to go for a walk and, as I nodded off, I noticed the midwives reading my magazines. It's funny, because even though I was in no state to be reading them myself, I remember feeling annoyed that they were looking at them before me. Sometime later I was examined again.

"Ten centimetres dilated!" the midwife announced.

I was so relieved, thinking it would all soon be over. Strangely, even though I'd read several pregnancy books thoroughly, I'd never thought too much about what happens straight after birth. I certainly hadn't realised I would have no chance to get over the birth because of the demands of looking after a newborn baby.

The gynaecologist came back into the room and said he was happy for me to try pushing, but he would allow only an hour for this and then we would have to go into theatre.

The next hour went quickly, with a variety of positions tried, but although I heard "I can see the head" many times, no baby appeared.

When my allotted hour was up, Stuart and the midwives put on theatre gowns and I was wheeled on the bed into theatre. Stuart was very tired and stressed by this time, and became even more so when asked to wheel the drip stand – which was still attached to me – as we raced along the corridor. I was really losing track of reality by then. This was partly because of tiredness and the unfamiliar environment, but also the disorientation of lying horizontal whilst being wheeled along a corridor.

I do remember a Robbie Williams song being played as we went into the theatre, and how bizarre that seemed. The gynaecologist who'd seen us earlier came in, and when everyone was scrubbed and ready to go, a second gynaecologist entered. Stuart remarked afterwards it was a bit like God had walked in, because everybody stopped what they were doing and only spoke to answer him. He examined me and instructed the original gynaecologist to try forceps first. A much kinder anaesthetist increased the epidural and a cut was made.

Kielland forceps were eventually used to turn the baby and I was told to push. Even though I could feel very little, I managed to do so.

"The head's out!" the midwife exclaimed, and then a minute later, "It's out!"

"It's out," I repeated.

And there he was: long and thin, and wearing the frown that we would soon come to recognise when he was displeased. Our beautiful son, Samuel, had entered the world.

CHAPTER 2

The First Few Days

~)

HE HAD THE BIGGEST EYES. They were deep blue with long, black lashes, and filled with love. He was put on my breast to see if he would latch on for a feed and he did so immediately.

"You're a natural," one of the midwives said.

The same thing had been implied when I was giving birth but it ended up not being the case. I've now learnt to be wary of such statements.

We lay looking at each other. It seemed so strange that this little person had been living inside me for the past nine months. Stuart had been holding him when I'd passed out earlier, and his abiding memory is Samuel alternating between the famous frown and yawning. This was probably due to the pethidine, which would have crossed from my bloodstream to his via the placenta.

As a result of the blood loss and epidural, I was given a catheter and fluid drip. I was then wheeled back to the delivery room with Samuel still lying on me. There was yet another change of midwives and it was now ten o'clock, Thursday night – twenty-four hours since we'd arrived at the hospital.

Time seemed to be speeding up and it was hard to account for the hours since Samuel's birth. I remember feeling scared of going to a normal ward and Stuart going home. Although the hard work was done, the thought of being left alone with my baby was terrifying. I just didn't have any clue about what I should be doing. I didn't feel at all with it and wanted to sleep, but when I saw Samuel's trusting little face looking up at me, I didn't feel I could put him down.

Eventually I was taken to the ward, but I was the only patient in the six-bay room. A wiry old Scottish midwife was introduced to me; I could tell she would take no nonsense. I found myself apologising to her every time I had to call her over. She put Samuel in the little cot next to my bed.

"Now lie down and get some sleep while your baby's sleeping," she instructed.

I'm sure I must have slept, but in no time at all I heard Samuel cry. I looked over at his cot and he seemed to have angled his head back to get a good look at me. His eyes were round, dark and huge in the half-light of the ward, and I could see such warmth in them. For the first time I thought he looked very knowing.

As I couldn't move due to the epidural, I pressed the call button. The midwife was there immediately.

"Yes?" she asked, as she puffed up my pillows.

"I think Samuel needs feeding."

She picked him up and handed him to me, and watched him latch on.

"Buzz when you've finished and I'll put him back in the cot."

I never buzzed her. Samuel just looked too cosy snuggled up to me. I swear I could almost see a smile on his lips! With his eyes closed I could see just how long those eyelashes were, and how dark. His head was also covered in dark hair. Over the next few weeks, a bald patch appeared and then, after three months, all the dark hair completely went and a fresh crop of golden blond appeared in its place.

Eventually, the midwife came back and said, "Let's put that baby back in the cot if he's finished feeding."

"Actually, I think I'll keep him here a bit longer," I said.

"Well, I think it would be better if you slept."

Of course she was right. I'd had a long labour, lost a lot of blood, and hadn't slept properly for days. But as I looked at Samuel sleeping contentedly in my arms I just couldn't move him; a feeling that became increasingly familiar to me. In the end, she agreed.

"Oh well, we *are* supposed to encourage bonding," she said. "I'll come back in a bit. See if you can sleep."

The pillows were all piled up high behind me for support when I was feeding Samuel, but were proving uncomfortable to sleep against. I tried to manoeuvre them into a better position without waking him. I wiggled down the bed as best I could, considering the epidural hadn't worn off and I had a catheter and drip attached.

Samuel and I spent the remainder of the night in this position, with him occasionally waking to feed and then going back to sleep. With hindsight, I realise I should have made the most of this quiet time to get the rest I so badly needed, and to build my strength up for what lay ahead. But it has given me a lovely memory and I enjoyed that special time getting to know this very important person who had appeared in our lives.

The next morning, the catheter and drip were removed and I felt a bit freer. When Samuel slept I left him with the midwife and had a bath. Afterwards, I dressed in a maternity skirt and felt disappointed when I looked in the mirror and realised I still looked pregnant. On top of that, my feet had swollen to twice their normal size and felt hot and sore. The combination of pregnancy and summer had also covered my face in freckles and my skin looked anaemic underneath. All in all, I wasn't looking my best! When I came out of the bathroom I couldn't find Samuel, but then I saw him at the nurse station in his cot.

"Did he cry?" I asked. I thought he was crying a lot, and only seemed happy when he was feeding.

"No, he's fine," a midwife assured me, "but we've moved you into the next bay. You'll be with some other new mums in there."

She said this like it was a good thing, but I felt anxious.

What if Samuel cries more than the other babies? I thought. *What if they notice I don't know what I'm doing?*

I wheeled Samuel in his cot over to our new bed, picked him up and cuddled him. The other mums all had people with them. It was getting late in the morning and there was still no sign of Stuart. This was completely expected; I have never known him to be on time for anything in the entire time we have been together.

I then realised Samuel's nappy needed changing. Baby poo is very runny and, as I hadn't changed him yet, I felt nervous doing so in full view of the other mums. I wished that Stuart was with me to help, but as he wasn't I just had to get on with it. I pulled the curtain around me. I had seen in antenatal classes that cotton wool and water are the best things to use on a newborn baby's delicate skin. However, the reality of using those little, fluffy balls was something of a farce. By the next day I was using baby wipes.

Whilst in the middle of changing him for the first time, he weed. I tried to get the nappy on quickly but it was too late. His sheet and blanket were covered. I'd got as far as changing his nappy and getting a vest over his head and arms when his screams of protest became too much and I had to settle him with a feed in order to calm him again. It had been a cool summer, but the days around Samuel's birth were some of the hottest that year, which only added to the heat I was already feeling.

Just at that moment, a midwife came over. She saw immediately the cot needed changing. "Can I help?" she asked.

I felt embarrassed that I'd not managed to change Samuel and the cot and give him a feed without getting flustered. When I look back now, I realise how hard I was on myself. I had been under the impression other people were coping just fine, so I should too. Now I realise that other people don't always cope and are often just covering things up. Also, what does it matter? Everyone's circumstances are different and some people really do have more to cope with.

The other three women on my ward all had their partners with them and all three babies were sleeping. Samuel was only fourteen hours old and, according to the books I'd read, should have been spending most of his time asleep. I was conscious that he was crying more frequently than the other babies on the ward.

When Stuart arrived I was leaning back on my bed feeding Samuel. He thought how strange it was to see a little head with dark hair snuggled up against me. In contrast to the reality of the situation, he thought I looked very natural lying there with Samuel. It just goes to show you can't second-guess how situations are actually perceived by others.

"Where have you been?" I whispered. This time it was me doing the frowning.

"I rang everyone to tell them about the birth."

Stuart had phoned our family shortly after Samuel was born, but it now transpired that he'd also called our friends to let them know of his arrival and, as the delivery had been difficult, he had felt compelled to go into details. Stuart certainly hadn't expected the birth to be so long, complicated and gory, and as the days went by I realised just how badly it had affected him. He told me how awful he'd found it seeing me in pain and not being able to help, and also how the sight of all that blood had played on his mind. He described it as being like a scene from a horror film. To be honest, I was so consumed at the time with what *I* was feeling that I almost laughed off his confession. Only later, on seeing Samuel go through painful procedures and not being able to help, did I realise how distressing my labour must have been for Stuart.

I think I was guilty of brushing aside Stuart's need to talk. But as Stuart is inclined to chat – his school reports described him as "a compulsive talker who does not follow instructions!" – we had a few words; this time about him not arriving at the hospital earlier. I'm not proud of that; it must have been distressing for Samuel sensing my anger. I'm sure mothers are not meant to feel anger in the first twenty-four hours after their child's birth, but anger was definitely what I was feeling then.

Those first few days were so different from what I'd imagined. When I'd thought past the birth at all I'd just envisaged holding our baby, cuddled in a blanket, and greeting our visitors. I certainly hadn't imagined Samuel would cry constantly when he wasn't on my breast, which was starting to be the case.

That afternoon my mother and her partner, Alan, visited. Samuel was peaceful during the visit and even slept in my mum's arms for a while. However, I didn't feel completely relaxed; I was very aware that Samuel could wake any time and need feeding.

My mother was as under Samuel's spell as I was when she held him that day. What I didn't know then was that when I was six months pregnant she'd had a dream in which she was looking after a baby, about a year old, who was lethargic and wouldn't eat. The dream seemed so real she'd felt sure it was a premonition. However, when Samuel was born healthy she put it out of her mind and just focused on enjoying him.

The fear she felt from the dream didn't reappear until Samuel was about four and a half months old. When looking at him one day, she instinctively felt that he had leukaemia. There was no reason for her to think this as Samuel was thriving – putting on weight, interacting and generally behaving as any baby his age should. My mother had had acute myeloid leukaemia seven years previously, so she told herself she was simply projecting her fears onto him from the memory of her own illness. Interestingly, however, she never once worried that my sister or I might suffer the same fate. Also, as leukaemia is not hereditary, she knew her fears were ungrounded. However, her overwhelming feelings persisted and stayed with her up until Samuel's diagnosis.

Just as my mother and Alan finished their visit that day I was told I was anaemic and given some iron tablets. In the evening my sister, Nancy, and her husband, Richie, visited us. It was while my sister was holding Samuel that I noticed he was putting his fist in his mouth. At the time I didn't realise this meant he was hungry.

By early evening I was shattered. Stuart held Samuel for an hour so I could try to get some sleep. He stood by the window and showed Samuel the rabbits outside, rocking him even though this compounded his back pain.

By now the other three women on my ward had gone home, but Samuel was crying a lot and I felt I needed the help of the midwives. The reality was that they hadn't paid me much attention. Even though I had mentioned that Samuel cried every time he was taken away from my breast, not one of them suggested he might be hungry. It seems amazing to me now that I didn't think of it, and a real concern that the midwives, with all their experience, didn't realise it either;

especially when they knew I was anaemic and the effect this can have on a woman's milk supply. As far as I was concerned, Samuel was being fed for several hours at a time with barely a break in between; whenever I called the midwife over I was reassured he was okay.

"He's latched on well," several different midwives said, which I interpreted to mean he was *feeding* well.

I managed a short nap before Samuel cried again. Looking back, it was clear he was in distress, but being a first-time mum I just didn't pick up on the signs. I feel that telling the midwives Samuel was spending a couple of hours at a time on my breast should have alerted them to a feeding problem.

That night, after Stuart went home, things got steadily worse. The Scottish midwife who had been on the night before was back, and this time seemed determined Samuel and I would spend the night in our own beds. In principle she was right, as we both needed sleep, but she didn't know Samuel had become more distressed as the day had worn on. I tried to settle him in his cot but he wasn't happy. Eventually, she came back. She seemed irritated to find me holding him again.

"That baby should be in his cot and getting some sleep," she said.

Again, I tried to put him down. She left me to it. When it became clear he wasn't settling, she returned.

"I can hear him right down the corridor, and there are babies down there with real needs," she said.

She picked Samuel up, more roughly than I would have liked, and swaddled him in his blanket. I was distressed at having my tiny baby taken from my arms and handled in that way. He looked at me with his big eyes and I could see his confusion and anxiety. I'm sure many people would argue you can't detect this in a child so young, but Samuel was always alert and expressive. I saw that look again several times when he was being treated for his illness, and it always made me want to cuddle and protect him. Of course all parents want to protect their children, but unfortunately the feeling of having failed in this is common for parents of children who have died.

Samuel did go quiet for a little while after being swaddled in his blanket, but again, he twisted his head round to look at me. Feeling guilty, I closed my eyes and tried to sleep, but when he cried again I picked him straight up for a feed. By about two o'clock in the morning, the midwife reappeared.

"Have you slept yet?" she asked.

"No. He just won't settle," I replied.

She looked at me for a while, as if unsure whether to say anything.

"I can give him a bit of milk," she said eventually.

She must have worked out that Samuel wasn't getting any milk from me, even though I was yet to realise it. I agreed, but it didn't stop me from feeling guilty. I had read all the books and heard the saying: *breast is best.* I'd also attended the breastfeeding workshop in preparation and had just assumed this was what I would do.

"I often see this with long, scrawny babies," she said as she took Samuel away.

I felt incredibly concerned as I watched him disappear from view, and worried if I was doing the right thing. However, I was desperately tired and needed some sleep. If a bottle helped Samuel to settle I reasoned it would be okay, just this once. I lay back down on my bed and, for the first time in six days, I slept. Not just a nap, but a proper, knocked-out sleep. I don't remember dreaming or stirring until the morning, when I woke to see Samuel in his cot beside me, sound asleep and more peaceful than in the whole time since he'd been born. I managed to eat a big bowl of cereal and a roll with butter before he woke.

When he did wake, the whole thing started again. He would feed for over an hour and then when he was taken off my breast he would cry. New mothers had now appeared on the ward and, again, they all looked like they were handling things really well.

I heard one mum on the phone: "Yes, I feel fine. He's just slept the whole time since I had him."

I remember thinking, *What am I doing wrong? Why won't Samuel sleep?*

Again, I called a midwife over and explained that Samuel cried when he wasn't feeding, and again she watched him latch on and told me he was doing fine. I must have gone through this with five or six different midwives, but apart from the Scottish one, none suggested he might be hungry. I was confused. For some reason, I just didn't connect all the facts and realise I wasn't producing any milk. Now I can't believe I didn't make the connection; especially when I remember how well he'd slept when he'd been given some milk from a bottle. But, being a first-time mum, it was all new to me and I just didn't have the knowledge to come to this realisation. The midwives, on the other hand, with their combined years of experience, must have seen this problem many times before. This, of course, makes me wonder why they weren't more helpful.

Even though the crying was getting worse, I didn't want to stay another night in hospital. All the other mums seemed to be coming and going in a matter of hours, and I felt I should be getting on with things by myself as well. I felt embarrassed I couldn't seem to settle my baby and didn't want to keep playing this out in front of an audience. I also got the impression from the Scottish midwife that she thought we were being a nuisance. I didn't want her being rough with Samuel again and so, that afternoon, we left.

It was nice to get out in the sunshine. After three days I'd had enough of hospital life. Little did I know how long we would be spending in hospital in just over a year's time.

Samuel, to our relief, fell asleep in his car seat. This was something he did whenever we went out for a drive; I think the motion of the car and the noise of the engine helped lull him off to sleep.

It was mid-afternoon by the time we got home and the temperature outside was in the high twenties. To get him away from the heat and the glare of the sun, Stuart took Samuel into the dining room, which is in shade at that time of day and the coolest room in the house. He put him down on the floor, still in his car seat, and we both just stood there, looking at him.

"What do we do now?" Stuart said.

"I don't know."

We both looked at our tiny, sleeping baby, curled up in his little seat. "It's a frightening thought, though, isn't it? That we're responsible for this child for the next eighteen years."

Stuart's parents, sister and two nieces were coming round in the evening, so he decided to walk into town to get some drinks for everyone. When Samuel cried, I picked him up out of his car seat and took him up to our bedroom. We lay together on the bed and I fed him. I think he must have got some milk because he raised his eyebrows up and down as he sucked, which was something I noticed him doing in the future when he was feeding from a bottle. The next thing I was aware of was the front door being slammed. Stuart was home and Samuel and I had both fallen asleep. It felt peaceful at that moment, and just how I wanted it to be. Unfortunately, it didn't stay that way for long.

Stuart's family arrived and, somehow, I found myself helping with getting drinks for everyone. My back was causing me real problems; something that became apparent as I tried to walk into the garden where everyone was sitting. Each step was painful and I felt exhausted. I regretted inviting everyone over. I just didn't have the energy and I was still worried about Samuel crying so much. All I wanted to do was sleep and have Samuel asleep next to me. I put on a fairly convincing act, but if I were to have that time again I would make sure it was just the three of us.

That first night at home Samuel cried continuously. None of us slept the entire night.

"Do you think he has attention deficit disorder?" Stuart said at one point. (Something he deeply regrets now!)

I was so angry.

"This is what babies do, Stuart. We have to get used to it!"

But, of course, I was wrong. Babies shouldn't cry that much, and when they do it's because something's not right.

By early next morning, Stuart had had enough.

"I'm calling the hospital. This can't be right."

"Don't!" I protested.

I didn't want them to think I wasn't coping. In the end, he called a breastfeeding helpline run by NCT – the National Childbirth Trust – and spoke to a woman who said she would come round to help in the afternoon. However, as the morning wore on we became more desperate. I sat rocking Samuel in his car seat, hoping it would have the same effect as the day before. Tears streamed down my face. He sat in his seat looking at me with big, wide eyes and I wondered what he was thinking. Stuart tried rocking him in his arms and singing to him, as he'd done when showing him the rabbits.

Before I'd gone into hospital, Stuart said that for the first few days following the birth I should be tucked up in bed with the baby whilst he brought me meals and looked after me. The reality seemed a very long way from that image.

At about eleven o'clock, my father and his girlfriend, Sue, turned up. The last thing I needed after a sleepless night was more visitors.

"Ahh, bless! You're still all podgy!" Sue said in her Yorkshire accent as she came through the door.

I might have laughed on another occasion, but my spirits were already low and her banter did little to lift them.

I took Samuel out into the garden and Sue and my dad followed. This time I didn't volunteer to get drinks; Stuart took charge of that. I was tired and dazed and it was hard to stay focused. Samuel was still crying constantly and kept putting his fist in his mouth. I attempted to concentrate on my father's conversation whilst trying to feed him. I could see Dad looked concerned.

"Perhaps your mum could help?" he suggested. He had been so insistent about coming over, but I really don't think any of us had expected those first days to be so difficult. "We won't stay long," he added.

I took Samuel back up to our bedroom after they left and rested with him on the bed. He was still crying and my back was becoming more painful with every movement. Stuart, who was feeling increasingly anxious, phoned the hospital and managed to get hold of the midwife. To his relief, she said she would come over.

When the midwife arrived, she explained that she'd been trying to call us all morning but the hospital had written our telephone number down wrong. As it was Sunday, the midwives' office wasn't open, so she'd not been able to double-check the number. It was a good job Stuart had called her or no one would have come out to see us. We felt like everything was going wrong.

"Samuel cries constantly," Stuart explained.

"Is he feeding well?" the midwife asked.

"I'm not sure," I replied.

Ridiculously, I still felt I was making a fuss and should just be getting on with things.

"Let me watch him latch on," the midwife said.

I put Samuel to my breast.

"He's latching on well."

"Look, we've been through all this at the hospital," Stuart said. "We've had five or six different midwives say that to us but Samuel is feeding for a couple of hours at a time and when he comes off he cries."

The midwife took Samuel off me then repositioned him. She watched him feed for about twenty minutes then took him off. He cried.

"I don't think he's getting any milk," she said. "He shouldn't feed for two hours at a time."

She asked if she could try and hand express some milk by massaging my breast. If we weren't so exhausted and concerned I think Stuart and I would have laughed at this. The midwife started massaging whilst I held a little bowl underneath to catch the milk. She kneaded my breast for ages, pushing and squeezing really hard. Eventually one tiny drop came out and plopped into the bowl.

"Well, you are producing *something*," she said.

"Is that it?" Stuart asked.

"This is colostrum – you don't get much of it. Your milk should come in properly in a day or two."

She was just suggesting I lie back in bed and try to feed Samuel again when there was a knock at the door. This time it was Stuart's brother, his wife and their three teenage boys. We had invited them before I'd given birth but, as much as I love them, I really didn't want to see them, or anyone, at that moment. I felt tired, fat and useless. My back was aching, I was hungry because I'd barely found time to eat, and I just wanted to burst into tears. Stuart went down to see them and asked if they could sit in the garden.

"I don't want to go down," I said to the midwife.

"Then don't. I'm sure they'll understand."

When Stuart came back up I told him I didn't want to see anyone.

"You *have* to see them. They've come a long way."

"No. I don't want to!"

I was crying now. Stuart looked flustered. He sat with me and tried to get me to change my mind. Samuel was still crying; poor little thing. He must have been exhausted and I was seriously wondering if I was up to motherhood. Eventually, Stuart agreed to take Samuel down to them whilst I stayed upstairs.

When he brought him back up I tried to give him another feed. I relaxed on the bed and, again, he latched on. He must have been so hungry. I'm not sure if he actually got some milk or if he was just so tired he would have slept anyway, but for whatever reason, he fell asleep for about half an hour.

"Do you think he's getting some food now?" I asked the midwife.

"I think he might have got something," she said.

She was actually a breastfeeding specialist and was keen for me not to give up. However, she did add, "If he cries continuously all night, you might want to give him a small amount of formula; just so you all get some rest."

On hearing Stuart's family leave, I put Samuel in his Moses basket and went downstairs. There was a beautiful vegetarian pie that our sister-in-law, Wendy, had made for us, together with some flowers which she'd put in a vase. It was so lovely and thoughtful of her that I felt guilty for not coming down and seeing them but, as always, they understood. Later, when I spoke to her, she said she just wanted to come up and hug me. With hindsight, that would have been nice. However, I'm not sure I would have stopped crying, and three teenage boys don't want to hear that! We set about having some of the delicious pie, but I'd only eaten about half my meal when Samuel started crying again.

Sunday night followed the same pattern as Saturday, with Samuel distressed for most of it. It seems awful to think of him so hungry and dehydrated in that August heat when we could so easily have given him a bottle. I had accepted the message that breastfeeding is better for your baby to such an extent I thought the exact opposite about bottle feeding; in my mind it had become akin to giving him drugs. By the middle of the night, Stuart had had enough and decided to make up a bottle. I protested and cried. I remembered the line drummed into us at the breastfeeding workshop: "Many mothers do not persevere long enough with breastfeeding."

I must persevere, I thought to myself.

This was ridiculous, as Samuel was clearly hungry and formula milk had to be better than no milk. Now I realise just how many children have been raised on formula and have grown up perfectly healthy.

Stuart said to me at one point, "Look around you. Can you tell who was breastfed and who was bottle fed?"

We gave Samuel thirty millilitres of formula milk, which he gulped down. His little eyebrows went up and down as he swallowed, and once he'd finished he looked so relieved. All three of us lay exhausted on the bed, looking at one another.

Stuart said, "Why on earth didn't we do this sooner?"

Samuel fell asleep for a couple of hours before waking again for another feed. This time I tried to breastfeed him. I did this for the remainder of the night, so that by morning we were all exhausted again. First thing the next day the same midwife that had seen us the day before arrived. We gave her the details of the previous night and she listened and checked Samuel. She then got her baby scales out and weighed him. In just four days he'd lost over 10 per cent of his body weight.

"I'm going to ring the hospital to see if they want him back in."

I was distraught and started to cry.

"I've not looked after him properly. Perhaps he should go back into hospital. I obviously can't care for him."

The midwife smiled and reassured me, "It's all right. You *have* looked after him, but we have to sort out this feeding issue."

The hospital decided we didn't have to return if we could get Samuel to put on weight over the next twenty-four hours.

"Shall we give him bottles, then?" I asked.

"I think you might have to," the midwife replied.

I think at that point both Stuart and I felt relieved we'd been "given permission" to use formula milk. Obviously, we didn't *need* anyone's permission. I suppose I felt the responsibility for this decision had been handed to someone else and, therefore, I hadn't failed by not persevering. I've since read in several books that being anaemic inhibits the production of breast milk, but either the midwives didn't know this or they chose not to tell me. Perhaps the nurses on duty hadn't read my medical notes and didn't even know I was anaemic. We can only speculate.

Breastfeeding is pushed so hard that it made me feel inadequate and a failure for not continuing with it. I now know many mothers who "persevered" for much longer than I did whilst their babies lost weight and both mother and baby suffered. How can it be better to let babies get malnourished – and for mothers to feel like failures – than to accept things aren't working and give the baby a bottle? Unfortunately, it is all too easy for mothers and midwives who have not experienced difficulties with breastfeeding to have little empathy or understanding for those that have.

The change in Samuel was amazing. After giving him his second bottle he lay on our bed, quietly looking up at Stuart whilst I rested.

He was so peaceful and calm, and I remember Stuart saying to him, "Sorry I thought you had attention deficit disorder, little man."

It was the first step to getting on top of this amazing new situation we were in. As I said before, seventeen years is a long time to be in a relationship without children, and suddenly having a baby in your life takes a lot of getting used to. However, from this day things slowly started to improve.

CHAPTER 3

The Weeks That Followed

~

THE CONGRATULATIONS CARDS LAY UNOPENED on the dining-room table. Washing-up was beginning to pile up in the sink and there was a big bowl on the side filled with water, baby bottles and sterilising solution. On top of that, my back was giving me so much pain I could hardly walk.

"We need help," Stuart said.

We'd decided to have some time alone after the rush of visitors the previous few days. Friends had sent texts asking to see us, but I had put them off. Samuel was much more content and would lie peacefully in our arms during the day, but still wasn't sleeping well at night and we all had a lot of catching up to do. So when Stuart acknowledged we needed help, I knew he was right.

"I'll call my mum," I said.

Mum never seemed particularly interested in babies and hadn't gone on at us to have children the way some parents do. However, when she met Samuel, she couldn't have been a more doting grandma.

I told her about all the problems we'd had over the past few days, and a couple of hours later she turned up with a steam steriliser for Samuel's bottles, and bags full of presents. Within an hour, the washing-up was done, the bottles were in the steriliser and we were, at last, opening our cards. I couldn't believe we had so many: about fifty in all. I had the same feeling just twenty months later when we had over double that amount, except this time the cards said "*With sympathy*".

It was lovely opening the presents and seeing the adorable baby clothes inside. Most I liked, but some were far too grown-up for a newborn baby, so Mum kept those to return. Luckily, she's a big fan of shopping, so choosing new outfits for Samuel was a joy to her on the days she wasn't spending with him.

Getting up the stairs to put the clothes away in his chest of drawers proved a problem. Every day the pain in my back had got worse, and by now it was so bad I couldn't lift my foot without agonising, shooting pains bringing tears to my eyes. I knew I couldn't go on like that, so I decided to talk to the midwife about it when she arrived for her visit later.

Jenny, the midwife who'd started my labour off so nicely with a lavender bath and back massage, arrived to see us at midday. I was pleased to see her and she gave me a big hug as she came through the door.

"I can't believe your labour went on so long," she said.

We told her all about it and Stuart said how he wasn't happy about a few things to do with the labour. We explained the problems we'd had with breastfeeding. I also told her how much pain I was in and she sorted it out right away by calling our GP, Dr Masters.

Jenny weighed Samuel and we were pleased to find he'd put on weight. When he was laid on the baby scales he didn't cry or make a fuss, but frowned at Jenny as if to say, "I'll put up with this providing it doesn't take too long." Even then it was evident who was in charge!

When Jenny left she agreed to come back in a few days with my birth notes to discuss why labour had gone the way it had. I also wanted to talk to her about how the midwives at the hospital dealt with my concerns regarding breastfeeding. I wanted this information fed back to the staff involved so that they might be more aware of feeding problems in the future.

It was only an hour or so later when Dr Masters arrived. He had been our GP for ten years, but in that time we'd hardly had need to see him. All that changed when we had Samuel. Nearing retirement, I expect he just wanted to ease gently out of his profession. Instead, he became intrinsically involved with our family and our son's last week of life. Despite the differences of opinion we sometimes had, we feel lucky to have had a GP who was prepared to come to our house and give us so much of his time and care. However, on this day he was yet to really know us. He came into the living room and sat down on a dining-room chair put there by my mother, who believed it would be better for my back. Actually, it was horribly uncomfortable to sit on for any length of time; I was glad Dr Masters sat there, because it meant I didn't have to.

"Right," he said slowly, looking at me over the top of his glasses. "So you hurt your back during labour." I told him how much pain I was in. I still felt weak as I stood there talking to him, and my skin looked a strange mix of very pale with dark freckles. I got the impression he was taking it all in. He listened and nodded. "I think we'll call the physiotherapy department at the West Suffolk Hospital," he said. "Can you get there for an appointment?"

It was the same hospital I'd given birth at and it wouldn't have been impossible to get there, but with a baby less than a week old, anaemia and impaired walking ability, it didn't seem that easy either.

"Could they come out to me?" I asked.

Dr Masters grimaced. (It is an expression of his I grew very familiar with.)

"Well… We could ask, couldn't we?" he said.

So he asked and, thankfully, we got.

A couple of days later, a physiotherapist arrived. She looked me over, made me stand and bend in certain positions, and concluded I'd torn some ligaments when I'd leapt out of the way of that ball just over a week ago. Being in labour and giving birth had increased the strain on my back and exacerbated the problem. She taught me some exercises that would help strengthen my supporting muscles, and told me to keep walking, as it would gradually heal.

Up until that point, walking around the house had presented enough of a challenge, but I was desperate to get out so was keen to follow her advice. I hadn't thought our house was small when there were just the two of us and I was out at work all day, but with Samuel's arrival, and everything that came with this little person, I felt the walls were closing in.

We had our first walk out one evening shortly after her visit. We strapped Samuel in a baby sling on Stuart's chest and set off to the Abbey Gardens. It seemed like weeks since our last visit and, in that time, I felt my world had become very small. I didn't realise then that I should have just been grateful to be in my own home, as later my world would become much smaller, revolving around one room in a hospital.

Unfortunately, on this occasion we only got as far as the end of our road. It took ten minutes to do a two-minute walk. I was so frustrated.

Gradually, my back got better. Our next walk took us all the way to the Abbey Gardens, and the one after that as far as the town. Three weeks later I was getting about normally. During this time, we got used to having another person in the house – one whose demands came before anything else. The days were peaceful; Samuel would either sleep in his Moses basket or we would cuddle him, sing to him or shake little rattles to amuse him. The nights, however, continued to be unsettled.

One evening, when Samuel was about five weeks old, we went to our neighbours' for drinks. Jonathan and Nancy had lived next door to us for three years and we'd become quite friendly. They had two little girls; the youngest was three months older than Samuel. We took Samuel in his Moses basket and, as he was asleep, we left him in the hall just outside the living-room door where it was dark and quiet. After a couple of hours, despite our good intentions, Nancy and I realised we'd talked mostly about babies all night. On overhearing our conversation, Stuart seemed to temporarily forget Samuel's whereabouts.

"Where's Samuel?" he said.

"In the hall," I replied.

He sighed with relief and I laughed.

"Did you forget we had him with us?"

"No, no," he lied. "I remember him – nice little chap."

Obviously, we were still getting used to having a baby in our lives!

That evening I told Nancy about the problems we were having getting Samuel to sleep at night. He fell asleep in the early evening and would sleep well for a few hours (so we always had the evenings to ourselves) but after about eleven o'clock he would wake every couple of hours for a feed and then take up to fifty minutes to get back to sleep. It was exhausting, but as Samuel was now bottle fed, thankfully Stuart could help with some of the feeds. I felt luckier than many as Stuart worked from home so, at his suggestion, we did alternate nights so each of us got a good night's sleep every other night.

Nancy told me about Gina Ford's *Contented Little Baby* book. She outlined the routine and said that her children seemed to fall into it quite naturally. I decided to give it a go and found Samuel's sleeping pattern did seem to naturally follow the routine during the day. It also helped us to work out how many bottles he should be having and when.

Up until then I'd offered him milk every time he cried, but found that he often wouldn't drink much. I was constantly washing up, sterilising bottles and making up fresh ones. By following the routine, I managed to get him to take a full bottle every time, which was more efficient. It also meant I wasn't constantly on edge, thinking he would cry any moment. He had long, undisturbed naps so he really was contented when he was awake. However, night-times continued to be a problem.

By now I had started going to the health visitors once a week to get Samuel weighed. I told them about the difficulties I was having with his sleeping and they said it sounded like he had colic. Stuart had already commented that he could feel gas travelling up Samuel's back when he tried to rock him back to sleep after a feed, so I thought it was likely. I never found the health visitors to be of much use for most of his life, but at this visit they suggested changing his formula. It was a good suggestion because there was a noticeable change in the length of time it took us to settle him after his milk; even though he was still waking every two to three hours, he fell asleep much more quickly. It must have previously been very uncomfortable for him to lie down. We were feeling tired and irritated because of lack of sleep, but I think it's sometimes forgotten just how exhausted the baby must be. We gradually got into a pattern of feeding him before he went to bed at seven o'clock, then again at eleven o'clock, then at two and five in the morning. Then he would wake for the day at seven.

I noticed early on that Samuel was a sociable baby. At just three weeks he would smile at me and at four weeks he was laughing. He would often take me by surprise with one of his little laughs. I might be gazing out the window or have my focus elsewhere, but when I looked back at Samuel in my arms he would be watching me, laughing away. He always loved studying people when they weren't looking at him. I noticed he did this throughout his life and particularly in his last week, when he would stare at people for ages with such a knowing look. I wonder if he was trying to take it all in and if he knew he only had a limited time left.

When Samuel had his obligatory six- to eight-week review, he wouldn't smile at Dr Masters. At the review the doctor will check how the baby responds to speech and language, and they do this by seeing if the baby will smile at them. Dr Masters gave it his best efforts, but Samuel just studied him with an inquisitive look. He was about to record a negative result, when I picked Samuel up and he gave the biggest, most beautiful smile. Obviously, our son was very discerning about who he smiled at!

The doctor also checks that the baby can support its head, by holding the child out along the length of their forearms, face down. Samuel did this perfectly and then tilted his head up even higher, as if seeking an extra mark for being so impressive.

"He'll pass his GCSEs with flying colours!" Dr Masters said.

Around the same time, my neighbour Nancy suggested that I attend one of the NCT coffee mornings. At the very first one I went to I got roped into helping out at their forthcoming sale. Two other mums, Heidi and Kirsty, sat at a big oak table drinking coffee and eating cake whilst their children ran round, dressing up and chasing the dog. Samuel sat in his car seat, following the action and probably wondering what to make of it all.

"We have an NCT sale twice a year," Heidi said.

"It's a good place to buy lots of nice, cheap clothes and toys," added Kirsty.

"If you help set up you can have first pick of everything."

"That sounds good," I commented politely.

"So, can we put your name down to help?" finished Kirsty.

They were like a double act, but they got results: three weeks later I joined about fifty other women sorting through the hundreds of bags of clothes and toys that people had dropped off to be sold. I bought lots of nice things, but it was the longest I'd been away from Samuel since I'd had him and it felt very strange. Stuart also found the morning difficult, as he'd never entertained Samuel on his own for that length of time. When I got home at just after one in the afternoon, he was frustrated he'd not managed to get Samuel out of the house between his naps and, consequently, was dying to escape. Whilst he was out for a walk, I tried out some of the things I'd bought Samuel.

First, I showed him the pop-up dinosaur books, which he loved and tried to grab. I got him to help me turn the pages, something he learnt to do by himself very early on and with such a delicate touch. (Months later, I caught him going through my diary, carefully turning each page and examining what I'd written – I wondered what had kept him so quiet!) Next, I strapped on the bumblebee wrist rattle.

He studied the thing with such contempt, then looked up at me as if to say, "What is this?" then back at the rattle.

He proceeded to shake his arm, and when he couldn't get the bumblebee off, frowned and lay there quiet until I could bear it no longer. I removed the rattle and never put it on him again.

By the time he was fourteen weeks old we were becoming quite settled in our routine. I was more confident taking him out, knowing he'd had his naps and feed and, therefore, shouldn't start crying uncontrollably. That was the theory, anyway, and, most of the time it was the case. But not when we went to the baby massage classes run by the health visitors. This was a four-week course held in a draughty church hall and, as the course began in the middle of a cold October, Samuel was not best pleased at being undressed and rubbed in oil.

Stuart and I had noticed at this stage what we called the "three-second warning". Samuel would turn his lips down in an upside-down U shape, his chest would rise and fall to inhale plenty of oxygen, and then he'd let out a huge cry. This was often done in protest at something he didn't like, which was the case when I placed my well-oiled hands on his chest at that first baby massage class.

"It's okay; don't worry," I whispered.

All the other babies were lying contentedly on their towels or changing mats, looking up at their mummies. But it was no good – Samuel let out a loud howl.

"Oh, Samuel!" Caroline, the health visitor, said as everyone turned and looked in our direction.

I picked him up and tried to comfort him, but he wasn't going to let me off the hook that easily. Whilst Caroline tried to get on with the class, I whipped a dummy out of my bag and popped it in his mouth.

"I'm so glad you did that," said Cate, my neighbour. She took a dummy from her own bag to give to her daughter, Megan, who was threatening to follow Samuel's lead.

Cate and I became good friends after that. We'd originally met at antenatal classes and had bumped into each other once afterwards. Megan was born three days before Samuel, and Cate had the good fortune to have Jenny deliver her at home. However, she was experiencing sleepless nights like me and had also resorted to a dummy to try and get her daughter to settle.

Stuart hadn't been at all pleased when I'd given Samuel a dummy to help him sleep. It was always something I'd said I would never do, but weeks of sleepless nights had changed my mind. He loved his dummy, but until he went into hospital he only had it to sleep with, and rarely outside the house. However, it became a real comfort to him in hospital and he wouldn't part with it, even when he was awake and playing. In some of the video footage we took in his last few weeks, we ask him to take his dummy out so we can see his pretty mouth, but he shakes his head vigorously and cuddles into me.

As the weeks went by, we settled into a routine of seeing my mum once a week, going to NCT coffee mornings and baby massage classes. I found out about another NCT group, which was for babies rather than toddlers, and started attending it on Tuesdays. It was at one of these that I met Nicky and her twins, Ben and Libby. I was just beginning to think everyone who attended NCT groups lived in huge houses, when I found out Nicky lived at the end of our street in a Victorian terraced house like ours. At one coffee morning, we discussed the problem of fitting housework around a newborn baby. I never thought I would enjoy such a mundane conversation! Nicky finally snapped us out of it by saying, "When I open my front door, tumbleweed blows out."

We got on really well, and Samuel loved the twins, who were eight months older than him. Once, when he was a bit older, Nicky said to me, "I've got my eye on Samuel for Libby; I think he'll make a great husband for her." We looked over at the babies and saw Samuel and Ben cuddling each other. "Or Ben," she added. "I hadn't thought of it but… as long as they're happy!"

As we got to know each other, I found out Nicky's job was a big part of her life. She worked four days a week at Addenbrooke's Hospital, organising the training and exams for new doctors and surgeons. It was where we would eventually spend much of our time and her visits, whilst we were there, were always comforting as she is such a warm, generous and entertaining person.

When Samuel was three months old Stuart's aunt, Kathleen, died. I didn't feel her funeral would be the right place to introduce Samuel to his extended family, so I decided to stay at home with him. Stuart later said that whilst he was there he suddenly thought how terrible it would be if Samuel died. He supposes he thought this because Samuel was so new in his life, but nonetheless it's interesting he thought of Samuel and not me. How awful and incredible that just seventeen months later Samuel did die.

Those first few months of Samuel's life were happy times, but very tiring. I wanted to press *pause* and take it all in; it was such a change from how our lives had been up until then.

It now seems unbelievable that he's not here. Sometimes things feel like they did before he was born, At others, ironically, it feels more like someone has pressed *pause* so we can catch up on our sleep before he comes back. But, of course, that's not the case.

We made mistakes in those early weeks. We should have focused all our energies on Samuel and not felt pressurised into having so many people round. It's funny because most of our family weren't actually putting pressure on us; we were just very aware they wanted to see him. Of course, it was the same when we later took him home from hospital, knowing his condition was terminal.

Some babies seem to sleep through everything, but Samuel never did, and I worry it was too much for him. Before I knew it we were attending activities or seeing people almost every day and, with hindsight, I don't think it was necessary. Stuart was keen to get me out of the house and with other people to talk to, but he's always been more sociable than me; I think he was imagining how he would feel in my situation.

I really enjoyed the times Samuel and I were able to just relax in the house together, but those times were few and far between. That being said, perhaps it was good we crammed so much into his short life. He was always a sociable baby, so hopefully he took pleasure from our busy schedule.

I enjoyed those first few months, but I often felt anxious. It was all so new, and Samuel's needs would change just as I had got used to doing things a certain way. I hated it if he cried or I thought he was unhappy, and I was always worried I wasn't doing things right. But the months that followed were genuinely blissful.

CHAPTER 4

The Blissful Months

~⌐

FINALLY, WE WERE GETTING MORE sleep. As recommended in the many books I'd now read, we replaced Samuel's two-in-the-morning milk feed with water, and after a couple of weeks he slept right through from eleven at night until five in the morning. This was a gradual process. I gave him milk if he rejected the water, but after a couple of weeks it had worked. I could cope really well with just one night feed, especially as he went back to sleep immediately afterwards. We would then get up at seven to start the day.

I was also beginning to feel more confident as a mother. Samuel had settled effortlessly into the Gina Ford routine, and it was easy to work round the times that he needed a nap or had his milk feeds. We had a nice group of friends, and clubs that we could attend. When the baby massage course came to an end, Cate and I agreed to continue meeting up on Thursday mornings. Samuel and Megan played nicely together and it gave me a chance to relax whilst he was occupied. Cate and I would chat although, being first-time mums, I think at least half our conversations revolved around babies!

Megan was just three days older than Samuel, yet I noticed straight away she was more active. At four months she was sitting unaided and at nine months was walking. I knew she had developed these skills much earlier than average, but I still noted the differences.

Samuel, however, said "Mumma" for the first time at five and a half months – again very early – so I told myself every child develops at different rates.

We have video footage of him where Stuart and I say to him, "Say Mumma."

At first he warms up to it: "Mmm… Mmm," then really goes for it: "Mum… Mum… Mum, mum, mum!"

Much to Stuart's annoyance, he didn't say "Dada" until he was eleven months old, but you can't have everything!

As time went on and he didn't crawl, or even roll over, I began to worry that there was something wrong, although I just couldn't pinpoint what exactly. He did sit unaided at six months (bang on average) which did something to allay my fears, and he began to get about by bottom-shuffling at eleven months. Sometimes I thought he was just skipping the baby stage, but at other times I worried. I couldn't put my finger on exactly what I was worrying about, as he was achieving his milestones and intellectually he was all there.

At about nine months old, when we were at Cate and Megan's house, he sat working out which shapes to put in the shape sorter.

"Did he just put that star in there?" Cate asked incredulously.

"Yes, he did!" I answered, also amazed.

"See, Megan? That's what you can do if you just sit still and concentrate," she said.

On another occasion, whilst I was getting him dressed, I said to him, "Where's your socks?"

Quick as a flash, he picked them up and held them high in the air. He had his "pleased with himself" little smile on his face. I was incredibly proud that he knew what his socks were at just nine months! So, I don't know if there was a problem this early on or if this was just the way he was. Certainly, as time went on, I think it is likely he was delayed physically because of the leukaemia, which caused pain in his legs and resulted in a lack of energy.

Samuel took absolutely everything in and, as he got older, I watched him studying the other children at the clubs we attended and I felt he was logging the differences himself. I know that sounds far too advanced for a baby, but he was very astute and noticed everything. It makes me sad to think he was suffering physically, and perhaps emotionally, and I didn't know. I wish constantly I could go back and make it better for him.

He was almost five months old at Christmas. We had invitations from all the family to spend Christmas with them, but I'm glad we decided to stay at home; the following year Christmas morning was spent in hospital with Samuel having chemotherapy.

Many friends and family members sent Samuel presents in advance of the day, and we were shocked at how much he'd received; it took us all day to open them. We had to keep stopping for breaks, as I think it was too much for him.

We'd just got through one huge pile when my mum and Alan arrived for dinner with a bag crammed full with yet more presents. He was such a well-loved baby, with a big family, that everyone wanted to treat him to something special. What made Stuart and I laugh was that the present he liked best was a reindeer finger puppet made from felt, which Mum had bought from a craft fair for fifty pence. He would giggle and giggle at the way the antlers flopped about as I wiggled the reindeer on my finger. He played with all his other toys, too, but the reindeer was his favourite.

On Boxing Day, it was Stuart's parents' turn to spend the day with Samuel and spoil him rotten. There were yet more presents for him to open and then I tried to put him down for his nap so we could eat dinner. But there was just too much excitement going on for him to sleep. There was the big tree in the dining room with all its sparkly decorations and lights, then there was the table with candles, and crackers with bangs and silly hats. Samuel obviously didn't want to miss out, so he ended up sitting at the table on my lap. It was as if he just couldn't believe what was going on, as he didn't stop giggling throughout the meal. He made us laugh so much that we all struggled to actually eat anything. He was such a happy child.

The arrival of the New Year presented another challenge, as I decided to start weaning him. Samuel was five months old, and the government guidelines recommend exclusive breastfeeding for six months. However, Samuel was bottle fed and, on top of that, my mother-in-law suggested he was hungry. After the initial difficulties we'd had with feeding, I didn't want him to go hungry again.

Just before Christmas I'd tried him on a few teaspoons of baby rice, but then he developed a cold – the only illness he ever had until leukaemia (Stuart always says he saved it all for the big one!) – and just wasn't interested in food, so we decided to wait until January.

As usual, I consulted many books and talked to friends before starting the process. On my first try, Samuel opened his mouth nicely and took the spoonful that was offered to him. Despite predictions that he was hungry, he didn't gobble this down before eagerly awaiting his next mouthful. Rather, he considered thoughtfully this new texture that tasted like milk but wasn't. We continued with a few teaspoons of baby rice at lunchtime for a few days before moving on to puréed carrot, which seemed to be the standard first proper food to try. It didn't go down well. He spat the carrot out and refused to touch it again.

With hindsight, weaning is where it all started to go wrong. Samuel never really took to solid foods, although I've talked to many mums who've told me their children existed on yoghurts and mashed banana for the first few years of life. Fromage frais was the only thing Samuel really liked, but he would also eat my homemade soups.

As time went on I became increasingly aware that he wasn't having the quantities of food that I'd seen other babies eat. I began to add lentils to the soup to increase the protein, and cheese and cream for calories.

But mealtimes were never easy. One morning I tried to get him to eat some baby cereal, but he refused it. My sister had stayed the night and sat at the table with Samuel, eating her own cereal to encourage him to eat. I then tried him with some pieces of fruit; again, he refused them. In the end I resorted to fromage frais, thinking it was better than nothing.

The kitchen is next to the dining room, joined by an archway. As I went over to the fridge and opened the door, Samuel leaned forward in his high chair to see round the archway. When he saw I was getting him his fromage frais he sat back in his chair and gave my sister a very satisfied smile. My sister said, "Somebody knows how to get their own way!" but I wondered if he was just being picky or if there was some other problem.

I knew what I was doing was going against everything the baby books advised, but it just felt wrong to force him to eat foods he didn't like.

One time, when I did keep pushing a particular food, he eventually said, "No." I was so surprised, as he was only about ten months at the time and I hadn't heard him say it before. I'm convinced now that Samuel's aversion to food was because of the leukaemia. Although the books I read are helpful, the advice they and family and friends gave just didn't apply to Samuel.

Because of the difficulties getting him to eat, I gave a lot of thought to nutrition, and I tried many different foods and ways to encourage him. There were odd occasions when I pushed him too far and I really regret this now, but I was desperate to get him to eat so he would grow well and have the energy to move around. I don't believe I gave him any kind of phobia about food, as I soon learnt it was better to be relaxed about it. I would just put some finger foods on his high chair tray so he could feed himself if he wanted.

As the months went by he ate less and less, but I know from talking to other parents in hospital that a poor appetite goes hand in hand with cancer, so I now believe this contributed to Samuel's aversion to food; perhaps from the very beginning.

Eventually food, sleep and everything to do with Samuel dominated my thoughts, and I still didn't feel I was getting it right. But at this stage in his life, just after Christmas, everything seemed to be going reasonably well and we were very happy together. Stuart was still working from home, although money was becoming more and more of a concern. However, we tried never to talk about it in front of Samuel and always just enjoyed our time with him.

Despite being at home and earning little money, Stuart kept to regular office hours when it came to running his business, so I had sole responsibility for Samuel during the day. At half past five, Stuart would switch off his computer and the three of us would spend some time together. Samuel loved music. We'd always played a wide range to him, from nursery rhymes to classical, from Madonna to Metallica, but it soon became apparent that he liked gentle melodies the best. So every evening, after dinner but before his bath, we put some music on and danced with him in our arms. ABBA became a firm favourite; as soon as the opening bars began his face lit up and a huge smile appeared. He seemed to relate to "Angeleyes" in particular; although really a ballad, he would tap out the beat by waving his arm in and out as if he were at a rock concert.

He always had his gorgeous smile on his face which said to me, "Yes, I'm very pleased with everything, thank you."

In February, when Samuel was six months old, we began attending Baby Bounce every Wednesday morning at the local library. Cate and Megan also came and we met many other nice people, including Cheryl and her son, Rowan, who was a month younger than Samuel. I wondered if Cheryl looked scary to Samuel, with her tattoos and piercings, but she had a lovely smile and children just accept people as they are. I'd seen her before, at the breastfeeding workshop, and knew she worked in the library. She had very strong views on letting the baby lead the way with regards to feeding and sleeping. I know the health visitors tried to discourage some of her ideas, especially co-sleeping, but I admired how she stuck to her guns, particularly later when I regretted following their advice about controlled crying. Over the months, I got to know Cheryl better, and she was incredibly kind to Samuel and me. She even visited us once in hospital, when Samuel was in the last month of his life.

Baby Bounce always started the same way, with the song "What Shall We Do with the Bouncing Baby?" sung to the tune of "What Shall We Do with the Drunken Sailor?" and then we would add things like, "We'll clap, clap, clap their hands" or "Tickle, tickle, tickle their tummies, early in the morning". Samuel loved it. Every Wednesday I would wake him up from his morning nap by opening his bedroom curtains and gently singing the opening bars of the song. As Samuel opened his eyes and stretched, he would bounce his little bottom up and down in time with the tune.

Before the music began each week, the babies would sit on a rug by a giant, cuddly octopus and play with the rattles and toys whilst the parents sat on stools around the edge. It was always very popular, and often there would be twenty or more babies and their parents. One morning, when Samuel was about seven and a half months old, I was busy chatting to Cate, whilst Samuel was sitting in the middle of the group on the floor facing Hayley, the lady who ran the group. Everyone was part of the way through the first song when I realised I hadn't picked Samuel up, unlike the other mothers who'd all picked their babies up, and he was now all alone in the middle of the floor. But was he bothered? Not at all. He was bouncing away by himself with a little smile on his face, quite enjoying the attention.

Around the time that Samuel and I started Baby Bounce, Stuart got a job. He'd been running his own business for seven years, but gradually business had tailed off and it was no longer paying enough to keep us all. We decided one of us would have to find work and, for many reasons, we felt it should be Stuart. Ever since Samuel was born Stuart had been applying for different jobs, but although he'd had interviews, he'd not been offered anything. His background was in IT, but after being at home for so long – coupled with the fast pace that everything to do with computers changes – his skills weren't up to date. To make matters worse, he just wasn't interested in the programming side of it any more and wanted to do something different.

After acknowledging that talking was his greatest skill, he decided he wanted to go into teaching. His preference was to teach philosophy but, as his qualifications were in computing and engineering, it seemed it would be a long road to get where he wanted to go, so that idea had to be abandoned. After a while, he decided to look for a job teaching computer skills to adults; he contacted all the local agents with his CV and a letter saying what he was looking for. But by February, with no job forthcoming, he had to accept anything to get us by financially.

So, on Monday 11th February 2008, Stuart started meter reading. It was a horrible time for him, as he had to work incredibly long hours for hardly any money. At the time Meter readers were paid for each reading they took which is fine if they are working on a large estate with outside meters. It's not so great if you are in the middle of the countryside, visiting difficult-to-find farms with tracks a mile long up to a house, where you have to find someone to take you to the meter. All this might take half an hour and you've just earned twenty pence.

This meant he wasn't even earning the minimum wage, but the company got around it by making the meter readers buy franchises, meaning they were self-employed rather than employees. Stuart became very dispirited and we really wondered if he would ever get a good job again. He did, but it took him until July. We then had just two months where everything felt great, before Samuel was diagnosed with leukaemia.

Throughout this time, my very good friend Lizzie would call to check we were all right, as she knew what a struggle it was for us. Lizzie and I had worked together for years when we were in our twenties, and she has always been so kind, giving us many useful things for Samuel. She gave him his little music box, which hung on the side of his cot all his life, whether we were at home or in hospital. Samuel's bath chair also came from Lizzie; we used to call it his throne, as he looked so important lying back in it, waiting to be washed. She also bought him clothes and many other gorgeous things.

It was particularly kind of her because she was struggling with her own enormous worry at the time: just before Christmas she had been diagnosed with breast cancer. She is a beautiful, young woman with three gorgeous children and a loving husband, and it seemed so incredibly unfair. When she called early one morning to tell me she'd found a lump, I could tell how worried she was, but I didn't believe for one minute it would be cancer. I agreed with her that she should get it checked out right away, but I just didn't think Lizzie would get cancer. I know this same delusion affects everyone, because none of our family or friends thought Samuel would die from his leukaemia.

A friend said to me that a young death is not what you expect, hope for or deserve, but nature has many paths. She is right, of course, but until it happens to you it is not something you even think about; it's always something that happens to other people. Another friend once told me life gets serious when you hit thirty. It certainly does.

Stuart made Lizzie a tape of upbeat music to take her mind off things, and she returned the favour over and over again when we were in hospital by sending us parcels with books and magazines for us and toys, balloons, a bubble machine and clothes for Samuel. One day, when we hadn't been in hospital long, she turned up with so many bags of presents she could barely carry them.

When money was really tight, I started gardening for a few neighbours. I had been doing this for a few years in my spare time but didn't know if I would continue once I had Samuel. However, needs must and I really enjoyed that bit of time to myself. I love gardening and can really lose myself when I do it, and often work much longer than I'm supposed to. Usually my mum would look after Samuel whilst I worked, but occasionally Stuart's parents would help out. My mum would always follow my routine, as she came round frequently and knew how easily Samuel would sleep if she stuck to the times. But when Stuart's parents came round he never seemed to settle.

Stuart's dad would say to me in his usual Captain Mainwaring style, "He doesn't want to sleep, Amanda. He's not tired."

No, not when Grandad's energetically bouncing him up and down singing "The Galloping Major" instead of giving him his bottle and calming him down! I think Samuel probably enjoyed all the fun, but he was always a nightmare later, and by bedtime he would be so overtired I just couldn't settle him.

One day, when my mum was looking after Samuel, she took him for a walk into town in his pushchair. She suddenly noticed him bouncing up and down and wondered what he was doing. Then she realised a car was coming up the road with its windows down and music blaring out. Most people would have found it annoying but Samuel just bounced along, enjoying the beat!

Occasionally, Samuel would join me whilst I gardened for the neighbours. This was fine in a garden with a nice lawn for him to play on, but not so easy when I worked in Margaret's gravel garden. As I wheeled him in his pushchair through the side entrance one afternoon, I looked at all the gravel and had visions of Samuel attempting to eat it.

"You're going to have to stay in the pushchair today, poppet," I told him.

Luckily, I'd thought to bring some books with me, so I wheeled him over to the garden table and placed a big pile of baby books next to him. I had just begun weeding when I heard the thud of a book being dropped on the ground. I turned and watched as he took the next book from the top of the pile. He turned the pages with efficiency and when he got to the end he sighed, as if the book just hadn't come up to scratch, before tossing it over the side of his buggy.

He then pursed his lips as if to say, "I'll persevere, but the next one better be good," before taking the next book from the pile.

After half an hour, with all the books now on the ground, he'd had enough. We went back home, and I had to go back that evening to finish off.

I was very keen to give Samuel lots of different experiences. I hoped to make him confident and self-reliant, but I don't think I needed to worry; he always exuded an air of quiet self-assurance.

We took him swimming when he was three months old, which he seemed to enjoy, although he wasn't sure if he should be playing in the water or drinking it. My sister and Stuart came along to his swimming sessions and my mum and Alan watched, so he was the centre of attention again. We knew he loved water as he really enjoyed kicking his legs in the bath as he sat back in his throne. As he got older, he would play with his boats. They had wheels on the bottom and Stuart would make them roll down the back of the bath.

"One, two, three... Wheeeee!" he would say, letting them go to splash into the water.

Samuel watched and copied, making the right noises but not actually saying the words; but sometimes he would forget when to let go so, "One, two, three," became, "Un, oo, ee, ee, ee, ee," and we would have to encourage him to let go!

In the evenings, after Samuel had gone to bed, Stuart and I would wonder at how our lives had changed. Now we had to clear away children's toys and sterilise bottles before we could sit down to relax, and we couldn't go out whenever we liked, as we had before. Our lives now revolved around someone else, but we loved it and found we could talk about Samuel endlessly – something that didn't change even after he died.

Sometimes Stuart and I would wonder what kind of adult Samuel would grow up to be. We could clearly see he was a very strong character who knew his own mind but who was also kind, always sharing his toys and food. He loved music and animals and enjoyed his swimming sessions. Neither Stuart nor I am sporty, but Samuel had a good physique, with a nice straight back and strong shoulders. We hoped to encourage him with sports, as we thought it would help him become a well-rounded individual.

Despite my concerns about Samuel's lack of energy, as soon as he learnt to walk with support, at eleven months old, he would go up and down the length of the house holding either Stuart's hands or mine. It made our backs ache, but Samuel really enjoyed it and he would have the biggest smile on his face from his achievement. I hoped then that I'd just been worrying unnecessarily before, as he now seemed so keen to get about. I still don't know, but he was so strong-minded that it wouldn't surprise me if his desire to walk took precedence over any slight pain or weakness he was feeling.

One day, in an effort to encourage Samuel with sport, Stuart decided to watch Wimbledon with him. I was out at the time, so they were having a boys' session together. I laughed when he told me, thinking, *Yes, very sporty – watching television!*

Stuart laid Samuel back on his lap and they concentrated on the game. Every time one of the players scored a point, Samuel clapped. We could almost hear him saying, "Well done, old boy!" – which rather suggested he'd have grown up to be a spectator, just like his dad.

He always seemed like an adult in a baby's body. Whilst he was watching the tennis he threw his dummy for the first time. It was as if he felt very grown-up and thought, *I don't need that.* In typical Samuel style, he didn't just remove it and put it down on the chair next to him. No. He chucked it across to the other side of the room without even taking his eyes off the telly. He never did anything by halves!

It was also apparent from an early age just how sociable he was. We used to laugh and say he was a man about town. Often he would ride around in his pushchair with his feet resting on the bar. He looked so laid back that many people would comment on it.

Wednesday in Bury St Edmunds is market day and coachloads of elderly people arrive to look around the town. One afternoon I took him to the Abbey Gardens so he could feed the ducks and go on the swings. As we circled the flowerbeds, the old ladies sitting on the benches around the perimeter waved at him and commented on how gorgeous he was. He leant back in his pushchair, put his feet up and waved back as if he was royalty!

He seemed to make friends wherever he went. I knew babies got a lot of attention, but it took me by surprise just how much he got. We would go into our local bakery several times a week for bread and he endeared himself to everyone there. He would go in with his feet up, looking so confident and laid back, but now I wonder if this was an early sign of his legs aching and the beginning of the leukaemia. If it was, I'm amazed at his bravery. He hardly ever made a fuss, and he had every right to do so if he was in pain or feeling unwell. He just stoically endured whatever was thrown at him and made the best of life. He is my constant inspiration.

Ever so slowly, the blissful months drifted into more difficult times. People have asked me when I thought the leukaemia began, but I can't make a clear distinction. The very gradual changes I noticed could have been put down to many things. I now look back at how often I thought he was teething, and wonder if it really was his teeth giving him difficulties, or something more.

The early symptoms were subtle, and as he was our first baby (and babies have trouble with eating and sleeping) it was very hard to detect. Even now I'm uncertain when it all began. As I mentioned before, weaning was very difficult and giving him any milk other than first-stage infant formula didn't seem to agree with him. But the first time I can really remember thinking something was not quite right was in May, when he was nine months old.

CHAPTER 5

Small Changes

MAY WAS A HOT MONTH. Although only the beginning of summer, the weather demanded shorts, T-shirts and a hat for Samuel. I even contemplated sunglasses, but seeing how he threw his hat off after just a few seconds of wearing it, I imagined sunglasses might suffer the same fate. I'd already wheeled over his hat with the pushchair several times; sunglasses wouldn't be so forgiving! I hadn't been able to resist a gorgeous little outfit for the beach, though, with a camper van appliqué on the front. One Sunday at the beginning of May we decided to go to Wells-next-the-Sea so he could wear it. It was Samuel's first trip to the seaside and Mum and Alan arranged to meet us there with a picnic.

I knew I would be changing his routine by going, but I had such a nice image in my head of how he would play in the sand and sea that I thought the disruption would be worth it. The day started off fine. Samuel slept some of the way in his car seat, which I thought meant he would be okay for the rest of the day. We parked the car in the town and met Mum and Alan. Getting to the beach meant a long walk or a ride on a small tourist train with open sides. We took that option and Samuel sat on my lap for the journey. He wasn't particularly happy from the word go and, contrary to my expectations, he didn't seem to enjoy the train ride.

I think most of us are guilty of having expectations of how you would like an occasion to be, but you can't control other people or get them to behave how you want, and to expect them to is unreasonable. By now I'd learnt that even babies are their own people and you have to respect them for who they are. Although I'd fantasised about what it would be like to have a child of my own, life with Samuel was always different from how I'd imagined. This was in part due to his illness, but also because he was such a unique, intelligent individual, who exceeded every expectation I ever had.

Samuel arrived at the beach in a slightly grumpy mood. This was not something we'd experienced before, as he'd always had such a happy demeanour and, although we all commented on it, it was easy to put it down to other things.

"Do you think he's teething?" my mother said.

Mum was always buying little packets of teething granules for him and it was the first explanation we all jumped to whenever something was not quite right.

"No, I think he's just tired; his routine's been altered today."

This became my explanation for all the changes right up to a few days before he was diagnosed. I have no idea (and neither do the consultants) if this was the start of his leukaemia, if something had been lurking undetected from birth, or if it came about just a couple months before the diagnosis. I suspect if a blood test had been done many weeks before the diagnosis (which came at almost fourteen months), it wouldn't have shown anything unusual. However, from my later experiences, I think this very slight change in his personality and subsequent sleeping pattern was the start of him not feeling well.

When we got home that evening Samuel found it difficult to sleep. I dressed him in just his nappy to keep him cool, as his room was well above the recommended eighteen degrees, but he kept waking, and each time I went into his room he had removed his nappy! Luckily, he hadn't had any accidents and I just dressed him again and gave him some milk to settle him, but it was still a very disturbed night.

At around that time I had changed his milk to second-stage formula, which contains iron. I had tried to do this at six months but noticed he woke more with it so, assuming it gave him tummy ache, I changed back. Now I began suspecting the same thing. We were on our third pack of it, and as each pack lasted about a week I'd thought he'd been tolerating it. I remember bumping into my neighbour Nancy along the tree-lined walk through the old cemetery on my way back from town.

"Did we keep you awake last night?" I asked her.

"No. Actually, Esther's been a bit difficult this week as well. I think it must be the heat."

"Maybe," I answered.

I told her about the milk and she agreed it might be worth changing back.

"What about a blackout blind?" she suggested. "Perhaps the light mornings are waking him."

That certainly seemed like a good idea. By now Samuel was sleeping well all night – only needing a feed at 11 p.m. before I went to bed – but as the mornings had been getting lighter he'd started waking earlier and earlier. I bought a blackout blind the next day and, after quite a lot of fuss, Stuart put it up. Initially, I thought these changes had made a difference, but the disrupted nights soon came back, only much worse.

In late June, when Samuel was almost eleven months old, he went for his development health review. This was done by a health visitor, but instead of going to the clinic where Samuel was regularly weighed, we had to go to the office. I was quite interested to see how he was getting on and, as it seemed a significant step in his life, my mum came along too. As I've said before, our lives really centred on him, so any chance for a discussion about this most important person got turned into a big occasion!

I remember feeling very proud as I told the health visitor that Samuel had said "Mumma" at five and a half months. When a baby is born the parents are given a little red book which charts the baby's development, with information about vaccinations, screenings, growth charts and so on. Looking back at the book now, I see that the health visitor has written "Good early speech skills". She has also written "Sociable baby" – which I was very pleased about – but mentions his small appetite. At the time I felt quite concerned about how little food he was eating. I mentioned it to the health visitor, but it didn't seem to be considered very important. Perhaps I didn't put enough emphasis on it myself; maybe more might have been done about it if I had.

I remember she asked what I was feeding him, and she had written in the book: "Good diet; taking finger foods". Perhaps what I was telling her was not uncommon. I left that day with a leaflet on encouraging your child to eat; I expect that in most cases a small appetite doesn't represent a larger problem. Looking back, it makes me realise I had concerns which I felt were serious enough to mention three months before he was diagnosed. It also goes to show that, to everyone else, Samuel appeared perfectly healthy.

A few days later, another big change occurred in our lives: my sister moved in. Her husband had just got a job managing a local farm, so they had to relocate from Norfolk. My sister worked for a large shop in Norwich, but was able to transfer to the chain's Bury St Edmunds store. However, the new jobs started before they could sell their house, so Nancy moved in with us. Richie stayed now and again, but went back to their house (which was over an hour's drive away) most evenings to look after their cat. It didn't help that they worked different hours. Richie started work sometimes as early as five o'clock but finished early, whereas Nancy started work at ten o'clock and finished at six. Overall, life was quite disrupted for them. However, I loved having my sister to stay and, although she didn't like being apart from her husband or her home, she is very glad that she was able to spend so much time with Samuel.

It was when she came to stay that Samuel started to wake in the night more frequently, and initially I wondered if there was a connection. At about six months he'd started to sleep through from eleven o'clock until seven in the morning, and then when he was about seven and a half months we tried to cut out the eleven o'clock feed. It was hit and miss, though, and if he woke I would feed him just to settle him back down quickly.

By the time Samuel got to eleven months, all the books I'd read indicated that he should be going through the night without a milk feed, yet he was beginning to wake more and more often. I assumed he must be hungry, so started feeding him again. I was conscious, however, that if I wasn't careful I could end up in a vicious circle: giving him too much food in the night with the result that he then ate too little during the day. I tried to increase the amount he was eating through the day to counter this, but it was a difficult balancing act, especially as his interest in food seemed to be waning at the same time. Of course, at the time I thought this was because I was overfeeding him in the night; it took a long time to work out there was actually a bigger problem.

Soon after my sister moved in, Samuel started waking between his bedtime of seven and eleven o'clock at night. He had always slept well between these times, so I was surprised when this new development continued night after night. Again, I concocted many theories. One night, Stuart's friend had been round and played with Samuel quite vigorously, right up until his bedtime. We had also given him a digestive biscuit, so that night I convinced myself it was a combination of sugar and excitement which had kept him awake.

Another night, Stuart worked late on the computer in the room next to Samuel's, so he became my suspect for that disturbed night. Around this time, Samuel also learnt how to pull himself up to a sitting position in his cot; I would go in and see him giggling away with his legs dangling through the cot's bars. My instinct was to praise him for this, as it seemed such an accomplishment and I could see he was terribly pleased with himself. However, I knew I had to be firm, so I laid him straight back down.

With my sister around as a distraction, I tried to remain upbeat about these changes, but as time went on they began to wear me down. Usually, he would fall asleep at seven, just as he used to. I would then make everyone's dinner, but just as we sat down to eat, Samuel would wake again. It began to take increasingly longer to settle him, and thirty minutes gradually became an hour and then two. Some nights I would bring Samuel back down just so I could eat – the television would distract him until he became sleepy – but I was always reluctant to do this as I didn't want to set a pattern. Looking back, it seems ridiculous that he could be awake for so long without me realising something was wrong. But initially, the minute I held him he stopped crying and he could be distracted easily by the television. He was also still following his routine during the day – having a two-hour nap at midday without waking.

I clearly remember being upstairs with Samuel, sitting on the little step that led to his bedroom, holding him and rocking him back to sleep. My back ached, but I thought it was important not to keep taking him out of his room; if he was just getting into bad habits this could only exacerbate the problem. It didn't help that family and friends were full of stories of babies and children attempting to get their own way by being downstairs in the evening. Of course, they were all trying to make me feel better as well as offering advice, but to me it just confirmed the problem was purely a psychological one.

Things were starting to get very difficult, but we kept thinking it was all part and parcel of having a baby and it would eventually settle down. Then, at the beginning of July, we had a huge boost to our spirits when Stuart got a new job. After hearing nothing from all the CVs he'd sent out to agents, he'd almost given up hope of ever finding a job that paid more than the minimum wage.

However, searching on the Internet one night he saw a job advertised for a software trainer for an energy management company. The next morning he rang the agents who were advertising the job, but they told him someone had already got to the third interview stage, so the job was probably his. However, Stuart asked them to forward his CV, and shortly afterwards they phoned to say the company was really interested. Stuart had to prepare a presentation – which he did on philosophy, as he figured everyone else would have done something connected to computers – and pretty much straight away they told him he had the job. There was one small fly in the ointment: the job involved international travel and, as Stuart's quite a home-loving person and we had a baby, this didn't appeal to him. When they said he was welcome to take his family with him, he accepted the job.

We'd almost given up hope of him getting a good job, and when he came to tell me it was like the final scene of *An Officer and a Gentleman*. I was working in Margaret's garden when Stuart turned up in his suit to tell me the good news. There I was, with mud on my legs, scratches up my arms from pruning the rose bushes, and a pair of secateurs in my hands, when Stu strolls up. He didn't pick me up and carry me off into the sunset, but I was just as happy as if he had!

To celebrate his achievement we decided to take Samuel to the zoo. Stuart's parents had bought us tickets for Colchester Zoo months before, but we'd wanted to delay going until we thought Samuel was old enough to get the most out of the experience. At almost one year old we thought the time had come. Samuel had already proved himself an animal lover with all the attention he gave to every passing dog, cat, squirrel or duck, so we thought the sight of lions, elephants and monkeys would really excite him. In fact, it was a blue stork that became the focus of all Samuel's attention that day. We still can't work out why; it looked little more exciting than a statue. However, something must have caught his attention, because when we went to lift him off the wall he was sitting on, he had the biggest bottom-wobble we've ever seen. This literally is a bottom-wobble: I picked him up under his arms and he wobbled his bottom in and out so much that I could hardly hold him. This was accompanied by much frowning but, as usual for Samuel, no crying.

The very next day, Monday 14th July, Stuart started his new job. But instead of things getting better for us they continued, ever so slowly, to deteriorate. Samuel's lack of interest in food was worrying me more and more. He still liked his fromage frais, but apart from that all he wanted was finger foods, and this seemed more for the novelty of picking things up rather than really wanting anything to eat. Initially, he quite liked sitting up at the dining-room table with me, but only if he could feed himself and I didn't try to push him into eating.

A few days before his first birthday Cate and I decided to take the children out for a picnic. We both packed up a lunch that included sandwiches, strawberries, yoghurt and organic crisps. Samuel sat happily on the rug and took things out of the basket. He and I watched Megan eagerly eat everything on her plate and then reach over and start on Samuel's. I remember his bemused look as he nibbled on a strawberry; I just couldn't get over the difference. I played it down, but the difference in their appetites really concerned me. I tried to encourage Samuel to eat a sandwich, but he really wasn't interested. I kept wondering why he wasn't hungry. Was I feeding him too much milk? Did he not like the food I was giving him? I'd tried giving him food I'd made, jars of bought baby food and meals in cafés. I had thought watching Megan eat might encourage him, but he just seemed to find it amusing and began passing her more food. I remember discussing it with Cate as she drove us back to Bury St Edmunds.

"It sounds like he needs more filling food during the day so he'll sleep at night," she said.

"That's what I've been thinking, but he just doesn't seem to want it."

"Maybe you need to make eating more fun for him. I'll lend you some of my recipe books and also a book on getting your baby to sleep, which is a bit softer than Gina Ford."

I collected the books the next time I saw her, and read them cover to cover, even though I was so tired all I wanted to do was sleep. It didn't help that Megan was so physically advanced, and Cate looked like Nigella Lawson. My inability to get Samuel to sleep and eat was making me feel about as far from a domestic goddess as you could get. Of course, like most new mothers, I was insecure about my parenting skills and I blamed myself for all the problems Samuel was having. I really thought I must be doing something wrong and reasoned that if I just read the right books and tried different things, eventually I would find the answer. We couldn't keep going on like this; I was getting overtired and every day seemed to take matters more and more in the wrong direction.

On 2nd August 2008, we had a nice diversion from all our worries: Samuel James Murray was one year old. It feels like such an achievement for both child and parents to get to that milestone. The first year of a baby's life is not an easy one, but despite the difficulties we were having we still felt as if a celebration was in order.

The night before his birthday, Stuart, my sister Nancy and I spent the evening blowing up balloons with "1 year old" written on them. We also pumped up an inflatable lion I'd bought to encourage Samuel to pull himself up and stand, as I'd been feeling slightly worried that he wasn't yet doing this. However, as he was happy to walk when holding our hands, I'd not said much to anyone about my concern; I can't even remember now if I'd mentioned it to Stuart. Also, I knew I was comparing him with Megan, who'd walked at nine months old, and I knew everyone would tell me not to compare because children are all different.

On the morning of his birthday, I opened Samuel's cards in bed with him whilst Stuart filmed the whole event. We were so involved in showing him his cards that at the time neither of us realised he kept looking at the camera and purposefully blinking. It looks so sweet when we watch it back now, as if he was having a good time regardless of what Mummy and Daddy were doing.

When we brought him downstairs his Aunty Nancy was waiting for him, along with the lion and balloons. He was so excited by the balloons that he became annoyed with us when we tried to get him to open his presents. On the video it now makes us laugh to see us three adults playing with his moving bop-along alien whilst he sits happily throwing the balloons in the air.

After the essential midday nap, we piled food into the boot of the car and collected our friend Angela. We stopped at a shop in town to collect more balloons – helium-filled ones for a table display – then headed to Stuart's parents' house for the party. We only had a small car and I can't believe we got four adults, a baby in a car seat, food, a birthday cake and balloons into it. When we arrived, Stuart's parents, Cynthia and Derek, had set up a table for all the food, and the rest of our family soon arrived and filled the table. I am really glad we made so much effort for his first birthday. Samuel was completely surrounded by all the people who loved him and he thoroughly enjoyed being the centre of attention (just for a change!) that day. He particularly liked being with his three male cousins (Patrick, Joe and Jonny; aged twelve, fourteen and sixteen), as they entertained him so well with the balloons, and his female cousins (Hannah and Ellen; aged nineteen and sixteen) who gave him endless cuddles.

It's lovely looking back at the photographs and video footage. As usual, Samuel was completely spoilt by all his relatives and friends, but I still think the balloons gave him more enjoyment than anything else. One exception to that might have been the little wooden trike bought by my mum. His face really lit up when it was wheeled over to him. We always laughed when he sat on it, as he would never push himself. Instead, he held his feet up and smiled his gorgeous smile at us until we were compelled to push him along.

Looking back at the video footage, I can see he puts his foot down every now and again to steady himself, which shows he was perfectly capable of pushing himself, but he must have thought, *Why bother when so many other people want to do it for me?*

Although we all had a lovely day, Stuart's sister, Debbie, did comment at one point that Samuel seemed to go off into a world of his own sometimes. I had noticed this myself; not just on his birthday, but on other occasions too.

Once, I'd been out with my mum in town and she'd said to me, "Samuel has such a lovely life; he's given so much love and attention and you never tell him off. He only ever gets positive feedback from you."

I just smiled and said, "I try," but in the back of my mind I thought to myself, *So why isn't he happy?*

Actually, it wasn't even that he seemed *un*happy. He was never a whiny baby, but he no longer seemed to be giggly or full of energy and, occasionally, he did appear lost in his own thoughts.

I also noticed on his birthday that he looked very hot. In fact, his hair was quite damp, which I thought was unusual. It was a muggy day and I felt hot myself, so I put it down to the weather, but I have since found out that hot sweats can be a sign of cancer.

At one point during his party I sat Samuel on the floor with me and tried to get him interested in his party food. He picked at it for a bit, and I think he quite liked the novelty of us sitting on the floor together sharing food from one plate, but he soon bottom-shuffled off to see everyone else.

When the cake was produced – complete with a candle shaped like a number one – everyone sang "Happy Birthday" to Samuel. He obviously enjoyed everyone singing and he sat very proudly as he listened to us all. However, he didn't understand the concept of blowing out the candle, and I felt terrible when I did it for him and he cried. So, of course, the candle was relit and everyone sang for him again!

"Can Samuel have a piece of cake?" Patrick asked afterwards.

"No, I don't think he better; it might be a bit too sugary for him," I answered.

I now can't believe I didn't let him have any. As time went on I became relieved if he ate anything at all, and in hospital the food policy was "anything goes". This advice came from the consultants, nurses, chef and nutritionists, because any calories were better than none; this quickly became my policy as well. At the time of his party I was still trying to follow a healthy diet. I had heard it was all too easy for children to take a liking to sweet food and then not eat their main meals, and I felt we were having enough problems in the eating department without adding to them.

Just a couple of days after his birthday, I took Samuel to the health visitors to be weighed. I was worried to see he had only put on three and a half ounces since his development review six weeks previously. This meant he had slipped down a centile. It says in the little red book that the child should be referred to a paediatrician if the curve veers upwards or downwards by the width of one centile band. Well, Samuel's weight had now veered downwards by one and a half centiles, but still the health visitor felt nothing was wrong, so I continued to blame myself.

I vowed to do more to sort out Samuel's feeding and sleeping issues. I asked many of my friends what they were feeding their children, and copied some of their ideas. I tried going back to baby porridge for breakfast – mixed with lots of formula as he was still taking all his milk – but he would have two or three teaspoons and then want no more. I then offered him cereal and even got one that contained chocolate chips, but again, he would only eat one or two teaspoons. I then tried fromage frais and, after that, some raisins.

I would often take him to a café late morning to have a warm cheese scone, which he would pick at, perhaps because it was a novelty for him. I tried so many recipes and found that he liked sweeter things best, or anything with cheese in it. My most successful meal was baby pasta mixed with a sauce I made myself from tomatoes, sweet potatoes, lentils (for protein) and cheese. I also found if I fed him in front of the television he would eat more, as he was concentrating on what he was watching. This went against everything I believed in. I never wanted to be one of those mothers who just left their children in front of the TV, so I played him educational baby DVDs to assuage my guilt.

On 12th August we had the opportunity for a break as Stuart had to do some training in Newcastle for a couple of days. My mum, sister and Stuart's parents offered to take it in turns to stay at our house and look after Samuel. The day before we went, I made a fish pie that Stuart's parents could eat with Samuel for lunch, as they were doing the first shift. I then got in many different foods and wrote a detailed list of when he should eat and sleep. In the morning I made up bottles of formula for him and then we left for Newcastle.

Stuart had booked us into a hotel overlooking the River Tyne; quite central so I could wander around easily. Almost as soon as we'd booked in he left for his appointment, so I had a few hours to do whatever I wanted before he got back. However, it was pouring with rain and I was exhausted. I was getting about four or five hours of broken sleep a night at this stage and that, coupled with the worry and strain of looking after Samuel every day, was really wearing me out. So, instead of going out, I ran myself a huge bubble bath and sank into it with relief. After wallowing in the water for some time, I dried myself and went to bed.

An hour later Stuart returned and we got ready to go out for dinner. Just before we did we phoned home to see how Samuel was. According to Stuart's parents, he was fine. He hadn't eaten the fish pie but had eaten a biscuit. He hadn't wanted to have a nap, but he had been playing quite happily with them and had worn Derek out by getting him to hold his hands whilst he walked up and down the house. We'd bought Samuel a little trolley filled with bricks to hold onto whilst he walked, but it took him a little while to get the hang of it. In fact, the first time he held onto the bar the trolley moved forward but his feet stayed put, so he ended up almost horizontal before we got hold of him and stood him upright again. After that he wasn't so keen, but Stuart spent many hours walking behind him, pushing his feet forward with his own so he would understand what he was supposed to do; eventually he got the hang of it. Anyway, even though

Cynthia and Derek weren't worried that Samuel hadn't eaten or slept much, I felt anxious that things weren't right.

That night when we went back to the hotel I looked forward to my first really good night's sleep in over a year but, typically, I didn't sleep well. I don't know if this was because of worry or if I had just got used to less sleep, but I was frustrated that I'd not made the most of the opportunity when it was given to me. However, I did feel better for the break and we both looked forward to seeing Samuel again and hearing how my mum and Nancy had got on with him during the night.

Samuel was standing on the sofa looking out the window when we pulled up to our house. However, unlike when he was younger, he didn't smile or take a great deal of interest in us when we came in.

"Well, don't seem *too* happy to see us, Samuel!" Stuart joked when we came in.

"Don't say that; he's probably just tired," I said, always eager to jump to his defence.

Obviously, we can now understand that when you don't feel well you don't particularly feel like smiling. At the time, I put this change in his personality down to him growing into the person he was going to become. But I did, on many occasions, think it was getting harder and harder to make him happy, despite putting more and more effort into it.

"How did he sleep?" I asked Mum as soon as we sat down.

"He found it hard to settle when we first put him to bed, so Nancy and I decided to bring him back down to watch *Emmerdale*."

She did look a bit guilty when she said this, as she knew I tried not to do it.

"Did he enjoy it?"

She laughed. "He was only down for an hour or so, then he had a bit more milk and then he went to sleep."

"Did he wake up in the night?"

"Yes. I think his teeth are bothering him. I gave him some Calpol and a packet of his teething granules and then he settled back down. He woke up early this morning, though, so I gave him some more Calpol and milk and he slept through until twenty to nine."

"Twenty to nine? He's always up by seven at the latest with me!"

I really envied my mum her lie-in; it sounded like she'd had a better night's sleep than I had. With hindsight, I now know it was the pain that woke Samuel, and the pain relief that was helping him back to sleep.

"I'm not sure if it's a good idea to be giving him all that Calpol," Stuart said.

"Well, you can't expect him to suffer if he's in pain, and I really think his teeth are bothering him," my mum replied.

"Has he eaten much?" I asked.

"Not a full meal – he's snacked on things. He's had a couple of fromage frais and a biscuit. Oh, and a few raisins."

Later that evening, Stuart phoned his parents to ask them how they had got on. They also reported that they thought he might be teething, as he didn't seem quite right.

In some ways I felt relieved to know he'd not eaten any better with our parents than with us, and it seemed the only reason he'd slept was because of the Calpol. For the next week I followed my mum's lead and gave him Calpol and teething granules, but by the bank holiday weekend, Saturday 23rd August, I was feeling so sleep deprived (as well as hormonal) that I was barely able to keep it to-gether. At one point I really lost my temper but, luckily, took it out on Stuart rather than Samuel. I shouted at him for no good reason at all and then stormed out of the house. I think I was gone for less than an hour and when I came back I apologised, but I do feel bad about my behaviour because the one who was really suffering was Samuel.

The next day, in an attempt to gain some control over the situation, I began a sleep diary for Samuel. This is how our night went that Sunday:

7.00 p.m.	Settled in bed without dummy
8.40 p.m.	Woke; comforted in cot with dummy
9.07 p.m.	Settled
12.10 p.m.	Woke; fed 4 oz milk; wouldn't settle
12.50 p.m.	Settled
1.40 a.m.	Woke; fed 3 oz milk; settled
5.30 a.m.	Woke; fed 3 oz milk; tried to settle for an hour; up 6.30 a.m.

The following day I also kept a log of what he ate and how he slept. The diary went like this:

7.30 a.m.	Breakfast – some raisins
9.00 a.m.	Napped for 1 hour 20 mins
11.00 a.m.	Snack ¾ base of a hot cross bun (my attempt to get him to eat some carbohydrates with his raisins!)
12.10 p.m.	Napped for 20 mins
1.00 p.m.	Snack ¼ slice of cheese on toast
3.30 p.m.	Nap 10 mins in car
5.00 p.m.	Dinner, in front of TV – small bowl of pork and mango (from a jar), 1 fromage frais and ½ a chocolate biscuit

As you can see, the routine I'd so carefully followed for the first year of Samuel's life was now in disarray. I was torn between waking him up from his morning nap (so he would sleep longer at midday) and thinking he desperately needed his sleep because he hadn't had much the night before. You can see from the diary that I attempted both methods. Unfortunately, I ended up feeling equally guilty that I'd done the wrong thing whichever way I tried.

We do have one nice memory of that weekend, however, as we took a trip to a boating lake near us called Lackford Lakes. After a little nap in the car, Samuel seemed raring to go and even held my hands and walked along the dirt track in hot pursuit of a pheasant that he felt he must befriend. It was such a cute sight. Another thing that lifted our spirits that day was Samuel discovering blackberries. What made it all the funnier was the sign as you enter the lakes saying: "Please do not pick the blackberries but leave them for the wildlife." Being a stickler for rules, I normally wouldn't dream of disobeying. However, that day I felt my son's needs were greater, so consequently Samuel left the lakes with dark red blackberry juice around his mouth and down the front of his T-shirt, and with such a grand expression on his face that we thought no one would dare question him!

The diary entries for the night of Monday 25th August were even worse than the previous night:

7.00 p.m.	Bed; wouldn't settle
7.30 p.m.	Settled in cot after cuddling on bed
8.00 p.m.	Woke; fed milk; gave Calpol; very upset
9.00 p.m.	Settled
9.40 p.m.	Woke; grizzled; went back to sleep
10.00 p.m.	Woke; covered with blanket; went back to sleep
10.20 p.m.	Woke; grizzled; went back to sleep
11.20 p.m.	Woke; fed milk; went back to sleep
12.00 a.m.	Woke; very upset; fed; cuddled

1.00 a.m.	Settled
4.30 a.m.	Woke; very upset; went in, gave water; tucked back in
5.15 a.m.	Settled
6.50 a.m.	Up

The next day, whilst I was trying to encourage Samuel to eat some lunch, my neighbour Nancy came round. Samuel was sitting in his high chair but wouldn't put his legs down; he balanced them on top of his tray instead.

I remember Nancy commented on it and said how funny it was, but I was at the stage of thinking, *Oh well, if it means he'll eat something then why worry?*

I told Nancy about the sleep diary.

"That's a good idea," she said, "because the next day you sometimes look at it and think, 'Actually, that's not as bad as it seemed in the night.'"

"Well, what do you make of this, then?" I asked and gave her my diary.

"Oh, no! That's bad," she said.

I had to laugh. "Yes, I thought so as well."

"I don't know what to suggest," she said.

"I'm feeling at a loss, myself."

Over the next couple of days I continued with my diary. Then, on the Thursday, my friend Sharon came round in the afternoon with her son, Austin, who was three months younger than Samuel. When she turned up I remember fighting back the tears. I was so tired all I wanted to do was sleep, but I had been unable to get Samuel to have his midday nap. Initially, I had been hopeful he would have a long sleep as he'd had what, for him, was quite a substantial dinner: a bowl of pasta and half a fromage frais. But afterwards he just wouldn't set-tle and kept crying. Perhaps part of the problem was my own anxiety. Samuel was always very sensitive and seemed to intuitively pick up on my feelings. I was desperate to sleep, so I'm sure I wasn't providing the degree of motherly nurture a sick child needs. But I didn't know he was sick; I just felt confused and frustrated.

I had tried putting him in the garden in his pram and rocking him back and forth, but it made no difference. Perhaps I should have given up and played with him, but I don't think he was in any mood to play either. By three o'clock, I tried putting him in his cot again, and it was shortly afterwards that Sharon knocked on the door.

"Are you okay?" she asked, looking concerned.

"I just can't get Samuel to sleep. He's not even having his daytime naps now and I just don't know what to do."

"He's playing you up, Amanda," she said kindly. "My boys were just the same. They get to this age and they start wanting things their own way."

"Maybe; I just don't know," I said.

"He's quiet," Sharon commented.

"Yes, that's strange. He's been crying for about two hours."

I went upstairs to his bedroom. The curtains were wide open and we had been talking noisily downstairs, but Samuel was sound asleep. I couldn't help smiling. He looked so gorgeous, but I also felt incredulous. All that time I'd spent rocking him and comforting him and yet he'd fallen asleep all by himself. I wondered if I was just mak-ing things worse.

"He's asleep," I said when I came back downstairs.

"They all try it on, Amanda. He'll be all right."

Samuel slept for two hours, but that night it was so bad I didn't even have time to write in my diary. I decided there and then that enough was enough, and I made the decision to book him a doctor's appointment. Maybe they would say it was teething or just a stage he was going through, but I suddenly wondered if he could have an ear or throat infection that was causing all these problems. I hated to think he might be in pain and I hadn't realised it. The next morning I telephoned the surgery. We couldn't get in with Dr Masters. However, there was an appointment available with another doctor later that day. I booked the appointment gratefully.

CHAPTER 6

The Referral

~

"HE'S GORGEOUS!" THE YOUNG FEMALE doctor said, as she tickled Samuel's tummy.

He smiled, enjoying the attention. He didn't seem as off-key as he had for the past few weeks.

"I'm not sure what's wrong with him, but he just doesn't seem right," I told her. "He's not eating much and he's waking up more and more in the night."

"Do you think he's teething?" she asked.

"Well, that's what my family say, but I'm a bit worried it might be something else, like an ear or throat infection. I don't want to think I've missed something."

She looked in his ears and down his throat.

"All clear there."

"So do you think he's just teething?"

"I think so. It can cause them problems sometimes. Have you tried giving him Calpol?"

"Yes. And teething granules."

"Does it help?"

"It does seem to help him sleep."

"Well, keep doing that, but come back if there are any more problems." She tickled Samuel again and he laughed. "You can come back any time," she told him.

When we left her surgery, I should have felt relieved, but I didn't. It just didn't seem to fit together. It seemed that either Samuel was really suffering badly with his teeth coming through, or he was just playing up. I didn't know anybody else whose child was waking this much in the night, but couldn't believe he was just being difficult. It didn't seem possible a child this young could deliberately act in this way, and I also couldn't see why he would. He always had plenty of attention from me, so it wasn't that he was deprived of love and affection. He also had his daddy and aunty living with him, giving him more attention. He had a very stable life and was never told off. I just couldn't work it out. Was it possible I was giving him too much of my time? Could it be that I needed to give him a bit of space to play on his own and relax? But, if that were the case, then why did he seem to want to spend more and more time just sitting on my lap? Samuel's problems occupied my every waking thought, but I struggled to find answers.

I discussed it with Stuart daily, but he had no more answers than I did.

On Sunday 31st August, my diary entries looked like this:

7.00 p.m.	Bed with dummy
8.30 p.m.	Woke; tried to comfort in cot
8.50 p.m.	Took out of Grobag and kissed; settled him down again and left room
9.08 p.m.	Went in and comforted

9.20 p.m.   Asleep
10.08 p.m.   Woke; comforted in cot
10.20 p.m.   Asleep

After this, Stuart has written the following:

"Don't let me ever hear you say you're not a good mummy: this diary says it all. I want to take you out of your Grobag and give you a kiss! I love both you and Sam with all my heart and this is exactly the right approach to get things back on track. I'm sorry if I've been preoccupied and not as much help as I should have been. Hopefully things will settle down and we'll be back on track soon. Well done, and I love you!"

It was little things like this that kept me going. Thank God we have each other. I don't know how a single parent would have survived this. But, then again, I know from experience that you do just survive, because you have to. You cope because you have no choice but to keep going. Although Stuart had apologised for being preoccupied and not helping as much as he'd like to, he was struggling with a new and demanding job, so he had every justification for having his attention diverted. Besides, as I had chosen to be a full-time mother, I felt the responsibility was mine.

We got through another weekend, and then another week, but things were no better. I contemplated going back to the doctors, but didn't feel they would say anything different. The health centre was open on Mondays and, although I felt the health visitors concentrated more on younger babies, I decided to see if they could offer any help. At this point, I still didn't think Samuel was ill, but I was very confused by his behaviour. I had read so many books about babies with sleeping and eating problems, and had tried nearly every technique suggested. It was now 8th September.

I wrote Samuel's name in the book then took a seat and waited for our turn. I was pleased when a health visitor who knew Samuel well called us to the table for weighing.

"How's Samuel?" she asked.

"Not good. Sleeping has become a big problem and I'm struggling to get him to eat anything."

She frowned and asked, "Is he teething?"

"I don't know. The doctor said that but I'm beginning to wonder if it's more than that."

I started to undress Samuel to weigh him.

"It's okay; you don't need to undress him. When they reach a year we just weigh them in their clothes."

We sat Samuel on the scales.   She frowned again.

"He's levelled off," she said.

"Now I'm really worried."

"Why?" she asked with a sigh.

"Because he's not eating. Something's not right."

I was so frustrated. I couldn't believe she'd sighed.

"They often level off at this age. They're up and about, running arou—"

"He's not."

"What?"

"He's not running around. In fact, he's not doing much at all. He just wants to sit on my lap."

"They all go through a clingy stage."

"It's not just that – he's not eating or sleeping. I don't know what's wrong with him."

She sighed again. I needed help more than anything. I thought that was the whole point of health visitors, but the impression I was getting was that they did little more than weigh babies and run baby massage classes.

"Okay… what's he eating?" she asked, reluctantly.

I listed the foods I tried to get him to eat and she listened, but I don't remember her suggesting anything else. I then told her about the problems we were having with his sleeping and how often he was waking at night.

"We can't keep going on like this," I told her. "I've read loads of books and tried lots of techniques but nothing's working."

"Have you tried controlled crying?"

"Not really. Just recently I've tried comforting him in his cot, but he's still waking just as much."

She handed me a leaflet on controlled crying.

"I think you'll have to be firm with him. If you try this method, it should take just a few days."

She wrote in Samuel's red book: "Clinic – weight static – discussed feeding – night-time waking – leaflet re: controlled crying given."

It's the last entry in his red book.

When I got outside, I opened the page where Samuel's weight had been recorded. He had lost four and a half ounces. Taking into account the fact that this time he was wearing clothes and the previous time he wasn't, then it was probably more. And this health visitor had treated us like we were a nuisance. It looked like we were on our own.

That afternoon I came up with another idea to get Samuel interested in food: I decided to get him cooking with me. I knew people did this with older children, and as he was only thirteen and a half months I didn't know if it was a bit ambitious, but anything was worth a go. I put him in his high chair and sat him in the kitchen. Next, I opened the fridge and took out a plastic tub with the blackberries that we had collected the day before, and put it on his tray. I then got out an ovenproof dish and put that on his tray as well.

"We're going to make blackberry and apple crumble." I don't suppose he understood what I was saying, but he smiled anyway. "You put the blackberries from this tub into this one," I said, demonstrating, "and Mummy will cut up the apples."

Straight away Samuel got on with his task, every now and again stopping to pop a blackberry into his mouth, which was what I hoped he would do. He was so delicate with the blackberries as he transferred them neatly into the dish. I stood alongside him, peeling and chopping the apples. After a while, I put the first piece of apple into the dish alongside Samuel's carefully placed blackberries. He had just taken a blackberry out of the tub and went to put it in the dish only to find a rogue apple piece messing up his careful design. He frowned, placed the blackberry in the dish, and then picked up the piece of apple. He held it up for inspection, frowned some more, then dropped it over the side of his high chair.

I laughed so much and, when he wasn't looking, put another piece of apple in the dish just to see what he would do. Of course, he did exactly the same thing. So I saved the remainder of the apple and only put it in with the blackberries when he had completed his important task and wasn't looking!

I was pleased that he did eat some of the blackberry and apple crumble, but he was hardly eager. It always seemed that he was just trying food as a new experience, rather than eating because he was hungry. And this was what bothered me. It wasn't just the small amount of food that he was consuming; he just wasn't keen on eating. It was as if he didn't have an appetite at all.

That night, for some reason – probably exhaustion – Samuel slept from seven o'clock until one in the morning. My diary entry reads:

7.00 p.m.   In cot; went down well without dummy

However, he woke at one and was awake for the next five hours until 6 a.m., then he went back to sleep until quarter to nine. This was my first attempt at controlled crying and it was terrible. However, the literature had explained that the first night can be bad and it would improve. I knew I wasn't supposed to be feeding him but, after two hours of crying with me going in as suggested, I decide to give him water: I thought after all that crying he must be dehydrated. At twenty to six I give him two spoonfuls of cereal and half a bottle of milk. Eventually, he slept.

During this terrible time, Stuart slept in the spare bedroom. My sister took the week off work so she didn't have to stay whilst we attempted the controlled crying. It was a daunting exercise to undertake as a mother, but worse than that, it remains one of my biggest regrets. Samuel was desperately ill. He would have been suffering from terrible headaches and pains in his legs. But instead of being cuddled and comforted, he was being left to cry, in the dark, on his own. If I could go back and change anything it would be that. My beautiful boy means more to me than anything, and I treated him like this.

But at the time I did it, lying in bed crying as I listened to Samuel's cries, I told myself it was for the best. I thought we'd run out of options. I had read about, and spoken to, other mums who'd tried controlled crying, so I reasoned it wasn't cruel. But it felt unbearably cruel. After nine painful nights of trying this technique, I vowed never again to do what authority figures dictated, if it didn't feel right to me. From now on, I would trust my better judgement.

So that day, Tuesday 16th September, I decided to go back to the doctors' surgery. I made an appointment to see an older, more experienced doctor, and I again racked my brains for a reason for Samuel's problems. I had noticed when changing him over the past few days he had some dry nappies. I didn't know the reason for this, but now I wonder if it could have been dehydration because I had stopped giving him milk in the night. However, at the time I wondered if he had a urine infection.

The doctor listened to my explanation of Samuel's symptoms and then asked to examine him. I undressed him and the doctor pushed down on his bladder to see if it was giving him any pain. I was pleased to see Samuel's personality hadn't diminished, as he frowned with annoyance. I did feel he was given a more thorough examination this time. The doctor also checked his throat and ears to see if there was an infection.

"Well, I can't find anything obviously wrong."

The doctor looked puzzled as he said this, and I waited for him to make a suggestion. "He looks like he might have a bit of a cold coming."

He thought for a moment.

"See how he is this week, and if there's no improvement, bring him back."

I walked out of his office, despairing. I was glad he'd checked Samuel over and, of course, I didn't want him to be ill, but clearly something was wrong. I just didn't know what. The next day I decided to phone the health visitors again. I left three messages on their answering machine, and sometime around midday a lady called back. My mum had just arrived to see us, and I sat on the sofa facing her as I took the call and tried to fight back the tears. I explained, again, how bad our nights were and that the controlled crying hadn't worked. I also told her about the doctor's appointments and how they had found nothing wrong.

I said to her, "We can't go on like this any longer; I'm beyond desperate."

She promised someone would call me back urgently to arrange an appointment to come over and sort out a sleeping solution. I left two more messages that week to arrange that appointment, but by the time someone came back to me Samuel had already been diagnosed with leukaemia.

That afternoon Mum and I took Samuel out. We stopped at a café and tried to get him to eat a cheese scone. He managed quite a few mouthfuls, which seemed to perk him up a bit.

Encouraged, I said to Mum, "Why don't we get him measured for some shoes?"

In some ways this was a ridiculous idea, as Samuel was doing little more than sitting on my lap. On the other hand, summer was fast turning to autumn and he would need some shoes. I reasoned he should have proper walking shoes as it couldn't be long before he would be walking unaided.

As usual, Mum was excited by the idea of a bit of shopping – especially if it involved Samuel – so off we went to Clarks to get his feet measured. I pushed Samuel in his pushchair over to the children's area. The shoes looked so cute and suddenly I couldn't wait to get him into a little pair and see him toddling about. Of course, with his lack of energy at the time, this was complete fantasy, but it was how I wanted life to be for him.

I saw two pairs of shoes I liked better than the others: one red and the other beige. They looked so trendy and I could imagine him trotting around in them. I handed them both to Samuel. His face lit up. Despite everything he must have been feeling, I got the distinct impression that he, too, wanted to be walking around. He knew immediately what they were and he let me get him out of his pushchair without a murmur. I now believe it hurt him every time he was picked up, so the fact that he didn't make a sound then shows me he was fully focused on having those shoes on his feet!

The assistant measured his feet, then we tried him in the beige shoes. He sat on my lap, looked down at his feet, and smiled. The assistant asked me to stand him on his feet so she could check they still fitted. As I put him down, he cried out. I picked him up then tried again. He really cried out this time and whimpered whilst the assistant felt his feet. I was worried by this behaviour, because he'd always loved standing and walking. Whilst I had noticed he was spending more and more time on my lap, I hadn't realised that now he didn't like standing up at all.

We decided on the beige ones and the assistant took a photograph of him in his first, and only, pair of proper shoes. I wanted him to be smiling in his picture so I tickled him as she took it, but I couldn't help worrying that, added to everything else, he now didn't want to stand on his feet. It's funny, but I must have kept this additional worry to myself, as Stuart said he had no idea about this until I mentioned it to the doctor the following Monday.

That week my sister had come back to stay after her break from work. The controlled crying had made little difference to Samuel's sleeping and waking times, so I was now back to rocking him to sleep whenever he woke up. This was difficult because I was so aware of keeping Stuart and my sister awake, knowing they both had to go to work the next day. During the week I resorted more and more to Calpol. It got so bad in the end that I was frantically waiting for the time to be up so I could give him some more.

Samuel had now developed a cold and looked quite pale. I decided to buy him a tonic to build him up. I chose one that contained iron and mixed it into his food and drink. However, he noticed the different flavour, so I was torn between giving him only a teaspoon of food mixed with the tonic as opposed to three teaspoons of food without tonic. As I offered him a spoonful of food I looked closely at him and wondered if he could be anaemic. He was always pale-skinned so it was hard to tell, but now there seemed to be no colour in his cheeks at all. It amazes me, looking back, that he didn't cry more or make a fuss. Instead, it seemed as if he was bravely bearing his pain, although at the time I didn't realise how much pain he was in.

On the Thursday morning, 18th September, after another night of no sleep, my sister volunteered to take Samuel out so I could catch up with my rest. We put him in his pushchair and before they went out the door I gave him a little malted milk biscuit to take with him. My sister took him to the park and put him in the swing. He allowed her to push him without making a sound, but he remained locked inside himself. She took him out of the swing and over to the aviary to look at the colourful budgies and parrots, but again, he didn't react. Then they walked around the town before coming home. When he came through the door he was still clutching his uneaten malted milk biscuit.

"How was he?" I asked.

"Quiet. I don't think he's very well. He's obviously got this cold but he really doesn't seem himself."

"I know." I sighed.

"Do you think it's just these sleepless nights, or his teeth, or…?"

I shook my head. "I don't know."

"Neither do I, but I felt really sorry for him. He didn't enjoy the swings, or the birds, or anything."

Nancy went to work and Samuel and I struggled on for another day. I was so tired I was finding it hard to stay focused and alert, but I continued trying to get him to eat and sleep.

The next day, we went to our neighbour's for the music group she ran, called Tadpole Tunes. This was only the third time Samuel had been, and I had been looking forward to him going regularly now he was old enough. Whilst we all sat round in Nancy's living room, waiting for the session to begin, I overheard a mother I didn't know talking about what a terrible time she was having getting her little boy to sleep. I latched on to the conversation right away, desperate to hear what she was saying.

"He's ended up in bed with me nearly every night," she said.

So far I had resisted this option, as I thought it would start a pattern we would never get out of, but I had taken Samuel downstairs some nights when things had got too bad as I was worried about Stuart and my sister getting no sleep.

"It's the easiest option," she continued, "otherwise I'll be up and down all night."

As I listened to her I thought maybe Samuel's sleep pattern was just a bad habit we'd got into. But, of course, this ignored all the other problems. However, it was easy at the time to convince myself I could resolve this on my own – especially as the doctor and health visitors didn't seem to think there was a problem.

If things are bad tonight, I'll put him in bed with me, I thought.

Samuel didn't enjoy the music session and just wanted to stay huddled up on my lap. Whenever I picked him up or moved him around he would cry out, although this was never loud and he didn't whine or cry constantly. Now, when I see children crying and moaning for no reason, I always think how bravely Samuel dealt with his pain. He never really cried or whinged – perhaps he didn't have the energy.

I think I'd become so used to Samuel being like this I didn't see just how unusual his behaviour was. At one point, our neighbour

Nancy came over and gave him a biscuit, which he took but didn't eat, and she looked at him with concern.

"Oh, Samuel!" she exclaimed.

I remember wanting to ask her what she thought. However, I know now that she never thought there was anything really wrong. However, just before his diagnosis she'd mentioned it to a physiotherapist friend, who suggested I push things with the doctors; she'd been taught that not eating and sleeping could be a sign of something serious.

That night followed our usual pattern, and I contemplated putting Samuel in bed with me but ended up taking him downstairs instead. He actually slept then, cuddled up on my lap, and I remember feeling glad we were no longer doing the controlled crying and I was now giving him some comfort. However, I didn't sleep all night, so first thing the next morning, as it was a Saturday, Stuart took over so I could go back to bed. When I got up, Stuart said he had tried to get Samuel back in with the doctors that morning but hadn't been able to get an appointment.

"Why do you want him to see the doctor again? He's been twice and they say nothing's wrong."

"I don't believe them; this isn't normal," Stuart replied.

"Maybe it is. A lady at the music group yesterday said her little boy sleeps with her most nights."

"I don't care what other people are doing. We can't go on like this any longer. You're shattered and I'm not getting much sleep either."

"That's why I keep bringing him downstairs," I said, tearfully.

"I know, and I'm really grateful, but I've got a new job and I'm struggling to concentrate."

"Do you think he's ill, then?" I asked.

Stuart sighed.

"I really don't know, but I think we're going to have to insist they look into things some more. Please call the doctor first thing Monday morning and get him in that night. I'll come with you and we'll make a fuss, if necessary."

I agreed, but part of me felt embarrassed at the idea of bothering the doctors again when we'd already been twice. I had hoped the health visitors would have come back to me before now so we could have sorted out the sleeping and eating problems because, at this point, I still thought that was all the matter was.

That evening we were going to our friend Graham's birthday party in Norwich, which meant we would be staying in a hotel for the night. My mum and Alan had agreed to look after Samuel at their house and I looked forward more than anything to a night's sleep. In fact, at the party I made people laugh as I mentioned it so often, whilst everyone else was just enjoying a night out.

The party was great and ended with us all with our arms round each other singing "Hey Jude" – the song which was number one when Graham was born. However, during the singsong our taxi had arrived, waited, and then left. This meant we had to walk the couple of miles back to our hotel.

That night, I didn't sleep a wink. Despite having had such a good time at the party, the minute I had some quiet time my mind went straight back to Samuel. All night I lay worrying about him, wondering what was going on and how things had got so terrible. At the same time, I felt annoyed with myself for not sleeping when I had the chance.

By morning I was in an awful mood. As I watched Stuart sleep past seven o'clock... then eight... then nine, my fruitless worry and frustration turned to anger. Stuart was hung over when he got up, so we communicated little to begin with. After breakfast I went on at him to get ready quickly as we had arranged to visit my grandma in her residential home on our way home. It was always difficult visiting Grandma, as she suffers with dementia and had now got to the point where she no longer knew who we were. I wasn't looking forward to going to the home but felt duty bound, as I love her and wanted to give her some comfort.

As usual, Stuart took ages getting ready, which left us little time for our visit. In the end, it got so late we realised we would have to miss seeing Grandma and go the following weekend instead. I was angry with Stuart for his poor timekeeping and this, coupled with another sleepless night and my worry about Samuel, meant we argued all the way to my mother's house.

"Where's Samuel?" I asked as soon as we got in the door.

"He's asleep. Sit down; I'll make you a drink," my mum said.

Stuart went off to the bathroom and I took a seat in the living room. My mum came through with a cup of tea.

"Did you see Grandma?"

"No. We didn't have time."

"Why not?" Mum asked.

"Don't be annoyed with me!" I snapped back. "I've had no sleep again…"

The tears ran down my face before I could stop them. It wasn't usual for me to cry in front of anyone except Stuart, so I felt awkward. But at the same time, I felt utterly exhausted and despairing. Mum hugged me.

"How's Samuel been? Did he sleep?"

"I gave him Calpol again, which helped him sleep a bit."

"Do you think it's his teeth?" I asked, still going over the same questions.

I noticed Mum looked a bit cagey.

"Well… there's definitely *something* wrong."

Just then we heard Samuel cry and I rushed upstairs to get him. I took him out of his travel cot and hugged and kissed him. Despite my exhaustion I was still glad to hold him again and we cuddled into each other. I took him back downstairs.

My mum had cooked a roast dinner and she put some in the blender for Samuel. As usual, he didn't eat it. For pudding, he was given a little bowl of strawberry jelly, which he had a few teaspoons of, and I remember thinking to myself that I must buy him some jelly when we went shopping. After dinner I sat on the floor with him, playing with the new toys Mum had got him whilst she and Alan told us how he had been. He'd been awake a couple of times in the night for over an hour at a time and Mum had given him Calpol and cuddled him in bed until he slept.

"I did feel sorry for him," she said. "He's obviously in pain."

"What shall I do?" I asked her. "I've tried everything."

"I think you need to take him back to the doctors again."

"We're going tomorrow," Stuart said.

"Good. I think you'll have to really push them to do some tests. He's not right at all. I got him to eat some malt loaf this morning and he played a bit with his toys so I thought maybe it wasn't anything serious, but once the Calpol had worn off and we took him out for a walk he became so subdued. He could hardly even smile when a dog came over to see him."

I felt sad as she said this, because Samuel loved animals and he always gave them a lot of attention.

"Do you think it's something serious?" I asked.

Even though I asked the question, I was still thinking in quite a limited way. I certainly wasn't equating serious with life threatening.

"He's very lethargic and he looks pale, don't you think?" Mum answered.

I nodded and said, "I wondered if he might be anaemic."

"I noticed he has a tiny bruise under his eye and look – there are a couple on his leg as well."

And then it hit me: leukaemia. Mum was trying to tell me she thought Samuel had leukaemia. I didn't say anything else and neither did she. I felt my heart and mind race. *It couldn't be leukaemia*, I thought. *Please don't let it be leukaemia!*

But Mum had had leukaemia herself eight years previously and I knew she recognised the symptoms. We left Mum's shortly afterwards and drove the twenty miles home. Stuart had heard the conversation but neither of us mentioned leukaemia. In fact, Stuart says he still didn't think anything along those lines.

The next morning I arranged another doctor's appointment. It was just six days since our last appointment, but this time we were go-ing to insist on tests. I specifically asked to see Dr Masters but, be-ing semi-retired, he wasn't working that day. I then asked to see Dr Rutherford, as I knew she had a good reputation. I was pleased when I was offered an appointment with her at the end of her list that day. Whilst Samuel slept I wrote a list of symptoms to tell her:

* Very disturbed nights for the past eight weeks
* Very poor appetite
* Listless – will not put weight on feet
* Has had a cold
* Much drier nappies; sometimes dry after three hours
* Has some unexplained bruising on legs and face
* Cries more – not the same child
* Sleep improves after Calpol
* Has lost weight: 19.75lb on 4/8/08; 19.31lb on 8/9/08
* Pale complexion

* Under guidance from health visitor, controlled crying tried. No improvement after nine nights. I was told it would take up to a week.
* He has never taken properly to solid food
* Has never been able to drink any other formulae than 1st infant
* He has gradually dropped lower on the weight chart after beginning solids

I put it in the pram bag ready for our appointment later that day. Looking at it now, I can't believe we didn't all spot the obvious long before.

That afternoon I had arranged to garden for my neighbour Nancy. We had an agreement that I would garden for an hour once a fortnight and in return Samuel would attend Tadpole Tunes. When we arrived Nancy said she was taking the girls out.

"Will Samuel be all right on his own whilst you garden?" she asked.

"He'll be fine playing in the conservatory as long as he can see me," I replied.

We got some toys out for him.

"Are you sure he won't try to get out?" she asked.

I was surprised at the idea of him moving from the spot that I had put him in, but realised this wasn't normal behaviour for a one-year-old. So, whilst talking to Nancy about the garden and locking up after we'd finished, in the back of my mind I was revisiting my mother's suggestion about leukaemia. I desperately didn't want him to have this illness and I felt fearful of the future, yet I wanted Samuel diagnosed with something that could be treated and cured so that our lives would change. It's a very strange thing to describe.

On a subconscious level I felt he definitely had leukaemia, but in the front of my mind I was still desperately searching for a less painful explanation.

Nancy took her children out and Samuel settled down in the conservatory to play. Her two dogs, both whippets, lay near Samuel, and whenever I went over to check him he seemed so calm and happy to have them near him. He played happily by himself for the full hour, and he remained in that calm state right up to the doctor's appointment. It was almost as if those dogs made him feel better in some way, because when we got home and I put him in his high chair and got him some bread and homemade soup, he ate more than he had done in ages.

Stuart came home at about ten to six.

"Who's this?" I asked Samuel as I heard Stuart turn the key in the lock.

He smiled at me then leant forward in his high chair to see round the wall and watch Daddy come in.

"Hello, little man!" Stuart said, picking him up.

"We've got to go straight to the doctors' surgery," I said. "Dr Rutherford's seeing us at the end of her list."

We put Samuel in his pushchair and headed into town. On the way, we found a shiny conker, which we gave him to hold. That little conker stayed on his high chair for ages after we went into hospital.

We checked in with the receptionist then sat in the waiting room. Dr Rutherford opened her door.

"Samuel Murray!" she called.

We wheeled Samuel into her room and sat down.

"This is the third time I've brought Samuel in for an appointment. Each time I've come in with a theory about what's wrong, but nothing's been found. I've run out of theories now, but I just know…" I looked at her and paused.

"Something's not right."

Dr Rutherford nodded and waited for me to continue.

"I've written a list of Samuel's symptoms."

"What are they?" she asked.

I started by telling her about his sleeping pattern and eating difficulties. I then told her how much weight he'd lost.

"He's very pale as well," I said, "and I've noticed these bruises on his face and legs."

I wanted to make sure she took us seriously, and wondered if she knew what I was implying by saying this. In some ways, I felt that to mention the word *leukaemia* would make me sound neurotic and, of course, I didn't want it to be that! I did want, however, to get him tested for it.

Dr Rutherford leant over and felt Samuel's glands. Next she looked into his eyes and then felt his stomach. I know now that this is what doctors do when they are looking for leukaemia.

"I've always bruised easily," Stuart said. "Maybe he just takes after me."

Dr Rutherford smiled, but it was a sad sort of a smile that didn't reach her eyes. I've seen that smile a lot now, from doctors, nurses and consultants.

"He doesn't want to stand any more either," I said.

"Show me."

I tried to get him to stand on his feet. He cried out and held his feet up.

"We could get some tests done here," she said, "but I think it might be better to refer him to a paediatrician."

"How long will that take?" I asked. "I've just booked us a break in a holiday cottage. We should be leaving this Friday."

This had been another one of my ideas to get things sorted out. I thought maybe a break away from the house, with Stuart spending time with Samuel as well, might just sort things out. Obviously, I was really clutching at straws by now.

"I'll get him in this week," she said, starting to tap a list of symptoms onto her computer. I noticed she headed the referral letter: "Urgent". "If you don't hear anything tomorrow, call the hospital or the surgery and we'll chase things up."

"Thank you," I said, feeling relieved.

I put Samuel back in his pushchair. Dr Rutherford turned away from her computer as Stuart and I stood. She leant forward, rested her chin on her clasped hands and looked at Samuel for a long time.

"Could he just be teething?" Stuart asked.

Dr Rutherford just shook her head and continued to look at Samuel.

"Can we keep giving him Calpol?"

"Yes." Dr Rutherford sat upright again. "Just don't exceed the dosage."

She seemed in no hurry for us to go.

"Thanks," I said, as Stuart opened the door.

Dr Rutherford just nodded.

We thought a lot about that appointment afterwards. I often wonder if she knew then what was wrong with Samuel and if she wondered what the future held for him.

CHAPTER 7

Tests

⁓

"ZOOM, ZOOM, ZOOM! WE'RE GOING to the moon! Zoom, zoom, zoom! We'll get there very soon! Five, four, three, two, one... Lift off!"

I picked Samuel up and raised him above my head for the lift off, just like all the other mothers. He let out a yelp. Hayley, the librarian running Baby Bounce, laughed.

"He loves this, doesn't he?"

I didn't like to contradict her. Yes, he *used* to love this song, but I realised the sound he made was from pain. I probably shouldn't have taken him to Baby Bounce that day, but my thought was that it would be the last time we would come. Samuel had been a regular attendee since he was five months old and I wanted him to go one last time. If my worst fears were confirmed, fun would be off the agenda for some time. So, that morning I had put Samuel down for his nap as usual at nine o'clock and when he woke up I gave him some Calpol and a biscuit and took him into town.

It was Wednesday 24ᵗʰ September, two days after we saw Dr Rutherford and the day of Samuel's appointment with the paediatrician at our local hospital. All that morning, whilst I was getting Samuel ready and when we sang the songs at Baby Bounce, I avoided any thoughts about leukaemia. In fact, I had successfully avoided all thoughts of it since our appointment on Monday evening, but my fear showed itself in my actions. Cate and Megan weren't at Baby Bounce that day, but Cheryl and Rowan were.

"Samuel's got an appointment at the hospital this afternoon," I told Cheryl after all the songs had been sung.

Cheryl had known all about my worries regarding Samuel's eating and sleeping, but knew nothing of my fear that he was seriously ill.

"I'm sure he'll be all right," she said.

"He's lost a bit of weight," I told her.

I felt like I was trying to prepare her for the bad news, although I didn't verbally acknowledge this – not even to myself. She looked concerned.

"Very much?"

"No, not much."

"I shouldn't worry. They're very good there. In fact, we've had to go there recently for Rowan."

She told me about Rowan and continued to try to reassure me. I just listened and said no more about Samuel, but my heart was pounding. On the surface I looked calm and ordinary, but my body was in fight or flight mode. This felt like survival, but not for me – for my son.

"Off we go then, darling," I said to Samuel, scooping him up. He cuddled into me. I watched the other children, now all trying to crawl or walk and follow their mums with exuberance and energy. The contrast was startling. I put Samuel in his pushchair and quickly walked away, afraid to dwell on my feelings.

"Let's go and see Rachel at the baker's," I said as I pushed him out of the library.

On the way, I stopped at the market and bought some grapes and bananas. I gave him a grape to hold as we went around the town and was pleased when he ate it. The fact that I was so happy to see him eating just one grape shows how little he was eating at this time.

At the baker's, the smell of bread and the friendly atmosphere were inviting. We joined the queue. When Rachel saw us she smiled warmly and gave Samuel a little wave. He gave a small smile but was too weak to wave back. We got to the front of the queue and I ordered our bread.

"Samuel's got an appointment at the hospital this afternoon," I said to her. "I just wanted to come in and let you know."

"Oh, no! What's wrong?" she asked.

I'd got to know Rachel from coming into the baker's and we always talked whenever she got the chance, but we'd never seen each other socially. She has since become a very close friend but, at that point, we just talked over the counter.

A few weeks before, she'd said to me, "I know this is going to sound strange to you, but Samuel has angels with him." She'd laughed at my surprise. "He's very special, you know." A few months after Samuel died, she reminded me of that. "I thought they were protecting him on Earth," she said, "but they were guiding him to Heaven."

I explained about Samuel not eating or sleeping well and that was the reason for the referral.

"He looks a bit pale," she said. "Come in tomorrow and tell me what the doctor said."

I said I would, but my stomach churned. I didn't want to think about what tomorrow would bring.

I pushed Samuel back through the Abbey Gardens and the old cemetery to our house. As I did so, I drifted off into a daydream. Suddenly, I realised in the dream I was telling members of our family that Samuel had leukaemia.

How horrible! I thought to myself. *What a terrible thing to think!*

I felt angry with myself for conjuring up such a dreadful scenario but, at the same time, I felt this was what was coming. It was as if I was experiencing two different thought patterns simultaneously: my normal self, which was being upbeat and logical, and at a deeper level my fears, which I was trying to keep hidden even from myself.

When we got back home, my friend Lizzie had attached a carrier bag to our door. In the bag were a card, a magazine, some chocolate buttons for Samuel, and some flowers. The card was to wish us good luck for our appointment that afternoon. It was so thoughtful of her and also incredibly perceptive. She said in the card to try not to worry, but she told me afterwards she'd been concerned when she'd called the day before.

She'd asked me then what I thought was wrong with Samuel and I just kept saying, "I don't know," but she'd picked up that I was thinking it was something serious.

Samuel looked exhausted when we got in. I tried to give him some lunch, then put him to bed for his nap. He went down easily after his milk; he must have been desperate to just sleep. I can't imagine how he was feeling. Hopefully, the Calpol had helped with the pain, but the last thing he probably felt like doing was being dragged around town and bounced up and down at Baby Bounce.

I put the flowers in a vase and got myself a sandwich. I flicked through the magazine Lizzie had dropped round. "My hair's a bit like Posh Spice's!" Lizzie had written in her card. I turned to the pages featuring the Beckhams and looked at the picture of Victoria. I was pleased that Lizzie's hair had grown back that much after her chemotherapy. After a while, I heard Stuart's car pull up outside our house. As he got out he waved at me through the window.

"Hi, babe," he said as he came through the front door. "It's nice to be home early. Chocolate buttons… Where did they come from?" he asked, picking up Lizzie's card. "I'll have some of them later."

"They're for Samuel," I said. "Shall I make you a sandwich?"

"Thanks. Where's the little man – in bed?"

"Yes. I'll get him up just before we have to go."

"He's always snoozing!"

Stuart was his usual upbeat self, which made things easier for me. He said after we'd had the diagnosis that at no point did he even consider leukaemia or anything serious. He was just glad we had the hospital appointment and were getting things sorted out.

When Samuel woke he was pleased to see Stuart, and I felt really guilty as he was smiling quite happily when we put him in the car. Recently he'd progressed from the baby car seat to his new upright one and he liked it very much. When we'd first put him in it and driven out of the shop car park he couldn't stop laughing. It was like he couldn't believe his luck, and he felt very important and grown-up. The only downside was that he stopped sleeping so much in the car; he could now look out the window, and never wanted to miss anything. We drove round to the back of the hospital, to the Rainbow children's ward.

"Just think," I said to Stuart, "there are some children in here who are really ill."

In the back of mind I was silently adding, *Please don't let Samuel be one of them.*

The consultant we were due to see didn't have an outpatient clinic that day, so we were told to go upstairs to the ward and we would see him there. We never did see the actual consultant. Obviously, Dr Rutherford hadn't given any hint about leukaemia in her referral letter, although she had asked for a blood test to be done.

Rainbow ward is one big, wide room with a nurse station to one side and about seven beds around the outside of the room. There was a rocking horse in the middle and a children's play area, with a little waiting area to the side. There was also a school room and a larger play area at one end, and clinic bedrooms down the other.

When we arrived we were taken to a private bedroom. After a short while, a young student doctor came to see us. As I explained

Samuel's symptoms to him I thought they sounded vague, and I suddenly questioned my earlier theory of leukaemia. That diagnosis suddenly sounded too enormous; not the sort of thing an ordinary family would have to deal with. I thought childhood cancer must be very rare, and cancer in a baby almost unheard of. I felt silly for even thinking Samuel could have something so serious. *Thank goodness I hadn't told anybody*, I thought to myself. *They would think I was completely neurotic and melodramatic.*

I undressed Samuel, laid him on the bed and sat with him as the doctor examined him. He asked lots of questions, but it was obvious he didn't have a clue what was wrong with Samuel. In the end he said he would ask the consultant's registrar to come in and see us. An Asian lady came in to see us and she, too, asked lots of questions. She deliberated whether Samuel could be coeliac or had an obstruction in his throat which was preventing him from eating properly. But the more she observed him the more she became convinced of her first diagnosis.

"He's presenting like a classic coeliac," she said. "They often come in very upset, having lost weight, and not eating well."

"Could he be anaemic?" I asked her.

"Quite possibly," she replied. "Is he always this pale?"

"He is pale-skinned, but I think he looks paler than normal."

"We'll get the blood test done. That will show up anaemia."

"If he's not coeliac, will you do an operation on him to look for a blockage?"

She gave a small laugh.

"Oh, I think that's a bit extreme. There are lots of tests we can do before then. I'll come back in a bit to do the blood test."

That was at about three o'clock; it was almost six o'clock before we saw her again. Luckily, Samuel was so tired he fell asleep on me for a while, and when he woke up we managed to entertain him with books and toys. At about five o'clock I asked the nurse if he could have some food. As the appointment had been for two o'clock I hadn't thought for a minute we would still be there for Samuel's teatime. It was difficult to know what to ask the nurses for as Samuel was eating so little, but they made up a bottle for him and gave me a yoghurt and an apple to feed him. Having since had experience of living in a hospital, I now know they keep jars of baby food in stock but, at the time, I didn't realise this; nobody volunteered this information.

"We should weigh him," the nurse said after Samuel had had a few teaspoons of yoghurt.

Baby scales were produced and I was worried to see he had lost more weight. I expressed my concern but the nurse just said, "I'll let the doctor know." At about six o'clock, the doctor returned.

"I'm sorry – I got caught up with another patient and forgot all about you!" she laughed, but Stuart and I weren't happy.

Samuel must have been the most ill patient they had on the ward and yet he was forgotten about. We didn't say anything that time, but as our experience of hospital life increased we became more vocal when things didn't go right for Samuel.

"We need to take him to the treatment room to take his blood," she said.

We followed her down the corridor where a nurse joined us. There was a tall plastic tube filled with water and plastic fish in the corner of the room. It was switched on and the fish danced up and down in the water. It was supposed to distract Samuel while his blood was taken, but it was noisy and he didn't like it. It was switched off and other toys were found as a diversion.

Samuel was sitting on my lap, half facing me with his left arm under my arm for the consultant to take the blood from his hand. I then had to press his head into me so he was looking the other way, whilst the nurse and Stuart tried to distract him. It seemed to take forever to take the blood and Samuel became very distressed.

It was so upsetting, especially as we couldn't explain to him why he was being hurt in this way, but then I thought, *At least that's over with and now we can go home.*

Up until that point, seeing Samuel have his blood taken was the most distressing thing I had ever witnessed. By the same time the next day, I had witnessed more than I would have thought possible. I felt utterly distraught by it all and I was only a bystander. What on earth did it feel like to be Samuel?

At just after 7 p.m. we gathered up our coats and Samuel's baby bag and left the hospital. It felt such a relief to get out into the fresh air.

"I hate hospitals," I said to Stuart as we came out the door and headed towards the car. It was getting dark and it was past Samuel's bedtime.

"It's all the hanging about. Can you believe they kept us waiting that long?"

"Well, at least we're going home now. Think of all the poor children who'll be in there for days. How will they confirm he's coeliac?"

"I think they're hoping the blood test will tell them some more."

"Poor little chap. That'll be a pain for him."

"No, it's fine. Waitrose has a whole aisle devoted to wheat-free foods."

"Really?"

"Yes. I'm just glad we know and now things will hopefully get better."

I felt completely convinced Samuel was coeliac. The doctor had said he presented like a classic coeliac and it certainly seemed to explain things. If eating caused Samuel pain, then no wonder he was refusing to eat, and if he wasn't eating much then he probably wasn't getting enough iron, which was causing the anaemia, which in turn was causing the fatigue. I felt like we'd been given our future back. I didn't tell Stuart about my earlier fears that now seemed completely over the top.

When we arrived back home I put Samuel into his Babygro and then into his Grobag. We put him in his cot and played his music box. It has a very melodic tune and lights come on and light up fish before fading off. Samuel loved it, and as it had been part of his bedtime routine since he was five weeks old he associated it with going to sleep. Stuart and I stood with our arms around each other, as we did every night until the tune finished, and then we both kissed him good-night. Samuel smiled back at us as we left his bedroom. Ten minutes later I peeped round the door to check on him – he was sound asleep. I sighed with relief. I felt so happy that he was going to be okay.

"I'd better phone Mum," I said to Stuart. "She's been worrying." My mum sounded terrified when she picked up the phone. "It's okay; they think he's coeliac," I told her. I told her all about the appointment and, as my voice was light-hearted and upbeat, I think she really believed that Samuel must be all right. She told me she had her two close friends with her, and I realised she was definitely expecting to hear the worst. I remember thinking both Mum and I had been very melodramatic. If only that were true.

After the phone call I put some dinner in the oven and Stuart had a bath. The phone rang. It was my friend Nicky. She had been over the day before and had seen how pale and lethargic Samuel had seemed. I remember her taking one of his socks off and squeezing his toes. I have now seen doctors do the same thing; it is done to check if the child has a serious infection that is causing all the blood to go to the vital organs. She had done this very casually at the time, almost as if she was playing with him, but I had picked up on it.

When I mentioned it after Samuel had been diagnosed, she admitted she had also feared leukaemia when she'd seen him. But then I had given him Calpol and a chocolate biscuit and he'd suddenly seemed like a different child, so she'd felt maybe it wasn't anything quite so bad.

I repeated our hospital experience to Nicky and she laughed and said, "Well, this might affect Libby – I mean if she's going to be cooking for Samuel when she's his wife." We joked about it, but Nicky did say at one point, "What a relief!" so I knew then she'd also suspected something serious.

I was just getting the dinner out of the oven when the phone rang again.

"We'll get to sit down soon!" I called out to Stuart, who was still in the bath. I felt upbeat after my conversations with Mum and Nicky and had convinced myself more than ever that Samuel was coeliac and that was the cause of all his problems.

"Hello. This is the doctor from Rainbow ward. Is that Samuel's mother?"

"Yes," I said.

I didn't think they were going to ring with the blood results until the next day, but at least that meant we didn't have to wait in for the phone call.

"I'm ringing to tell you that Samuel's haemoglobin levels are low."

"So he's anaemic," I answered.

"Yes." She paused and then said slowly, "But his haemoglobin levels are *very* low."

My breath caught in my throat.

"He's got leukaemia," I said.

"We think he might have – yes."

I didn't want her to confirm it and I didn't want my suspicions to be correct. The word "leukaemia" had not been mentioned by anybody until now, and I didn't want it to be true. My stomach clenched; my heart pounded.

"You need to bring him back to the hospital."

"When?"

"Straight away."

"I can't believe this."

I started to cry.

"Can you get your husband?" I continued to cry.

"Please put me on to your husband."

I rushed through to the bathroom where Stuart was still in the bath.

"They think Samuel's got leukaemia," I told him.

He sat up quickly and took the phone. His eyes were wide with shock. I heard him talking and asking questions but my head was filled with things we had to do. I had a physical ache in my chest and my whole body was shaking. I switched off the oven and then raced upstairs to pack an overnight bag. I threw in my pyjamas and dressing gown, knowing instinctively we would be staying the night. I rushed back downstairs – I would pack Samuel's things just before we went so he wouldn't be disturbed for longer than necessary. Stuart was out of the bath and drying himself.

"They only said he *might* have leukaemia; they won't know until they've done more tests."

"What else could it be?" I asked while frantically serving up dinner.

"Are we eating dinner?" he asked.

"We must. We don't know when we'll next eat."

"He could just be anaemic."

"I knew he had leukaemia," I said.

"Did you?" Stuart looked confused. "I didn't. I didn't think he had anything seriously wrong."

We took a few mouthfuls of our food but neither of us could stomach it. We put the plates in the kitchen.

I should wash up, I thought. But the doctor had said we needed to get back to the hospital straight away, so I left them on the side and hoped my sister wouldn't mind washing up for us when she arrived in the morning.

Nancy had recently started going home with Richie at the end of the day and then coming to ours early the next morning, as she felt we had enough to contend with without her being there as well. Suddenly I thought to ring her; to let her know we might not be there when she arrived. I was in tears the minute I spoke to her.

She could barely take in what I was saying, but I later found out she'd said to her husband just that evening when they were driving home, "You don't think Samuel could have leukaemia, do you?"

I now know my friend Angela had also said the same thing to her husband. It's strange to think how many of us shared this fear and yet none of us had voiced it. I suppose we were all too frightened.

I made up a bottle for Samuel and packed two empty ones. I then went quietly into his room to pack nappies, baby wipes and a couple of spare Babygros. He was sound asleep. More than anything, I didn't want to wake him up and take him out of the safety of his home. When we were both ready and the bag was packed, Stuart said he would get him.

"Don't get him out of his Grobag," I said.

"I won't," Stuart said as he hugged me.

"Now starts a nightmare," I said as we left the house.

I didn't know then that I wouldn't see my home again for six weeks.

CHAPTER 8

The Diagnosis

~⌒~

WE BUZZED AND WAITED. STUART held Samuel in his arms as we all looked expectantly through the glass panel. It seemed strange to be back there so soon and I wondered if Samuel felt annoyed or confused to be taken out of bed and brought back to the hospital. Eventually, a nurse opened the door. The ward was in darkness apart from a few reading lights. It seemed a different place from the busy, noisy ward we'd left just two hours before. The nurse led us past the nurse station and sleeping children to the room we'd been in earlier. I felt terrified at the thought of what was to come. I expect Stuart did too, but neither of us showed it.

"My name's Lorraine," she told us. "I'll be looking after Samuel tonight."

We carried Samuel back into the room, now lit by a side lamp, and sat on the bed. An old-fashioned metal cot had been placed alongside it. The doctor we'd seen before came in and explained that she'd finished her shift, but another doctor would be with us soon.

"He'll take more blood and do some tests," she said. "Then, first thing tomorrow morning, Samuel will go by ambulance to Addenbrooke's Hospital for a bone marrow aspiration to determine exactly what's wrong with him."

After she left the room, Stuart said, "I don't think he's got leukaemia."

"Don't you?"

"No. I know he's anaemic but I don't think he's got leukaemia."

"I thought they seemed pretty certain."

"Let's just wait and see."

"I hope you're right," I said.

After a while, a male doctor came and asked us to go back to the treatment room with him. We followed him through the dark, quiet ward, strangely aware of the other patients sleeping and how abnormal it was to be there.

"I'm going to put a cannula in Samuel's hand," he said. "We can use it to take blood and then later to attach a drip."

We positioned him on my lap as we'd been shown earlier, and the doctor pushed the needle into his hand. Blood shot from his vein. We know now this is often a sign that a patient is low in platelets, which means the blood doesn't clot properly. He fiddled with the cannula for a long time, trying to position the needle into a vein strong enough, but Samuel became very agitated. Eventually, he said he'd have to try the other hand. We manoeuvred Samuel round and he tried again. Samuel tried to wiggle himself free. He didn't cry but was clearly distressed. When he looked up at me, I could see how tired and ill he was. His face was white and his big, blue eyes were filled with fear. He must have wondered why we were allowing something painful to be done to him; it was something we struggled with also.

The cannula was eventually fitted. Samuel snuggled into me and we sighed with relief. We were allowed to return to our room and I gave him some milk to calm him after his ordeal and to get him settled for sleep. We desperately tried to remain upbeat for Samuel's sake, but all the while our hearts pounded, and the thought that he could have leukaemia circled our minds. Time seemed to go very fast and, before we knew it, it was one in the morning. Lorraine came in to see us again.

"The doctor wants Samuel to have a chest X-ray."

"Oh, no!" I said. "Can't he go to sleep now?"

"I'm sorry; Addenbrooke's have asked for it. They need to know if the leukaemia has affected his internal organs."

We took in this new piece of information. The thought of leukaemia was bad enough – surely there wasn't going to be something else wrong as well? And then I realised she had mentioned leukaemia as a fact.

"Has he *definitely* got leukaemia?" I asked.

"Nobody's told us for certain, but they're pretty sure he has."

"Couldn't it just be anaemia?" Stuart asked.

"They'll know more after they've looked at the blood tests, but as far as I understand it, Samuel's last blood test showed leukaemia cells." She put her hand on my arm. "They'll be able to explain it so much better at Addenbrooke's tomorrow."

Stuart and I just looked at each other. I could see the shock and anxiety on his face.

"They're very good at treating leukaemia nowadays; the success rate in children is quite high." I didn't know how to respond. The thought of Samuel not being here was unthinkable. "And he won't be in hospital all the time," she continued, "but the treatment is over three years."

"Three years!" I repeated.

Thoughts of him going to school with no hair flashed through my mind: *He'll look different; he'll struggle to keep up with the other children; he might not be able to play with his friends.*

It all felt like it was happening too fast. This wasn't the life I'd imagined for my beautiful son.

We walked along the corridors of the hospital; all empty except for the occasional cleaner silently buffing the floor. It seemed like a different place from the hospital I'd given birth at less than fourteen months earlier. Then, I'd been full of hope and optimism – now I sensed a desperate fight for survival. We sat on some chairs outside the X-ray department.

"I feel sick," I said.

Lorraine produced a sick bowl and I sat with my head in my hands. Before long, they called us through.

"Can you sit Samuel on the table and undo his Babygro?" the radiographer said.

I did as he asked, but Samuel was obviously frightened. The room seemed vast, sterile, and filled with equipment. This was not the sort of place a child usually visited.

"Can everyone else come behind the screen?" he said.

"Can I stay with Samuel?" I asked.

"You'll need to wear this," the radiographer said, handing me a lead-lined apron.

I put it on, and whilst the X-rays were taken I sang "Twinkle, Twinkle, Little Star" to try to distract Samuel. It didn't work – he held his arms up to me. He wasn't crying but he was making frightened little noises.

"Look, darling, look at the camera. You're going to have your photo taken," I said, facing him forward again.

The image was taken and Stuart quickly came round from the screen and picked Samuel up whilst I got rid of the apron. We walked back to the clinic room. It wasn't long before the doctor appeared again.

"I'm pleased to say his internal organs all appear normal."

We were relieved, but it seemed a small positive compared to the huge list of concerns we now had.

"We're going to give Samuel a fluid bonus through a drip, so it goes directly into his bloodstream. It should make him feel slightly better before his trip to Addenbrooke's tomorrow."

"Then he can go to sleep," I said – more of a statement than a question.

"Yes. I'm sorry we have to do all this, but we're following instructions from consultants at Addenbrooke's."

Perhaps, in light of Samuel's having leukaemia, my worry about him getting sleep seemed out of place, but I was always concerned for his well-being. At that moment he was a desperately tired, frightened, ill little boy and I wanted to take away those negative feelings in whatever way I could; the only way I knew how was to get him to have some sleep.

Lorraine came in shortly afterwards with a drip stand and a bag of fluid. She hooked it up and tried to attach it to the cannula the doctor had put in Samuel's hand earlier. After fiddling with it for a while, she apologised and explained it wasn't working and another one would have to be fitted. It was difficult to remain calm. All we wanted to do was pick Samuel up and take him away from all the horrible things that were happening to him. He had been asleep in his cot with the sound of the television and smells of dinner wafting up to him, homely and comforting. Now he was in hospital and being kept awake whilst distressing, painful procedures were performed on him. It seemed terribly unfair that our baby boy should be suffering so much and, at that moment, it was hard to rationalise that all this was for his own good.

The doctor came back and said, "I'm so sorry. I'll try to attach the cannula here so we don't have to take him back to the treatment room."

Lorraine helped the doctor and eventually the cannula was refitted and attached to the drip.

"All done, Samuel," the doctor said.

Samuel took his dummy out and threw it at the doctor! Stuart and I laughed with relief.

"Sorry about that!" Stuart said.

Our little boy, who wasn't even fourteen months old, must have felt so ill and upset, but he never lost his fighting spirit. We were so proud of him.

Eventually, we were allowed to get some sleep, but the night was a very disturbed one. After everything that had happened it was no surprise that Samuel was unable to settle. I asked Lorraine if he could sleep in my bed with me, but she said they didn't really allow that in case he fell out. Instead, she raised my bed up to the same height as his cot and put his cot bars right down. I slept half in my bed and half in Samuel's cot, with him cuddled up to me, and Stuart stretched out, fully clothed, on a camp bed at our feet.

It's impossible to describe the level of fear you feel when you know your child has a life-threatening illness. It was also impossible to comprehend how we would live with that knowledge for a prolonged length of time. One minute my mind raced ahead to possible outcomes, both good and bad, and the next minute I was reliving the past, wondering when and where it had gone wrong and if there was anything I could have done to prevent it.

The hours passed slowly. From time to time Stuart and I talked. At other times we must have fallen asleep, only to be woken by the nurse coming in or Samuel waking up. At half past six I got up and went to the bathroom to get washed and dressed. We'd been told the night before that the ambulance would be with us very early and I wanted to be ready. I don't remember if we even had a cup of tea, let alone any breakfast, but I gave Samuel some milk whilst we waited.

"I'll go home and pack some clothes," Stuart said. "I'd better call my parents and let them know what's going on, then I'll drive straight to Addenbrooke's."

I nodded. The reality of what we were going through was sinking in and I felt so fearful. But I had my baby boy to think of, and I had to remember that I was the parent. I reminded myself to stay calm and in control in order to look after Samuel properly, and to give him the comfort and security he needed.

The ambulance crew arrived – a man and a woman. They were practical, upbeat and competent – everything you would want at a time like that. They told Stuart how to get to Addenbrooke's, and where to go when he arrived. Then they strapped Samuel into a car seat and attached it to a stretcher on wheels.

Lorraine kindly said she would come with me, despite the fact that she'd worked all night and her shift had ended. Then we were off, out through the Accident and Emergency department to the ambulance waiting outside. The cold air hit us as we walked through the door. It was going to be a bright, sunny day, but it was only eight in the morning and the day hadn't yet warmed up. Doctors and nurses were arriving for their shifts and there was already a sense of briskness about the place.

Samuel was efficiently manoeuvred into the ambulance. Lorraine and I climbed in and we pulled away immediately. Samuel was calm – perhaps tired or resigned to this new development – and Lorraine and I sat to the side of him, belted into seats which had been pulled down from the wall. We drove quickly to the outskirts of town and then, as we approached the roundabout that would take us onto the A14 towards Cambridge, I heard the siren come on.

"We're being blue-lighted to the hospital," Lorraine said, probably sensing my shock at the sense of urgency.

Blue-lighted. This new expression went round and round my mind. I felt like I might cry.

This is serious, I thought. *Samuel's life is threatened – he might die.* I breathed deeply.

"Are you okay, poppet?" I said, leaning forward and stroking Samuel's little hand. He turned his head and looked at me. I looked into his wide eyes, filled with expression, and not for the first time I thought how old he seemed.

Shouldn't he be crying? I thought.

He seemed so serene. Maybe he felt too ill to cry.

As we came into Cambridge we hit rush hour, but I was amazed to the see the cars pull over to the side of the road for us. I had been the one in the past pulling over for an ambulance, and now we were in the ambulance. To me, Samuel didn't appear any different from how he'd been for the past couple of weeks, so I didn't think of our situation as an emergency. But, of course, it *was* an emergency: his life was in danger and I was starting to understand what a terrible position we were in.

Addenbrooke's Hospital is over thirty miles away from Bury St Edmunds, but we arrived there quickly. Samuel was taken out of the ambulance and Lorraine and I followed the crew through a maze of corridors. Then time seemed to pause as we went into a lift and waited for it to reach our floor. As the doors opened, I saw colourful mosaics of people dancing. They stretched the length of the corridor and reached from floor to ceiling. For a moment I was taken aback by this stunning artwork that was so alien to the hospital environment. But then I was presented with a different image: as we entered C2 (the children's oncology ward) I saw photos of children attached to the wall. These children, of all ages, had no hair and no colour in their cheeks. Most of them had tubes coming out of their noses. The children looked ill; they looked like they had cancer. I looked at my beautiful Samuel and realised with a jolt that he would soon look like them.

"Morning! Samuel Murray!" the ambulance driver called out with a practised, friendly voice that jarred with the speed and urgency with which he pushed Samuel along the corridor.

"This way," the nurse said with a smile as she led us to a room with four beds.

We were taken to a corner of the room by the window. There, waiting for us, was a large, blue-and-green cot. It looked bright and modern with a control panel to make it go up and down or tip backwards and forwards. It couldn't have been more different from the one on Rainbow ward. I had originally felt fear at the thought of going to Addenbrooke's Hospital. It was further away and unfamiliar. I'd got used to Lorraine and the room we'd occupied, and didn't want to change. But I sensed straight away on ward C2 that we were in a very professional environment. There was a busyness about the place, but the nurses were friendly and everyone looked like they knew what they were doing.

The ambulance driver unstrapped Samuel from the car seat and handed him to me. I cuddled him into me and, before I could stop myself, I started crying.

"You've been holding it in all night," Lorraine said, putting her arm around me.

"You're in safe hands here," the ambulance driver said. "They'll look after him."

And then it was time for everyone to go, and Samuel and I were left on our own. I looked around the room. There was a chair next to the cot and pale-blue paper curtains separated the four beds. To the other side of the cot was what looked like a wardrobe, but I later found out was a pull-down bed for parents. Over each bed was a TV on an arm that could be directed any way you chose. Opposite us were a young teenage boy and his parents, and next to us was a boy of about four, who was walking around confidently, pushing his drip stand and telling his mother what to do. In the other corner was a little girl with a full head of hair, who was obviously testing her parents and the nurses to the limits. I later found out she was the only patient on the ward without cancer.

One nurse said to me months later, "It's always the children who are the least seriously ill who are the most demanding... and the same goes for their parents!"

I sat on the chair with Samuel and waited for someone to see us. A few minutes later a lady dressed in black trousers and a bright-blue T-shirt came over.

"Hello, I'm Lisa," she said with a friendly smile. "I'm one of the play workers. Would you like me to show you round the ward?"

"No, thanks. I haven't seen a nurse yet but I wouldn't mind a cup of tea, if that's possible."

Lisa went away and came back quickly with a cup of tea for me and some books and toys for Samuel.

"Someone will be with you shortly," she said. "Does Samuel like music? We're holding a music club in a couple of hours in the play-room, if you want to join us."

I felt like the new girl at school. I knew Samuel would be having some tests, but I had no idea what those tests would involve or how long we would be here for. I didn't know then, as Lisa probably did, that we would be on that ward for a very long time.

I sat with Samuel and showed him the books. I wished Stuart would hurry up, but I had the feeling we would have a replay of when

Samuel was born and I had waited all morning for him. In fact, it was a couple of hours before he arrived, having spoken to our families, packed a bag and driven to Addenbrooke's. In that time I'd met Lisa, a nurse and the anaesthetist.

"I've spoken to my parents and your mum. Your sister had phoned her last night so she already knew. She's on her way over here with Alan and Nancy," he told me.

After a little while, a slim, stylish lady came into the room. She had golden-brown skin and was wearing a colourful scarf over her hair. As she walked through the door she was looking through some medical notes and talking to another young lady.

"Hi, I'm the doctor. My name's Boo."

"Boo?" I repeated.

I saw her lips twitch at the corner and her eyes twinkle.

"Yes," she said. "So… you're feeling a bit shocked, I expect." We agreed. "Let's have a look at you, little man. A bit pale."

The other lady started writing in the folder.

"Let's have a look at your eyes. Oh, yes. What about your toes? Shall we have a look at them?"

She undid his Babygro and took out his foot, squeezed his toes, then tickled his feet.

"How's that tummy?" She pressed down on his stomach.

"Nice and soft. We're going to get him to theatre shortly," she said. "We'll take some bone marrow from his spine and then we'll be able to tell exactly what we're dealing with."

"Has he definitely got leukaemia?" Stuart asked.

"He's definitely got leukaemia, yes, but there are different types and we need to find out which one he's got."

Stuart breathed out. I could feel his fear.

"We're going to put a line in his chest at the same time," Boo continued. "This means we can take blood from him easily without using a cannula. We can also give him a blood transfusion, which he desperately needs, and we'll be able to give him chemotherapy."

"Oh, God!" I said.

Stuart put his arm around me.

"I know this is hard, guys," Boo said. "We'll get him down to theatre as quickly as possible and then you'll be able to see Mike – that's Samuel's consultant – and he'll be able to give you a lot more information."

"My mum had acute myeloid leukaemia but she's okay now," I said.

"Did she? Well, we think Samuel has ALL – that's acute lympho-blastic leukaemia. It's more common in children. But we'll know for sure when he's had the bone marrow aspiration."

"The treatment for that is three years?"

"It is. It's six months for AML, but that's as an inpatient."

"Yes, it was with my mum," I said, trying to take it all in.

"Now, have you seen these nasogastric tubes all the kids have got in?"

"Yes," I answered wearily.

Stuart looked around at the other children to see what she was talking about.

"We'd like Samuel to have one. We use them to put milk feeds through at night and to give medicines."

"Why does he have to have a night feed?" I asked.

"We really need to get his weight back up so he can cope with all the treatment he'll be having. The trouble with chemotherapy is that it makes everything taste horrible and it just deadens the kids' appetites. He'll never eat enough during the day to give him all the calories he needs, so the night feed does a really great job at topping him up. He's also going to need loads of medicines and they can all just go down the tube so you don't have to battle with him to get him to take them."

Stuart and I looked at each other.

"Is it painful?" Stuart asked.

"No, and the great thing is, if we do it when he's in theatre he won't feel anything. It's the best time to do it. Nose tubes are a great invention – they're brilliant from our point of view."

We reluctantly agreed to Samuel having a nasogastric (or NG) tube as well as everything else.

"We'll come and get you in a couple of hours, so have a wander around the ward, visit the playroom, and don't let him have any more to drink or eat. Okay?"

"Yes," we both replied.

We were trying to be sensible. We were trying to deal with this new, frightening reality, but we felt as if we were being led down a road, at terrifying speed, that we desperately didn't want to go down. We had been existing on just a few hours' sleep a night for weeks. On top of that, Stuart was trying to cope with a new, demanding job. And it didn't seem that long since Samuel was born. Now our lives were being turned around again; only this time, for the worse.

We did as Boo said. We walked around the ward and visited the playroom. We even sat in on the music group and sang along with the songs in an attempt to distract Samuel. All the while we attempted to take in that he had leukaemia. *Our baby had cancer.* We wondered how this had happened and if we'd done something wrong. We tried to come to terms with the fact that Samuel would have to have chemotherapy; that our boy would feel more ill than we could imagine; that he would lose his hair; and, ultimately, he would go through all this with no guarantee he would live. We thought all this whilst we sang nursery rhymes and shook tambourines and smiled at the other parents.

As we came out of the playroom, we saw my mum, Alan and Nancy at the door to C2. The pale oak doors have round circles cut away for the windows, and we could see them looking through. My sister said to me recently those doors became so familiar to them, as everything on the ward eventually did, but, at that time, everything felt strange. She remembers clearly looking through those circles and seeing us on the other side of the door, like she was witnessing us in a different life.

Nancy had bought Samuel a little cuddly lion that made a strange-sounding roar when you pressed its tummy. Samuel took it and cuddled it and loved it, as he did anything soft and furry, whether a real animal or a toy.

By now it was lunchtime, and as Samuel always slept between twelve and two I thought I would try to get him to have a nap. This was when I discovered how difficult it was going to be to get him to sleep in hospital. At home it had been hard enough in the last few weeks, but at least there I had the familiar props that signified to him it was time to sleep. Here, without his own room where I could draw the curtains and play his musical fish box, I had next to no chance. But I attempted it anyway and lay him down in his colourful cot.

One of the books I'd read to him that morning showed children playing peek-a-boo. Now, in his cot, he proceeded to show me how he'd taken it all in, despite feeling tired and ill, by covering his eyes and playing peek-a-boo with me. My heart lurched for him. His smile was warm and his eyes filled with love and I felt an overwhelming surge of pride and love for him.

An hour or so passed and, of course, with all the stimulation going on around him, he didn't sleep, and then we were told theatre was ready for us. We were given a small theatre gown, printed with colourful clowns, to put on Samuel. Then he was wheeled to theatre with Stuart and me walking by his side. Nancy, Mum and Alan said they would wait for us on the ward.

It was a long walk, and we had to go up one floor to get there. Once there, Samuel was given anaesthetic through the cannula in his hand. A few moments later he was asleep. He looked so beautiful, cuddled up into us with his golden-blond hair and rosebud lips. We were told the surgeon would use a long needle to take a small amount of bone marrow from his spine. This would make him feel a bit sore for a day or two, but the anaesthetic would numb it for a while. After they had performed this procedure, they would insert a Hickman line (a small tube) into a vein in his neck, which would come out through his chest. From this they could give and take blood and give him fluids and chemotherapy. This was to be the last time we would cuddle him without that tube.

Stuart and I were given a bleeper that we would be contacted on once the operation had been done. We were told we could go anywhere in the hospital with it, so we used the opportunity to have some time by ourselves to try to take in what we had all been through in the last twenty-four hours.

"In a way, I'd prefer him to have AML," Stuart said as we walked down the stairs. "That way he'll only need to have treatment for six months."

"Yes. That would mean he would still be under two when it's all finished."

"He wouldn't even remember it," Stuart said.

"But isn't ALL the better one to get? The one they have more success with?"

"I don't know. I think it's all quite treatable nowadays. Your mum had AML and she's okay now."

"Yes, but I think it's different for children. Although the lady in the bay next to us with the little boy said ALL is meant to be better, but she's known children to have been diagnosed with AML and go into remission in the time that her son's had the illness, so she thinks it can't be that bad."

We walked into the concourse where we'd been told we could find something to eat. There we saw a hairdresser's, a clothes shop, a newsagent's, a general store, a Body Shop, and several restaurants and cafés. It seemed huge at the time, but after living at the hospital a couple of weeks it felt incredibly claustrophobic. "I can't believe we're even talking like this," Stuart said. "This time yesterday, the idea that Samuel could have any type of leukaemia was unthinkable to me."

We walked around the concourse, but it was impossible to take anything in. We didn't want to be there; we wanted to be at home, living normal lives. Eventually, just as we were starting to get more panicked than we already were, the bleeper sounded. We rushed straight out of the concourse and almost ran up the stairs to theatre. I had a bottle of milk with me to give to Samuel as soon as he woke up, as he hadn't had anything to eat and very little to drink all day.

As soon as we walked into theatre, we heard him. He wasn't crying, but he was making the little noises we knew meant he wasn't happy with things. We were taken to a curtained-off area and there, behind the curtain, was Samuel, lying in a cot frowning whilst a young theatre nurse tried to entertain him. We picked him up, cuddled him and gave him his milk. After a little while, the surgeon came out to talk to us.

"It went very well. We've inserted a single lumen line through a vein in his neck into his chest and you'll see the line coming out of the chest wall. We've also taken some bone marrow, which will be analysed by Samuel's consultant, and from that he will determine which type of leukaemia he has."

We thanked the surgeon and left the theatre. Normally, if your child has an operation you would feel pleased it had been successful, but we knew the operation that Samuel had just had was only the beginning. At the very minimum he had six months of chemotherapy to go through and he could have three years – and that was providing nothing went wrong. At this point, I couldn't help remembering a boy I'd been at school with who'd battled cancer all his life, with endless operations and rounds of chemotherapy, only to die at seventeen. I didn't want that life for Samuel.

When we walked back through the doors of C2, Nancy, Mum and Alan were standing in the corridor.

"You've been moved," Nancy said, after they'd fussed over Samuel. They showed us to another room, called A Bay, which was closer to the nurse station. "Apparently, they wanted Samuel a bit closer to the nurses tonight as he's just had an operation," she said.

Again, we were next to the window, and I noticed the young teenage boy who had been opposite us in the last bay had also been moved and was now next to us. At about five o'clock, my family decided it was time to leave as my sister had a long journey back to her house. We promised to call them once we'd had the official diagnosis, but we all felt quite sure he had the standard ALL, which meant that, although the treatment was over three years, the survival rate was high, with four out of five children surviving.

We settled into our new bay and found CBeebies on TV. This was to become Samuel's favourite escape from the new reality he found himself in, and was a godsend to us. I now laugh when I think about how I didn't want him to watch TV before he was ill, and compare that to the hours he spent glued to it. But it calmed him and was the best distraction he could have.

"Hello. Stuart and Amanda?" a man with a soft Scottish accent said. We looked up. "My name's Mike Gattens. I'm Samuel's consultant." We shook his hand.

Despite his position, he had an approachable manner and I liked him immediately.

"If you'd like to follow me to my room we can have a chat about Samuel."

I went to take Samuel with me, but then Mike added, "Perhaps it would be better to leave him with Jo."

I noticed the nurse standing a bit behind Mike.

"He'll be fine with me," she said with a smile. "Hello, Sam." She took him from me. "You're gorgeous, aren't you?"

Samuel made a little whimper and held out his arms to me.

"I'll be back soon, darling." I said. "BB and Woof Woof will look after you."

I gave him his favourite cuddly toys and he immediately hid his face with them. He stayed like that until we returned.

We followed Mike to his room near the entrance of C2. I have now become used to the feeling of dread that runs through every part of your body when waiting to hear potentially bad news. I am used to it, but experience has only made it worse. As we walked, I offered up prayers to a God I wasn't convinced existed. We walked and talked and smiled like this was normal. But, inside, we felt sheer dread. Mike opened the door and Boo was inside waiting for us. She sat on a bench at the back of the room next to a window, although it was now dark outside. She had one leg dangling down and her arms loosely folded over her other knee. She tried to smile at us.

"Hi, guys," she said.

Mike indicated for us to sit down. He sat opposite and looked at us. I knew immediately it was worse than they'd first thought.

"It's not good news, I'm afraid. Samuel has a very rare form of acute myeloid leukaemia called M7." Mike paused for us to take in this information. "AML is a form of cancer that affects the cells producing myeloid blood cells in the bone marrow, and M7 affects the platelet precursors. The leukaemia is also in his central nervous system, which means it's going around his brain."

I don't know if we were expected to cry or if Mike just wanted us to digest this information. I suppose everyone reacts differently and he has seen it all.

"Can you treat him?" Stuart asked.

I felt like I could hardly breathe.

"We have a treatment plan for him, yes," Mike said.

I breathed out as Stuart reached over and took my hand.

"He'll be given four rounds of chemotherapy over the next six months. We'll also inject chemotherapy directly into his central nervous system through the fluid in his spine. This will be done twice a week over the next six weeks."

"That sounds a lot for a baby to go through," I said with desperation. Mike just nodded.

The room remained quiet. I wanted an alternative. I felt that if I stamped my foot enough and made a big enough fuss, like a child having a tantrum, then someone – God or the authorities or *someone* – would put it all right for us.

"I feel like he'll go through all that and die anyway," I said.

"If you think like that, you'll never get through it," Mike said.

I was shocked. I didn't expect him to be so blunt, but it was the kick I needed. After a minute, Mike continued. "Samuel will be an inpatient for most of this time, but if we can get him home for the odd weekend between the four chemotherapy sessions, we will."

"Why does he have to stay in for his treatment with this type of leukaemia?" Stuart asked.

"The chemotherapy used to treat AML is very aggressive. Samuel is likely to become very ill and will need a lot of supportive care – such as intravenous antibiotics and blood and platelets, which can only be given in hospital."

"You can stay with him," Boo added, looking at me. "There's a pull-down bed next to every patient bed for a parent to sleep on."

"Can we both stay?" Stuart asked.

"You can stay for tonight on the ward," she said. "After that, there's a house in the grounds for parents of seriously ill children to stay in. I'll let the nurses know you are interested in staying there and they'll arrange it."

"I know it's a lot to take in," Mike said. He gave us a half-smile that I would become very familiar with; it was a smile filled with sympathy. "Do you have any questions?"

"When will you start chemotherapy?" Stuart asked.

"The first bag will be put up tonight," Mike replied.

I look back on this and think we should have been grateful. We should have been grateful that we live in a country where expert care is given to seriously ill children without the parents having to pay for it. We should have been grateful that doctors and nurses dedicate themselves to caring for and curing their patients. But at that moment I didn't feel grateful. I felt as if my precious child had been taken away from me, and I was struggling to accept Samuel's condition and the reality we now had to live with.

CHAPTER 9
A New Reality

~~~

THAT NIGHT WAS A DIFFICULT one. Stuart and I shared the three-foot-wide pull-down bed, attempting to sleep top to tail. Samuel was given painkillers that should have helped him, but he was so upset with everything that had happened in the past twenty-four hours that he still couldn't sleep. At about ten o'clock, a very nice nurse called Mel put him in a pram and wheeled him around the hospital in an attempt to get him to sleep, so Stuart and I could finally have something to eat. After about forty-five minutes she came back. Samuel was still awake.

"He'd almost dropped off when I took him into the concourse. I think it must have been too interesting for him, though, because he sat himself back up and had a look around. He doesn't want to miss a thing, does he?"

We laughed.

"He certainly doesn't," I said.

Eventually, he did fall asleep, but every few hours Mel came in to see him and take his blood pressure and temperature. On top of that, all three patients in the room had either chemotherapy or blood going through a drip, which meant when the bag was empty and needed changing a loud bleep would go off that was impossible to sleep through. Bleeps would also go off if the lines became squashed or moved in the wrong way. When this happened, the words "downstream pressure" would appear on the pump. Consequently, nurses would be coming and going throughout the night to see to all the patients. Sometimes a conversation would take place with the parents (which you tried not to listen to) and at other times children would cry with pain, which was more difficult to ignore.

Whenever Mel came over to see Samuel, I would jump up to help her and make sure he knew I was there for him so he didn't get scared. I kept this up for the first few nights, but after a while both Samuel and I grew used to the constant interruptions and we would try to ignore them. That's not to say he stopped waking up, because he didn't. In fact, not a night went by in the whole six months that he didn't end up in bed with either Stuart or me for part of the night. But he would ignore some things, like having his temperature and blood pressure taken. Of course, Stuart and I barely slept all night, but as we were in a room with other patients and parents, we didn't talk. Instead, we lay awake, going over everything that had happened and coming to terms with things in our own way.

I battled with my fears for most of the night. Images of a baby's funeral went through my head. I felt sick and I couldn't stop my body shaking. I loved Samuel more than anything in the world, and this was my worst fear. He was so young and brimming with potential. He'd barely started in his life and he had so much to experience, so much to enjoy, and I wanted to teach him things, take him places and, most of all, make him happy.

But I took on board Mike's message that I had to think positively to get through this, and I realised the doctors wouldn't have a treatment plan for Samuel if they didn't think there was a chance he might get better. I also knew the treatment would be harsh and Samuel would feel very ill. The thought of what he'd already been through in his little life upset me enormously, and I knew the next six months were going to be incredibly difficult for him. It would also be difficult for us, his parents, watching him go through it. But if all went well, then after six months he would be better and he could go on to live a normal life. However, there was a long way to go to get there, and not only did Samuel need us to give him love, support and encouragement, he needed us to stay strong and be positive as well.

As time went on, we realised we would also have to fight his corner when things went wrong or if his emotional needs weren't being met. Luckily, neither Stuart nor I (nor Samuel, for that matter!) am afraid to speak up if we think something is not right. But it wasn't always easy – especially if it meant questioning Mike or someone else we respected.

The next morning we were asked to see Mike again in his room. The previous evening he'd talked to us about a clinical trial, which involved the choice of drugs used in the second half of treatment being randomly chosen between two recognised routes: either the traditional British treatment plan or the American one. This clinical trial had been running for six and a half years and was nearing completion. To date, no significant differences were found in the outcome of either route, so it didn't seem we had anything to lose by taking part in the trial. Also, we would be helping in clinical research. So, when we went in to see Mike, we agreed to Samuel being involved in the trial.

"After our discussion yesterday, do you have any further questions about Samuel's condition or the treatment plan?" Mike asked.

"His condition sounds very serious," I said.

"It is," Mike agreed.

"Does he have a chance of surviving it?" I asked, tears springing to my eyes.

"He has a good chance," Mike replied with conviction.

I smiled. It was the best thing he could have said.

"Well, if you're going to be that positive then so are we. We can't imagine life without our little boy and we'll do anything we can to get him better."

Mike returned my smile. "Well, if that's everything, I just need you to sign the consent forms for the clinical trial and we'll get on with treating him."

When we got back to Samuel, Stuart's parents, Cynthia and Derek, were waiting for us. Both Samuel and Cynthia were crying. I initially felt panic, wondering what had happened, but then Cynthia hugged me.

"I'm sorry; it's seeing little Samuel look so ill. I cried and that made him cry."

I picked Samuel up and Stuart hugged his mum. I decided, there and then, that we would to have to set an example if we wanted the whole family to be positive.

The weekend was busy with visitors and Samuel's treatment. On the Saturday he was very sleepy, probably from the combined effects of chemotherapy and painkillers, so I lay on the pull-down bed for most of the day, with him cuddled into me. Feeling me there beside him, I hoped he would feel safe enough to sleep. Whilst Samuel slept, Stuart's sister, Debbie, and his brother and sister-in-law, Graham and Wendy, came over to see us. Knowing it would be a lot for Samuel to cope with if he woke and saw them all at his bedside, we asked them to come one at a time.

"You're being so brave," Debbie said.

"Where's Graham and Wendy?" I asked.

"They're in the parents' room, talking to Stuart. We've bought you some ready meals, so Stuart's labelling them and putting them in the freezer."

The parents' room was located next to the entrance of C2 and housed two sofas, a television and a kitchen area. There was no cooker, as this was deemed a safety risk, but there was a microwave and a large fridge and freezer. Stuart's family had kindly bought supplies of ready meals for us so we didn't have to spend a fortune buying all our meals on the concourse.

Once they'd gone, Samuel was given a blood transfusion and another fluid bonus. As he still had a cannula in his hand, the blood was given to him through that whilst the fluid was put in via his Hickman line. It takes roughly four hours to give a patient a blood transfusion, depending on their weight and tolerance, but after only three hours we were both shocked and pleased to see the transformation in him. Suddenly he had all this energy. He was a normal one-year-old again and he wanted to play and be like other one-year-olds. And he didn't want to be in a cot in a hospital with horrible things being done to him. In a flash, he pulled the cannula out of his hand and the tube from his nose.

"I can't believe he just did that!" I said, amazed and worried at the same time.

"I'll get a nurse," Stuart said, rushing off.

I picked up the cannula and tried to stop it dripping blood whilst checking Samuel's hand. Luckily, he just had a small scratch where the needle had been. Then I noticed the colour in his hand and realised it hadn't looked like that in a long time. I noticed also the colour in his cheeks and the little smile on his lips that had also been missing of late. Kelly, the nurse, followed Stuart over.

"Don't worry," she said. "He's actually had quite a lot of that blood, so it should have done some good."

"I think it has – it gave him the energy to pull that cannula and nose tube out," I answered.

"A bit of improvement, then," she said with a smile as she fiddled with the buttons on the pump to turn it off. "He doesn't need the cannula back in as we can use the Hickman line from now on, but I'm afraid it does mean he'll have to have that nose tube put down again whilst he's awake."

"Oh, no!" I hadn't thought of that. Kelly unhooked the bag of blood from the drip stand and put it into a blue plastic tray. "Can't it wait until he's next in theatre?" I asked.

She looked sympathetically at me. "I don't think so. That won't be for quite a few days and he might need a lot of medicine before then."

"I'm sure I could get him to take it by mouth."

She looked doubtful, but Stuart answered for her: "I don't think he would like that very much. How long does it take to put the tube down?"

"Seconds," she answered.

"Oh, I don't know…"

I looked at Samuel. I knew it wouldn't be pleasant and he had been through so much already. Also, he did look very pleased with himself for getting rid of it! I wondered if he felt like he'd taken a bit of control back. It's lovely now to think of him like that, as over the coming months we would all become worn down with the treatment and it became harder and harder to fight our corner.

"Don't forget he has to have his night feeds," Kelly said. "The doctors are really keen to get his weight back up."

I knew I was beaten with this.

"Could he keep it out for tonight and have it put back down tomorrow?" I asked.

I suppose this didn't make a lot of sense to her, but I wanted Samuel to keep his confidence. I knew we would have to hold him down when it was put in again and I was already worried about the psychological effect all this treatment and staying long term in a hospital would have on him.

"I suppose that would be all right," Kelly said. "I'll let the doctors know."

Over the weekend, knowing we were in for the long haul, we tried to familiarise ourselves with the ward and being inpatients. With Samuel feeling a bit better, we made the most of his newfound energy and took him to the playroom. In there he could forget the awful treatment and get on with being a child again. Holding our hands, he walked around inspecting all the brightly coloured toys and watching the other children play. The plastic multistorey garage (which was taller than him) quickly became a firm favourite. He would stand holding on to it and put cars down, one at a time.

"Un, oo, ee!" he would say, just as he did with his boats in his bath at home, before letting go and giggling as he watched them whizz down the spiral track.

For the next few nights Stuart wasn't allowed to sleep at the hospital (an exception had been made the first night), so he had to return home. This was difficult for both of us in different ways. It meant Stuart was able to get some much-needed sleep, but he found it incredibly hard to leave us each night and return to an empty home. In the living room, by the front door, were Samuel's new shoes. On the tray of his high chair was the conker we had collected on the way to see Dr Rutherford less than one week ago. There were Samuel's clothes in the wash, his bowls in the cupboard, and his spoons in the drawer. Everywhere there were reminders of how life had been before Samuel was diagnosed and our lives changed forever.

Hospital life was difficult for Samuel, who wanted to sit with me constantly and was even afraid to go to sleep in case he woke up and found me not there. On the one hand, he was a completely dependent baby – and a seriously ill one at that. On the other, he was very aware of his circumstances and was vigilant in checking what was happening to him. He clung to Stuart and me, thinking of us as his only safety, and stopped going to everyone else, including my mum, who had helped look after him since birth. In fact, it was a great loss for our families, who were used to cuddling and spending time with him. And neither of us got much sleep, which was disorientating and left me feeling even more emotional.

On Sunday morning Kelly arrived, thoughtfully carrying a tray with a cup of tea and toast for me, as she could see it was impossible for me to leave Samuel for long enough to make it myself.

"Right, little man. How are you?" she said, bringing over a syringe with Calpol in it. "Do you think you'll be able to get him to take this orally?" she asked.

"Yes. He doesn't mind Calpol." I picked him up and rested him on my hip. "If we got his weight back up, do you think the doctors would agree to him not having a nose tube?"

She looked doubtful. "Possibly, but it's not just his weight. I know he's only having Calpol at the moment, but in the future he'll probably be on quite a lot of drugs and it's so much easier for them to be put down the tube. I had the tube put down myself when I was training and it's not too bad if you do it really quickly."

She took a digital ear thermometer out of her pocket and put a new plastic tip on the end.

"But didn't it make you feel sick?" I asked.

"It makes you gag, but if you go past that bit in your throat quickly, the feeling only lasts for a few seconds."

She put the thermometer in his ear, and when it bleeped she took it out again. I noticed Samuel taking in exactly what she was doing.

"It's fine," she said, looking at the display.

"Won't he feel it in, though? I mean he obviously didn't like it or he wouldn't have taken it out."

"They can feel it to start with, but they quickly get used to it. We've asked the older children how it feels and they all say not too bad after a couple of days."

She got the green blood pressure cuff from a stand at the side and switched on the machine. It made a bleeping sound, and as she came over with it Samuel held his arm up for her. I was amazed how quickly he was picking up what to do. Kelly wrote down the readings on a small piece of paper then removed the cuff.

"I'll come and get you in a few hours and we'll go to the treatment room and quickly get that tube down."

"Okay." As she walked away, I said to Samuel, "I tried, poppet."

Luckily, he had no idea what I was talking about. Later that day we found out exactly what it was like when we took Samuel to the treatment room to have the tube put in. Stuart carried him and he actually looked quite pleased to be getting out of his bay and going somewhere different. When we got in there we sat him on my lap.

"Look, son, look at the planes," Stuart said, pointing up at the mobile above our heads.

Samuel looked up and gave a little smile. Kelly held up a white tube and measured it against him to see how far she should push the tube down to make it go into his stomach. Too far and it would go past his stomach; not far enough could mean it ended up in his lungs – either way would be dangerous. Samuel watched carefully as she measured the tube, looking down as she held it against his belly button. A piece of tape was stuck to the side of his face and he frowned and made a little noise to show his disapproval. Then Kelly quickly fed the tube up his right nostril and down his throat. As predicted, he gagged as it hit the back of his throat. He brought his hands up and went to pull the tube out, but I grabbed hold of his arms and held them down. It was horrible. It went against all my instincts as his mother. I wondered what kind of confusing messages I was sending him. The tube was laid across the piece of tape on his cheek and another piece of tape was put on top to cover it. The end of the tube was curled up and taped to the back of his Babygro.

"All done, poppet."

I hugged him tightly and kissed him.

"Well done, little man," Stuart said.

I have to say, Kelly was right. It did only take seconds, but she was also the best nurse on the ward at doing them. Our later experiences were not nearly so good, with one completely terrible, upsetting attempt.

On Monday Stuart decided to follow up on the idea of living on-site. He had mentioned it on and off to the nurses over the weekend, and it seems in that time a message had been left for the manager of the house. Stuart had just brought it up again with Boo on her ward round, when the assistant manager turned up to see him.

"Hi, I'm Jane," she said as we shook hands. "I understand you'd like a room at Acorn House?"

She was a jolly lady with a big smile.

"I would," Stuart answered. "At the moment I'm driving home every night and then in again the next morning. I know it's only a sixty-mile round trip, but it means I'm not here first thing in the morning when Amanda needs me."

"And I expect you could really do with some help first thing in the morning with the little one," she said, looking at Samuel fondly.

"Yes. I can only get a cup of tea and something to eat when Samuel's asleep, and I can't keep expecting the nurses to do it for me. They'll be getting fed up with me soon!"

"Well, we've got fifteen rooms at Acorn House and they're usually all booked up, but someone left this morning so I've booked you in."

"Oh, that's great!" Stuart said with relief. "Does that mean I can have it from tonight?"

"It's yours already," she said with a laugh. "Would you like to have a look round?"

"Yes – fantastic. Do you mind?" he asked me.

"No, go ahead. I'll have a look later."

Samuel and I watched *In the Night Garden*, his favourite programme, whilst Stuart looked at our new home. Acorn House is owned by the charity The Sick Children's Trust, whose patron is Michael Crawford. It's run entirely on donations and is free for parents to stay in for however long their child is in hospital. It costs on average thirty pounds per night, per room, to keep the house running, and the small donations that we gave them, when we could afford it, couldn't have come anywhere near what we used.

"It's lovely," Stuart said when he returned. "You'll really like it. It's modern with a big kitchen, a nice playroom and a lounge. We've got a bedroom on the first floor with a bathroom next door. I've got the keys here. Why don't you wander over and have a look?"

He picked Samuel up from my lap and Samuel whipped his head round, anxious not to miss what Upsy Daisy was up to. Stuart explained where the house was and I went off with the keys to find it. It felt lovely leaving the ward and the hospital building, even though I was still in the grounds. It was my first trip out of the building in five days. I felt like a prisoner on a day trip! Back in our old life, Samuel and I went out every day; sometimes twice a day. Our routine would be a baby club or a trip into town in the morning, a lunchtime nap, followed by a walk in the park or coffee at a friend's in the afternoon. Now we were confined to a hospital bed and it felt claustrophobic and restrictive.

I've always felt an intense need to be outdoors, to connect with nature, and to be in natural daylight. I also felt it was very important for Samuel, and right from birth he spent a lot of time outdoors with me in his Moses basket and, as he got older, watching me whilst I gardened. Now we were living with air conditioning and fluorescent lighting, but at least we were next to a window which let in a lot of natural daylight and sunshine; whilst I had that I could cope with the restrictions that had been placed on my life.

It seems awfully selfish to think like that when Samuel was so ill, but it's difficult to live in that environment twenty-four hours a day, for weeks and months at a time. Not only did I feel an almost constant fear for Samuel's life, but my old lifestyle had completely gone and what had replaced it felt like a prison sentence. I had little say about what we did with our day, our nights were filled with constant interruptions and, unlike the doctors and nurses, who undoubtedly have a hard job, I couldn't go home at the end of the day. There were no weekends off or nights out.

Whenever I felt like I couldn't live another day on the ward, I reminded myself of what Samuel was going through: everything I was, plus he had leukaemia. He was having chemotherapy and frequently felt sick. He needed to sleep more than I did and yet he was getting nowhere near the recommended amount a one-year-old needs.

There were nights when I would be up for hours, rocking him to sleep, almost hallucinating from tiredness. I would repeat over and over to myself, *Samuel feels worse*, just to remind myself why I had to keep going.

But now I was leaving not only the ward, but also the concourse! The feeling of being outdoors in that lovely September sunshine gave me so much pleasure and I wanted desperately for Samuel to experience it. I really appreciated that walk to Acorn House that morning.

Acorn House is situated near the nurses' quarters, just a little way from the hospital, but completely surrounded by trees. The leaves were now turning wonderful shades of orange and red. The building was two storeys high and built of pale gold brick with large windows. It was built in a U shape, with a courtyard in the middle with benches, and pots filled with purple and gold winter pansies.

I let myself in. The manager's office was on the right-hand side where Jane was sitting at her computer, and there was a window seat where a big Winnie the Pooh had made itself at home. Later, when Samuel was well enough, we would bring him to Acorn House, and he would always want to sit with that bear whilst I took off his shoes and coat.

I followed the corridor round to the left. There was a lounge with two leather sofas, a bookshelf and a widescreen TV. It was far nicer than the parents' room, where the fabric sofas were covered with stains. The kitchen was huge, with two ovens, two microwaves and three sinks, plus two long tables. I felt like we'd moved into the *Big Brother* house. Outside the back door was a children's play area and the kitchen also connected to the playroom. Through the door at the other end of the kitchen were the bedrooms and a laundry room. The laundry room was very useful, as Samuel needed frequent changes of clothes and would often go through four or five outfits in twenty-four hours, as the chemotherapy gave him diarrhoea.

Room 15 was upstairs in the corner. Two single beds were pushed together to make a double. This didn't matter to us, however, as we only slept at Acorn House together for one night in the whole six months and, even then, Samuel was in the middle of us! Opposite the bed was a built-in sink with a wardrobe either side, and in the corner was a wicker chair. It had been furnished simply but tastefully. So this was it: our new home and a bolthole from hospital life. We were very grateful to have it.

"I agree; it's lovely," I said to Stuart back on the ward. He was holding Samuel but had moved away from the TV to talk to our neighbours. I noticed Samuel had a Bourbon biscuit in his hand and I wondered where he'd got it. *That's an improvement*, I thought.

Samuel looked at me and smiled, then took a bite out of the biscuit. He looked very pleased with himself. Chocolate biscuits were not something he'd had a lot of in the past, but now we had to get his calorie intake up I suspected they would quickly become part of his new diet.

"We've just got into Acorn House," Stuart explained to the mum of the teenage boy, who was our neighbour.

We'd spoken to the boy, Adam, a few times over the weekend when he was on his own, but hadn't had a chat with his parents yet.

"That's lucky. I've heard it's very nice," she said.

"It is," Stuart replied. "It's a real relief getting in there. Just imagine if I had to pay for a bedsit somewhere – it would cost a fortune."

"We couldn't afford it," I said.

"No, but I would hate to be away from you both. I'm just really glad they've got a place like that."

"Yes. I expect years ago parents wouldn't have been allowed to stay on the ward either," the mum said.

I looked at Samuel and shuddered at the thought of leaving him.

As we returned to our own bed, Adam said, "You're very brave, Samuel." "And *you're* very brave, Adam,' I responded.

We quickly made friends with the other parents on the ward. It was impossible not to when you lived in such close proximity to each other. Talking to the other mums and dads was often the thing that got you through another day. Unlike with old friends, who were kind and supportive but had no real concept of what you were going through, with parents on the ward you didn't need to explain. They knew what it was like to get no sleep night after night, they knew what it was like to live out of a suitcase, and they knew what it was like to live with the fear and worry of a life-threatening illness. You didn't have to explain. They had also watched their child in pain, being given chemotherapy and morphine, and they had also wondered if their child would still be alive this time next year. But most of the time we pushed away thoughts of the future.

I reminded myself of the chance Samuel had every day for the first week or so, reliving Mike's words, "He has a good chance", to keep feeling positive. Soon I noticed a strange thing: all the parents on the ward had the same attitude.

Life didn't get much more serious than this. Childhood cancer is frightening, restrictive and painful, but it could be worse – at least our children were alive. And, whilst they were alive, we could all keep battling to get them better and to get back to normal life. However bad it got, there was always hope and that desire for a better future.

Towards the end of the day on Monday, Samuel was given another X-ray. This time it was easier, as a mobile unit came to our bay.

"What's this for?" I asked.

"Samuel had a slight temperature earlier and the doctors want to see if he has an infection."

"Oh, I didn't know," I answered.

After that, I made it my business to find out all Samuel's temperature readings. It's amazing what experts we eventually became on his treatment. A month down the line I'd got my sister to get us a digital thermometer, after noticing many of the other parents had them and were taking their children's temperature themselves. It was also essential for any time spent at home. But at this point, I didn't even ask where they thought the infection was, and I also wasn't prepared for the seriousness of these infections.

An image was taken of Samuel's chest, and as he just had to lie in his cot this time, it didn't seem nearly as frightening for him and he didn't make much fuss.

At around six o'clock that evening, just in time to see *In the Night Garden* for the second time that day, Stuart returned. At the same time Mick, the chef, appeared, dressed in a brightly coloured chef's outfit with cartoon animals on his trousers.

"Hello, Sam. What are you watching – Igglewhatsit?"

"It's Igglepiggle, isn't it, Samuel?"

Samuel smiled at Mick, as if to say, "Of course it's Igglepiggle!"

"How about something to eat, young man?" Mick said.

Samuel looked at Mick, but then his attention was drawn back to the television where Upsy Daisy had now joined Igglepiggle.

"He's not really eaten much over the weekend," I said. "We've tried him on a few bits and pieces and whatever we've eaten, but he seems to just prefer his milk."

In fact, I'd been finding it very hard to find things for him to eat. He was at that in-between stage of weaning, where he had outgrown puréed food but wasn't ready for grown-up food. However, there was no chance of me making anything from scratch, so we had to rely on things we could buy.

"Well, I work Monday to Friday," Mick said, "and I can cook whatever you like at any time of the day between ten in the morning and seven at night."

"Fantastic!" Stuart said. "Can you do me a Chinese?"

Mick laughed.

"Only for the kids. You'll have to get your own!"

"Back to the takeaway, then," Stuart said.

"Now, how about a bowl of chicken soup? That should be easy enough for him to eat, and if I do him some bread and butter he can dunk it in himself."

"That sounds great. Thank you," I said.

After that, Samuel decided Mick was a friend. As I said earlier, Sam was very vigilant and quickly worked out who was nice and who was likely to do nasty things to him. So, anyone in a blue uniform got a wary response, whereas Mick and Hazel and Maureen, the cleaners, got a little wave. I think Mick came top of that league table, but then he had the added advantage of keeping Bourbon biscuits on him, which Samuel became rather partial to!

That evening, Samuel seemed slightly more peaceful. Stuart had brought his musical fish box and some of his own blankets, and when we put him in his cot at seven o'clock and played his music, he fell asleep, just as he had done when we were at home. Before that day, Stuart and I had spent the evenings holding Samuel until he fell asleep.

"You'll go mad if you don't get some time away from this bed," Sophie, one of the sisters on the ward, said as she came over to check on Samuel. "Remember, you're in here for a really long time and it's hard for all of you. We're here; we'll keep an eye on him and if he wakes up we'll come and get you."

Stuart and I looked at each other.

"We could go to the parents' room," Stuart said.

"Have you had any dinner?" Sophie asked.

We laughed.

"I don't think we ever eat before ten at night," Stuart said.

After a week or so, we learnt to bring our dinner to Samuel's bedside. That way at least we got some food, and I think Samuel quite liked us all eating together. But for now we decided to go to the parents' room together for the first time to have something to eat.

That night we took our baby monitor with us, but the range was too far and it just crackled, so either Stuart or I would go back every fifteen minutes to check he was still asleep. The nurses also kept an eye on him.

After a few weeks, we became more confident about leaving him with the nurses whilst he slept, and would even go across the grounds to Acorn House.

It was nice to get away from the bed, and it was amazing what a laugh we had with the other parents. Nobody would have believed that we were on a children's oncology ward, but if they listened in they would have heard the most distressing topics being discussed.

Many of the parents had other children at home, so would have to be there without their partners. The advantage of this, though, was that they could swap with their partners and return home for a few days to experience normality. This break would give them the strength to get back to the ward and do it all again.

We learnt that Samuel was the youngest patient on the ward and the second youngest they'd ever treated for cancer. Elsewhere in the country there have been other babies with cancer, some of them younger than Samuel, but it's very rare.

The only other parents who were staying as a couple were Sarah and Nick, who were there with their son, Oscar, who was a year older than Samuel.

Oscar quickly decided Samuel was going to be his friend, but for a long time Samuel was too ill to do much other than watch him. There was one funny occasion a few months on, when both boys were at home but came in for day-patient appointments. They sat side by side at the little table in the waiting room and were given Play-Doh and rolling pins to play with. Oscar set to work, diligently rolling out the bright pink dough, but Samuel took his rolling pin and bashed his Play-Doh flat.

"No, Samuel. You do it like this," Oscar said, demonstrating.

Samuel watched Oscar, pursed his lips in a way that I knew meant he wasn't going to be told what to do, and returned to bashing his Play-Doh.

But that was in the future, when things were going well. We still had a long way to go to get there and already it felt never-ending.

After we'd eaten, Stuart said to me, "Why don't you stay at Acorn House tonight?"

"Oh, no; that's your place."

"No, it's not. It's for both of us and you haven't slept properly for weeks."

"Is it just weeks? It feels like forever."

"Well, it's probably getting on for a couple of months, and that's a long time to exist on just a couple of hours' sleep a night."

"You're right, but I'm so tired I don't think I'll ever wake up again."

"Then have a lie-in. Catch up a bit. Me and the boy might, too."

"You'll be lucky!" I laughed. "The nurse will be round taking his blood pressure at seven."

I saw fleeting hesitation on Stuart's face.

"No, you go. You deserve it."

So that night I went to Acorn House and had the luxury of a bath and a full night's sleep without interruption. And, unlike before when I'd had the chance to sleep but had instead spent the night worrying about Samuel, on this night I didn't worry, knowing he was finally being treated and had "a good chance" of getting better.

CHAPTER 10

Settling In

~

WHEN I THINK BACK TO Samuel's illness, what strikes me most is
how quickly things changed. Within a week we'd gone from nobody
believing my fears, to a life-threatening diagnosis.

By the Tuesday, we were just beginning to accept our new reality
when, once again, everything changed. I was woken that morning in
Acorn House by a knock on my door. I had been in a deep sleep and
it took a moment or two to realise where I was. Panic gripped me and
I jumped out of bed and rushed to the door. My friend Nicky was
standing there.

"I'm so sorry," she said.

Tears ran down her face as she hugged me.

"Come in," I said, feeling relieved, although the adrenaline continued to flow through me. "It's okay. We're okay. I'm just glad they
know what's wrong with Samuel and they can treat it."

"You sound so positive," she said, sitting down on my unmade
bed. "Did I just get you up?"

I laughed.

"Yes, but don't think I'm lazy – I haven't slept for weeks."

"I know, you silly thing." She hugged me again. "I was so worried he had leukaemia, but when I spoke to you and you said he was
coeliac, I thought that made sense and I was relieved."

I was shocked that another person had suspected Samuel had leukaemia.

"I didn't realise you thought that," I said. Then I remembered her looking in his eyes and squeezing his toes, just as I'd seen the doctors do. "I'd better get to the ward," I said, suddenly feeling worried. I stood up. "Stuart will be wanting to get washed and dressed and he's probably desperate for a cup of tea."

"Okay, but I'll come and see you a bit later, if you don't mind." She wiped her eyes. "I was going to be so strong!" she said with a laugh.

Nicky left and I quickly got dressed. My feelings after a night at Acorn House always followed the same pattern: I would generally have a worry-free night, knowing Samuel was being well looked after, but as I walked towards the hospital my mind would start whirling again and I'd worry about what I was going to find when I arrived at the ward. By the time I reached the busy concourse, I would be so desperate to check on him that I would feel stressed by people standing in my way and would race round them, the fear clearly visible on my face. Samuel was safe in Stuart's arms when I arrived. I picked him up and cuddled him.

"How was your night?" I asked Stuart.

"It's quite hard to sleep, isn't it?" he replied.

I nodded.

"Is Samuel all right?"

"Yes, but he woke up a lot. The nurses come in all the time, except when you bloody need them! Samuel's machine was bleeping for fifteen minutes last night before anyone came in to see to him."

"I know it can feel like forever, but there's only three nurses on for seventeen patients."

"Well, it's not good enough. It keeps everyone awake, including Samuel. He's hardly getting any sleep. I think they forget he's one, not ten."

I agreed. It was a conversation we ended up having many times; not just between us but also with the nurses. However, although many were sympathetic, I think Samuel's age was often forgotten when it came to his treatment. It wasn't just his sleep at night that was disturbed. Up until we went into hospital he had two naps during the day as well: one between nine thirty and ten and another between twelve and two. Now the morning nap seemed to coincide with the doctors' ward round, so either he didn't get it or he was woken up by a doctor prodding his stomach or trying to look in his mouth.

After breakfast, Stuart went to Acorn House to have a proper wash and get changed. I was glad he had the week booked off work, although I dearly wished we were all in the holiday cottage in the Peak District, where we should have been, rather than in hospital. I was already dreading the idea of coping on my own all day, every day, and having no one to talk to. He hadn't been gone long when the doctors appeared for the ward round.

"How are you this morning?" Mike said as he walked over to us. Boo and another doctor followed. Mike pulled the curtain around us. He took the stethoscope that was hanging on the end of the cot and listened to Samuel's chest. "The X-ray that Samuel had done yesterday shows some shadowing on his lungs."

I don't think I ever got used to hearing serious, shocking news about his condition. In the past, when I'd watched *Children in Need* or any big appeal, I'd been under the misconception that those parents had accepted their lot, but it's simply not true – you always feel shock.

"What does that mean?"

Mike sat down on the bed next to me.

"Well, it would suggest a chest infection; possibly pneumonia."

"That sounds worrying," I said.

"We need to start him on some antibiotics straight away, which we'll do intravenously and orally."

"How did he get pneumonia?" I asked.

"Well, as you know, chemotherapy attacks the good cells as well as the bad and, effectively, leaves Samuel with no immunity. Therefore, it leaves him vulnerable to all sorts of infections." He gave me that half smile which I saw so often – a smile that didn't reach his eyes, which were now looking at me sadly. "It's why we're so vigilant at checking his temperature. It's our first indicator of an infection, and the quicker an infection is detected the quicker we can get some treatment going."

"I see," I said, trying to remain calm.

"He's been experiencing diarrhoea as well, hasn't he?" Mike asked.

"Yes. Is that a reaction to the chemotherapy?"

"Quite possibly. But it could also be a bug, so as a precautionary measure he's going to be moved into his own room and be barrier nursed."

I must admit, not knowing what barrier nursing entailed, I was just pleased we were getting our own room. Thinking purely about the bleeping machines, I envisaged a better night's sleep for all of us. However, as the weeks went on and the realities of barrier nursing made themselves known to me, I desperately wished to be back in that ward with the other children and parents and all their bleeping machines!

By the time Stuart came back, carrying two cups of tea, our belongings were already being moved into J Bay, which was opposite the nurse station.

"We're moving," I said as he walked over. "We're having our own room."

"That sounds good," Stuart answered, handing me a cup of tea.

"Well, yes, but actually it's because Samuel has an infection."

Remembering how I'd felt when Mike suggested that Samuel might have pneumonia, I carefully explained the conversation we'd had so Stuart didn't worry too much. "Poor little chap!" he said, leaning over and giving Samuel a kiss. "I've had a chest infection before and it's really painful. It feels like your chest is on fire, so goodness knows how bad pneumonia must feel."

The way parents are told about developments in their child's condition is very matter-of-fact, no matter how terrible the news. Obviously, it would be normal for a parent to worry if their child had pneumonia, but this was just an additional concern for us as Samuel's main condition was leukaemia. But, once I'd got over the shock, I realised this infection was a complication for the consultants but not an uncommon one. Of course, people can die from pneumonia, or any infection – and many of the children on our ward had infections that took them into intensive care – whilst there was hope we focused on it.

J Bay was a large room with a window overlooking the playground. Initially, I thought this was lovely and I thought how nice it would be for Samuel to watch the children, but after a day of being in there I realised no one went outside, and also the room never got the sun. In fact, there was a canopy over the window which always made it look gloomy outside, even on the sunniest days. However, it was private and it gave me some control over Samuel's sleeping, as I could close the curtains and turn off the lights to help induce sleep.

After one particularly awful day, when Samuel had been woken up every time he fell asleep, I finally vented my annoyance at the nurses, so a sign was made for the door to say Samuel was sleeping and not to disturb him unless urgent. I'm sure I didn't make a good impression that day and I wonder if the nurses thought I was being a bit precious, but I'd made a vow to myself that I would always do what was best for Samuel, even if it meant I made few friends. Samuel was a baby – more than that, he was an extremely sick baby and he needed sleep. He wasn't a machine that could just be fixed, and he had needs other than medicine that had to be met. As many of the nurses were young, most of them didn't have children and they just had no idea how much sleep a baby needs.

Many people have said to me, "Babies will sleep when they need to," but Samuel couldn't just fall asleep when he needed to. He felt ill, unsettled and anxious, and all these factors made getting him to sleep extremely difficult. So when I had just got him to sleep after an hour of soothing and rocking him, it was hard to stay calm when a doctor, nurse or cleaner walked in and woke him up.

I realised what barrier nursing meant when the first nurse came into our room wearing gloves and a disposable plastic apron over the top of her uniform. If the diarrhoea was caused by a contagious virus, rather than as a result of the chemotherapy, then the doctors and nurses had a responsibility to protect the other vulnerable patients on the ward. To do that they would wear aprons and gloves and wash their hands thoroughly after seeing Samuel. It does make you feel a bit like a leper, but we understood the reasons.

Another way they protected the other children was by not letting the barrier-nursed patient out of their room, and this was something I found very hard to cope with. If you imagine waking up in your bedroom and then not being allowed out all day and all night, that will give you some idea what it's like. If on top of that you know it's sunny outside, but the room you are in looks dark and gloomy, and day and night you are constantly disturbed by nurses, that will give you an even better idea. And this went on for weeks, not just one day.

It was far worse for Samuel. The chest infection made breathing difficult, but one of the nurses showed us how his cot could be tilted so he could sleep with his head higher than his feet, and that helped him to breathe a bit more easily.

The chemotherapy, which he was due to have for ten days, made him sick, and the diarrhoea gave him horrendous nappy rash. These sores were large, open wounds which looked like burns. The chemotherapy he was given was so toxic that Stuart and I were told to wear plastic gloves when changing his nappy, as his wee would burn our skin. Obviously, Samuel had no protection, so his skin was red raw. I cannot stress enough how upsetting it is to know your child is suffering so much. No wonder he couldn't sleep!

I was determined to do something about the terrible nappy rash, so each day we kept his nappy off as much as possible and laid him on incontinence pads, which we could change as soon as he weed. The doctors prescribed a thick barrier cream that we used constantly, and after a couple of weeks the nappy rash cleared up and his bottom looked like the soft, squashy little bottom a baby should have. We kept up this routine whenever he had chemotherapy, and he never did get nappy rash again, so that was one discomfort off the list.

We wanted to do anything we could to make Samuel more comfortable and to make his life a bit more pleasurable. We loved him so much. He wasn't just a baby to us; he was a little person who had a big character and a lot of fighting spirit.

After a few days, we were pleased to see not just the antibiotics but also the chemotherapy begin to take effect, and by Saturday night Samuel was sitting up and smiling and interacting once more. As a treat, the children are given a meal from Burger King once a week, which is great for the older kids, but we were slightly unsure about Samuel eating all that salt. However, we needn't have worried, because he took one small nibble of a chicken nugget then put it back in the box as if it was the most distasteful thing he'd ever been given. To compensate, we gave him an equally unhealthy Kit Kat, which he loved, and we have the most wonderful video footage of him eating it.

As the camera's video screen, as well as the lens, was directed at him, he saw himself as we filmed. He lifts his arm up to put the Kit Kat to his mouth, sees the person on the screen do the same thing, frowns, moves his arm again, just to confirm this person looking at him really is him, and then begins to play up to the camera! He puts his face right up to the lens and pulls a funny little face, then laughs and waves his arms around. At the time we just thought it was really cute. We've since watched a documentary that said children don't recognise themselves until they are between eighteen and twenty-two months. Samuel was fourteen months old at the time. We always knew he was advanced!

On Sunday we were told that the contents of his nappy had been tested and no contagious viruses had been found, so the cause of the diarrhoea was put down to a side effect of chemotherapy. Therefore, it was decided he was well enough to come out of J Bay and go into C Bay, which is a two-bed room. It's one of the better rooms and I was relieved we were to go next to a window. Being cooped up for so long was making me obsessive about getting some daylight. It also meant we could take Samuel into the playroom, and I was pleased he could get out a bit more and see the other children. I resolved to take him in there straight after the doctors' ward round the next morning. Stuart was going back to work the next day, after being off for eleven days, and I knew it was going to be difficult to occupy Samuel by myself, so I was really glad we were no longer barrier nursed and wouldn't be stuck in one room.

That evening I stuck Samuel's cards to the wall beside his cot and tried to make this new bay feel a bit more homely. I was getting used to life on the ward and was feeling a bit more confident about coping on my own once Stuart went back to work. However, that evening Samuel was very unsettled and it was difficult to get him to sleep. When we finally got him off, we went to the parents' room and ate dinner, but when I came back to check on him he'd had terrible diarrhoea again. I got him changed and one of the nurses put a small bottle of sterilised water down his NG tube to keep him hydrated. Not daring to leave him again, I decided to go to bed and Stuart went over to Acorn House.

The next morning, Stuart came over early, bringing me tea and toast, and yoghurt for Samuel, before he left for work. It was a beautiful, sunny day and I got chatting to a mother, Helen, and her teenage daughter in the bed next to us. Samuel fell asleep on my bed at about ten o'clock, so I asked Helen if she would watch him for me whilst I got myself a drink from the parents' room. I was just sitting back with Samuel, reading a magazine and drinking my tea, when the doctors walked through the door for their ward round. As the months went on and the doctors and I became used to each other, I started to ask them to come back later if Samuel was sleeping, but at this point I was too worried about keeping them waiting.

On Mondays and Fridays the consultants and doctors had a meeting before visiting the children, then they would come round in a group instead of in pairs, as they did on the other days. Samuel woke up from his lovely sleep in the sunshine to find seven doctors all staring at him. His little mouth immediately turned down (giving them the three-second warning!) as he looked at them all and then he let out a cry. I picked him up.

"Sorry, sorry!" Mike said. "We won't stay long."

I don't think he realised the damage had already been done and there was no way Samuel would go back to sleep after that.

"We're a bit concerned that Samuel had diarrhoea again last night. I think it might be better to get him back into a single room and barrier nurse him again."

"But we only came out yesterday," I said, feeling confused.

"I know, but we can't take any chances."

"But I was told his nappy had been analysed and no viruses were found."

"Yes, but that was done on Saturday; he might have picked up something by now."

"Really?"

"I know it sounds unlikely, but we have to be cautious."

So, before I knew it, I was unsticking the cards from the wall and one of the nurses, Mary, was carrying my bags to another room. Poor Samuel never did get to the playroom, and I had to leave the company of both another mother and the sunshine.

F Bay added to my nightmare: it was a small, dark, single room with no window. It was originally a cupboard, but it had been turned into a bedroom when space was limited, and had stayed that way.

"I can't stay in here," I said to the nurse as soon as I walked in. I felt claustrophobic and trapped. A prison cell would have had more appeal.

"Samuel has to be barrier nursed, so you'll have to," she said, putting my bags down. "Make sure you keep the door shut," she said as she walked out of the room.

Most of the nurses were completely approachable and sympathetic, but not this one. She was older and stern looking. I later learned she'd been given the nickname "Scary Mary" by some of the parents, as she had a reputation for her cold, unhelpful manner.

I sat Samuel on my lap and put on the TV as a means of distraction. I didn't want him to sense my anxiety, but I felt like a caged animal in that room. Being in hospital undergoing chemotherapy is a horrendous life for a child anyway, but to have no interaction with other children or any outside stimulus was even worse. TV helped, but there's only so much of it you can watch and there was nothing else to do. I don't know why a window was so important to me, but without any daylight I felt I would go mad. I decided I would have to ask to be moved the next time Mary came back in. An hour later she was back.

"Samuel's medicines," she said. She placed a grey cardboard tray containing five syringes of medicine onto the table together with some litmus paper, two empty syringes, and a bottle of sterile water. We'd only been in hospital just over a week and up until then the nurses had always given Samuel his medicines. I looked up at her, feeling confused.

"All right?" she asked, going to walk out.

"I've never given him his medicines before," I said.

She stared at me.

"Well, all the other parents do."

I was taken aback.

"Then you'd better show me how to do it," I said.

She sighed.

"Right, I'll do it."

"I don't mind doing it, but I can't if I've never been shown."

She didn't answer me. Instead, she roughly pulled off the tape that was holding Samuel's NG tube to the back of his Babygro. I felt upset and concerned. I didn't know all the other parents gave their children their medicine, and no other nurse had asked me to do it.

"Show me how to do it, then," I said, worried that I wasn't looking after Samuel properly.

"No, it's fine. I'll do it for you."

She took the end of Samuel's tube and drew up some of his stomach juice using one of the empty syringes. She then dabbed a small amount onto the litmus paper and checked the colour it turned against the chart. This was to check his NG tube was still in its proper place in the stomach.

Suddenly I felt angry. It was bad enough being in that room, but now I was being talked to like a prisoner as well. I was the mother of a seriously ill child! Samuel's illness was hard enough to cope with without this nurse making things worse.

"Once you've done that, I'd like to speak to one of the doctors," I said.

She looked slightly anxious.

"Oh, would you? Why's that?"

I noticed her tone of voice had completely changed.

"Because I'm not happy about a few things and I'd like to discuss them with a doctor," I answered.

She put the medicines down the tube and followed them with some sterile water to wash the tube through.

"Okay, love, I'll just see if anyone's available. Can I get you a cup of tea?"

"No, thank you, just a doctor," I answered.

When the doctor arrived, I asked if we could move to a room with a window.

"I'm afraid there aren't any rooms available," she said.

"I'm really struggling to be in a room without any natural daylight," I said.

The doctor looked sympathetic.

"I'm sorry. I know it's not a nice room, but we really don't have anything else available."

I sighed. I felt desperate, but it looked like I didn't have a choice. I was just going to have to think of Samuel and try to get us through this time.

"I understand, but when another room becomes available can we have it?"

She assured me we could, but it was six days before we were moved, which felt like an eternity, and even then it was because I saw for myself that a room was empty and asked to move into it. I didn't complain about Mary, but I never did tell her what I had wanted to talk to the doctor about, so she kept up her pleasant act whenever she was around us. However, I know other parents did put in complaints about her. Sometime later she was moved from C2.

We got through that first day with the help of a big stack of books. I sat and read to Samuel, but it was a lot of hours to fill. The next day was better as Lisa, the play lady, came in for an hour, bringing with her a big play mat for Samuel to sit on and lots of toys. He particularly liked a caterpillar that crept along by itself, and he giggled as it inched its way around his room, making funny little noises as it went. As he was barrier nursed it meant any toys or books we borrowed from the playroom would have to be thoroughly washed before other children played with them, so the toys Lisa brought with her that day stayed with us for the next few weeks, much to Samuel's delight.

That evening our friends Angie and Len came to visit. The idea was that once Samuel had gone to sleep, we were going to treat ourselves to a pizza on the concourse. It's sad to say, but our social life was in such a state of ruin that we were actually excited by this prospect. We were, however, slightly worried about going out of the ward, as up until then we'd not gone any further than the parents' room. We told the nurses where we were going and asked them to come and get us, or call Stuart's mobile, if Samuel woke up. The concourse is only a few hundred feet away from the parents' room, but it seemed like a big step to be taking.

Samuel took a long time to get off to sleep that night, so Stuart sat with our friends whilst I rocked him and played the wave setting on his musical fish box. Eventually, after about an hour, he dropped off and I carefully laid him in his cot and crept out of the room. It was great to see Angie and Len, but our minds were so full of Samuel we found it hard to relax and enjoy their company. We'd been with them about fifteen minutes and had only just ordered our pizzas when Stuart felt he should check on Samuel.

"I can't unwind until I know he's all right," he said. "He's been so ill these past few days and I'm worried no one will hear him if he wakes up."

So Stuart left me to fill our friends in on the last couple of weeks whilst he went back to the ward. After ten minutes our pizzas arrived, but Stuart still hadn't returned.

"I think I'd better see what's happened," I said, assuming Samuel had woken again.

"Well, have a bit of your pizza first and then you can take over," Angie said.

I had a few mouthfuls, but it was difficult to relax. Suddenly Stuart came rushing back.

"Something's wrong with Samuel," he said. "They're getting the doctor but he's not breathing properly."

"Just go!" Angie said, and we ran back to the ward.

When we got back there were nurses in his room.

"He's okay," one of them said. "He was making a strange sound when he breathed, but I don't think it's serious."

"It sounded terrible," Stuart said. "Like a seal's bark. I thought he was having an allergic reaction to the antibiotics."

Soon after, the doctor on call came in and examined Samuel.

"I think he has croup," he said. "Keep him as upright as you can and we'll keep a close eye on him."

It really amazes me how little fuss Samuel made as he dealt with one illness or infection after another. He didn't cry; he didn't get upset; he just bravely got on with living.

"I'll sit with him for a while and get him off to sleep. You get back to Angie and Len and have your pizza," I said.

Stuart went back to our friends for a short while and had his dinner, and I sat up with Samuel. Eventually he fell asleep and I put him back in his cot, which I'd tipped so his head was higher than his feet. However, lying down made his breathing worse again, and after a few hours I heard him make the same terrible sound that Stuart had mentioned earlier. I called the nurse in and she said she would ask the doctor to see him again.

It was about four in the morning when the doctor on call arrived, and he decided to get a more experienced doctor to examine Samuel. I was glad he was being cautious and my concerns were being listened to because, as ridiculous as it sounds, I worried for a long time about being too demanding. As I got used to hospital life and Samuel's condition, I began to trust my instincts more, and found the doctors always took my concerns seriously.

After the more senior doctor had examined Samuel, it was decided that a nebuliser should be used to loosen the phlegm on his chest. A mask that is fitted over the patient's face and a vapour is pumped into it, which the patient breathes in. Different medicines can be put into the vapour, depending on the patient's condition.

A lovely nurse called Liz came through straight away with the nebuliser. I lay Samuel back in my arms and Liz started the machine. She attempted to put the mask on his face but he became very frightened, and although he didn't cry he was clearly distressed. The vapour released smelt strange and the machine made a loud noise that must have increased his anxiety. Again, I worried about holding him down and wondered if he thought we were trying to harm him.

"It's okay, darling," I repeated several times as I fought to keep the mask over his face.

With an older child we would have been able to explain what was happening, but it must have been extremely frightening for Samuel. It only took a few minutes, but in that time we both got wound up and stressed. When the mask was released I saw Samuel relax in relief, and I'm ashamed to say I burst into tears. I really wish I hadn't reacted like that, and had instead just comforted him. I expect the lack of sleep contributed to the overwhelming emotions I was experiencing. However, I did try to learn from this, as it felt better all round when I controlled my emotions; I learnt to, where possible, just take a really deep breath. But I am proud to say my little boy showed what he was made of, as he quickly turned to his tearful mother, glared at Liz, and then gave her a big kick as if to say, "That's for upsetting my mummy!"

"I'm so sorry!" I said to Liz. Of course I don't advocate violence, but I was amazed, yet again, by Samuel's fighting spirit. I cuddled him into me. "It's all right, poppet. Mummy's just being silly. It's all done now."

Liz accepted my apology with her usual good grace and Samuel, at last able to breathe better, managed to get some sleep, albeit in my arms in my bed. Liz propped the pillows around me and I tried to doze, but I wasn't very successful.

The next morning Samuel was due to go back into theatre for his fourth dose of chemotherapy in his lumbar spine. The treatment felt relentless and torturous and I had the strongest urge to pick him up and take him home, away from all the painful, distressing procedures. I didn't, of course, because I knew the reality was he wouldn't have lived for very long if I'd done that.

It was decided that Samuel would be last on the list, as he was barrier nursed and that way theatre could be thoroughly cleaned after him. This meant he wouldn't go into theatre until about eleven in the morning, and consequently wouldn't be allowed to eat or drink anything until midday, after the procedure. Again, I felt that his age wasn't being taken into account; it must be bad enough for a ten-year-old not to eat or drink anything when they are feeling ill and thirsty, but at least they would be able to understand why. With Samuel, I had to use distraction to stop him becoming too distressed – not easy when you are in a small room with limited entertainment options. On top of which, of course, he still had croup; a horrible illness on its own, let alone in conjunction with leukaemia.

Eventually, the theatre porters came to get Samuel and I carried him as they wheeled his cot round to the small theatre in the day unit. Whenever I went through the double doors to the day unit, I always envied those children and parents who could come and go with their cancer treatment and didn't have to stay on the ward. It seems funny to me now that I envied them rather than healthy children, but I think it was because I felt so far removed from normal family life. These families had lives that were just a slight improvement on mine and, therefore, it felt obtainable.

The day unit had six beds, a small theatre, a waiting room and three consultation rooms. The staff in the theatre were always friendly and seemed to understand how hard it was to leave your child there. Somehow Samuel always seemed to know that something was about to happen to him, and he would become anxious. He would look up at me with his big eyes and shake his head, but I knew this procedure should rid his central nervous system of leukaemia, which would rid him of the painful headaches. The theatre staff were quick to administer the anaesthetic via the Hickman line, which made it easier, and then, as he dropped off to sleep, a mask was put over his face to give him oxygen. I always thought how gorgeous he looked as he seemed so peaceful and, unlike normal sleep, when he was anaesthetised he didn't have his dummy in and I was able to see his beautiful rosebud lips.

"Give him a kiss, Mum," the anaesthetist always said, which was my cue to put him in his cot and go. "We'll look after him."

I never wanted to leave him, but I was aware that the theatre staff needed to get on with their jobs. The procedure took about fifteen minutes and gave me just enough time to grab a cup of coffee and something to eat. I would then race back through, usually just as they were wheeling him out of theatre in his cot, surrounded by all the cuddly toys people had bought him. Initially, the nurses would wake him up to make sure he was okay, but he was always terribly upset when he was woken this way, so after a while I asked them to leave him to wake up naturally, even if it took an hour or more.

That afternoon Stuart's parents came to visit. Stuart had seen me on his way to work that morning and I'd practically begged him to take the morning off as I was so tired after another night without sleep. I was also worried about distracting Samuel prior to his procedure, and I knew it would be a stressful day. But, of course, Stuart felt he couldn't take any time off work as he'd only just started there; he didn't want to jeopardise his position. Instead, he asked his parents to come in for a while so I could go to Acorn House and have a sleep whilst they babysat. They were there waiting when Samuel, still asleep, was wheeled back to the ward, so I sneaked off for an hour whilst they looked after him.

I was grateful to them (and all our family) for coming in so I could do that every now and then. It wasn't an easy journey for them, involving travelling on the Park and Ride, but they did it even in terrible weather. I never stayed at Acorn House long, however, because I worried about Samuel waking up and finding someone different there. On this occasion I needn't have been concerned; he was still asleep when I returned. When he woke up, I lifted him out of his cot carefully so as not to pull on his line, and gave him his milk. He must have been very hungry, as it was about ten hours since he'd had anything to eat. Once he'd finished his bottle, I carried him to the play mat whilst wheeling his pump over with my other hand.

"Look, poppet. Nanny and Grandad are here to see you," I said. Samuel gave them a little smile.

"Would you like a biscuit, darling?" Cynthia asked, offering him a packet of digestive biscuits.

He looked in the packet, then cheerfully took one out and nibbled on it. After we'd all taken a biscuit, Cynthia put the packet on the play mat beside Samuel. He took a few more mouthfuls then put the biscuit down so he could get on with playing with his toys whilst we all chatted. After a while, he reached over to the packet and helped himself to another one. I saw Derek look slightly disapproving but, after all Samuel had been through, I didn't want to upset him by insisting he finish the biscuit he'd already started. Besides, I knew that part of the appeal of the biscuit for Samuel was taking it out of the packet, and I was just glad to see him eat something and enjoy it. However, when it came to Samuel doing it a third time, Derek could contain himself no longer.

"Now, come on, young man. Finish that one before you take another one."

"Ooh, Derek!" Cynthia said, giving him a glare.

I looked at Samuel, expecting to see a downturned mouth. Instead, he pursed his lips and frowned, as if Grandad had been very naughty.

"There you are, poppet," I said, offering Samuel the packet.

He took out a biscuit, looked purposefully at his grandad, took a bite, then turned his head away with his nose in the air.

"I'm sorry, Samuel," Derek said.

Samuel looked back at him, took another bite of his biscuit, then turned away again quickly. This time he even bottom-shuffled round so his back was facing Derek. Much to our amusement, he kept this up for about an hour with Derek periodically apologising to Samuel.

I sometimes wonder if I was setting myself up for trouble if Samuel had lived, but his life was so far removed from normality that I think it was acceptable to spoil him a little. He needed to know he was loved and could rely on me, and fun and treats were in short enough supply.

The terrible diarrhoea Samuel was experiencing continued, although an infection was never found. It kept us barrier nursed and confined to that room, which I'm sure is not good for either the parent or patient's mental health. On top of that, there was concern that he was not getting all the essential nutrients or calories he needed. He was still fed milk each night through the NG tube, but this was a delicate balancing act. Too much made him sick and contributed to the diarrhoea, but not enough meant he went short on calories and would lose weight. Although he wasn't active enough to use up many calories that way, cancer itself burns calories, so it was always difficult to keep his weight stable. Samuel was underweight when he was admitted, so his weight was always a concern.

To counteract this, doctors can prescribe a type of feed called TPN – total parenteral nutrition – that is fed intravenously into the blood via the Hickman line. TPN contains all the essential vitamins, minerals and calories that a patient needs, but it does have drawbacks. It increases the chance of an infection in the Hickman line, and also uses up the line twenty-four hours a day, which makes giving intravenous antibiotics, chemotherapy, blood and platelets difficult. It was difficult for the doctors to balance all his needs as it meant that he had to be off TPN if the Hickman line was needed for anything else. It also meant he was tethered to the pump twenty-four hours a day.

By the fourth day in F Bay (or, as I was now calling it, the cupboard) I was obsessed with the idea of getting Samuel outside. Of course, he was incredibly sick and maybe I was projecting my own needs onto him, but I felt sure he would feel just a little bit better in himself if he could get some fresh air and see the sun.

That day the doctors came round a little later for their ward round and Samuel was already midway through his lunchtime nap when they turned up. The room was in darkness apart from a side-light I had on to read by as I sat by his cot. The doctor gave a light tap on the door.

"Is he sleeping?" he asked when I opened the door.

The doctor's name was Amos. I hadn't met him before, but had noticed him because he always wore a colourful bow tie. I'd also heard other parents mention how nice he was.

"Yes, he is," I answered.

I hesitated, torn between thinking I should let him come in and get on with his job and wanting him to come back later.

"That's fine. We'll come back."

"Oh, thank you!" I said, surprised and pleased that I didn't have to ask.

"Are you okay? Have you any questions?"

"Well, actually I do, but I don't think you'll be able to do anything about it. I was wondering if there was any chance I could take Samuel out? I know he's barrier nursed, but I just think it would do him so much good."

Amos nodded and said, "It's a lovely sunny day out there." He considered for a moment. "You'll have to go straight through the ward and concourse without stopping, and just stay in the grounds, but I think half an hour would be all right."

"Really?" I felt like an excited child. "The only other problem is he's supposed to be on TPN twenty-four hours a day."

"That's okay. We'll just make it twenty-three," Amos replied, in his laid-back way.

I was ecstatic. I couldn't wait to get Samuel out. So, whilst he slept, one of the nurses got me a buggy and we lined it with sheets that could be put straight into the wash when we returned. Mick, the chef, even joined in by showing me how to put the buggy in an upright position, and Hazel and Maureen, the cleaners, told me where to put the sheets when we returned. Then, when Samuel woke, he was taken off his machine. I felt such a sense of freedom! For the first time in ages I could pick him up and cuddle him without having to negotiate the different tubes that were attached to him. Before anyone could change their minds, I wrapped him up in a big blanket and strapped him into the buggy. Samuel looked up at me and smiled.

"We're going outside, poppet!" I said, and wheeled him out the door, down the corridor, through the ward, out of the hospital and into the sunshine. I bet he couldn't believe it after two weeks of being cooped up indoors! "This is nice, isn't it?" I said as I wheeled him along a path towards a grassy area where medical students were sitting eating their lunch.

I looked down at him – he was taking it all in. I pointed out the birds and squirrels, just as I did back at home in the Abbey Gardens. I pointed out the berries on the trees and colours of the leaves and, just for a little while, life felt normal. I was so very grateful to Amos for letting us out that day. I hope it cheered Samuel up a bit. It certainly saved my sanity.

CHAPTER 11

Towards Home

~

By Saturday, we'd been living in the cupboard for six days and had now been in hospital for a total of seventeen days. I felt like part of the furniture. We still had no idea how long Samuel would be an inpatient so I tried, as far as possible, to live in the moment, and at that moment I was just grateful it was the weekend and Stuart was there to help. We'd also had some good news: Stuart's employers had generously agreed that he could work from the hospital two days a week. This was fantastic as it meant I could have the odd night's sleep at Acorn House, and Stuart would be able to spend more time with Samuel.

That morning, Graham and Wendy and one of their sons, Joe, came to see us. In fact, they came nearly every weekend, and it was particularly kind as it took them a couple of hours to get to us. They always brought food and drink to help us out for the week and never took any money. Thank goodness we had lovely families like that to support us. I can't imagine how hard it would have been to do it all on our own.

As I walked to the parents' room that morning to get us all a drink, I noticed that J Bay was empty and the cleaners were moving the furniture about and giving the room a thorough clean. I hung around the nurse station until one of the nurses came over.

"I've just seen J Bay is empty," I said to Carol, the ward manager. "I was wondering if we could move into it."

"Sorry; I've got another patient coming in today who'll be going in there."

I felt momentarily deflated, but the thought of Samuel and me staying in that small, dark room pushed me to take a stand. In my opinion, we had well and truly taken our turn in the cupboard. I could see a window from where I was standing and I wanted it!

"I spoke to one of the doctors earlier in the week and she said as soon as another room was free we could have it."

"Well, that would mean we'd have to move all your stuff out of your room and then clean that room as well."

"We'll move everything, then the room will just need cleaning."

"I don't kn—"

"It's really important to me to have a window and I'm sure the doctors would agree that the patient's mother should be happy. We're expecting to be in here for a long time."

"Oh, okay." She sighed. "If you move everything."

I rushed back to our room before I'd even made the drinks. "We can move! We're going back into J Bay."

"Is that a better room?" Graham asked.

I think they'd been shocked to find us living in a cupboard when they'd come in that morning.

"Yes, it's where we were before," I said. "It has a window. But we have to move everything ourselves."

It took no time to move with all of us doing it. To make things easier we took the cupboards, which were on castors, from our room as well as Samuel's cot and all his toys, our small suitcase, and the various bags we'd acquired. As I saw the cleaners go into F Bay, I momentarily felt a pang of guilt about the patient who would end up in there, but I hoped it would be someone who'd come in for just a short stay and not someone like Samuel, who was in hospital for the long haul.

The next few days were better ones for all of us. We were still barrier nursed, but the doctors were slightly more flexible and allowed us to take Samuel out for fresh air once a day, if he seemed well enough. I don't know why they suddenly allowed this, but one of the doctors did say fresh air might help with the croup. The contents of Samuel's nappy were still being tested and no contagious viruses had been found, so that may be another reason why they were a little more lenient.

With the help of visits from family and friends, and the extra two days a week that Stuart was able to be here, the days were bearable. Samuel kept up his brave fight with the help of lots of cuddles from us and distractions like visitors, toys, books and, most importantly, the television. The characters from his favourite CBeebies programmes had taken the place of all the small children he used to spend his time with and had become his new friends.

"Eh oh!" – learnt from the Teletubbies – suddenly appeared in his vocabulary, and he could hum the theme tune to *In the Night Garden*, even though he barely spoke any words.

But nights were still difficult. If there were no interruptions, I could usually get him to sleep by eight, then Stuart and I would spend a couple of hours together in the parents' room to relax and have a meal. It was always busy, so we would have to wait our turn for the microwave and to wash up. We were hardly ever alone. If we wanted time to ourselves to talk, we would walk around the concourse. Later on, as Samuel got better, we risked going to Acorn House, but it was hard to relax knowing we'd left Samuel alone in his room. On one occasion he was sick whilst we were away and the nurses had to call us. We felt so guilty coming back and seeing him being comforted by someone else, but the nurses were always kinder to us than we were to ourselves, and encouraged us to take time away.

Some nights were more difficult than others, and there were times when we didn't eat until eleven at night. In our first week back in J Bay the croup lingered, as did the chest infection which was still not properly under control. At the same time, Stuart and I both developed heavy colds; probably the result of not eating or sleeping properly. Usually parents are asked to stay away from the ward if they have a contagious illness, but the doctors agreed our absence from Samuel would have a worse effect on him than our germs, so we were allowed to stay with him as long as we kept away from the communal areas.

During this time, our friends Glenn and Nicola came to visit us. Stuart was at work at the time, and with everything that was going on I had forgotten they were coming. Samuel was having trouble breathing again, so Boo asked one of the nurses to give him another nebuliser. This time I asked the nurse not to completely cover his face with the mask, but to hold it above him so he wouldn't be so distressed. To make him feel more relaxed I lay on the bed with my face close to his, so it would seem like we were having it done together.

"Look, Mummy's having some, too," I said, trying to raise my voice above the loud hum of the nebuliser and Samuel's fearful cries.

Just at that moment our friends appeared at the door.

"Oh, not a good time," Jo, the nurse who'd shown them to our room, said.

I think Glenn and Nicola wondered what they'd come into. If they'd been under any false impressions of what life was like on a children's cancer ward, they saw the reality of it that afternoon.

"This would put me off having children," Glenn said as he saw tired, stressed parents looking after sick, frightened children.

The trouble is, nobody plans for their life to be like that. When we fantasised about having a baby, we didn't for one minute imagine the life we were now leading. We loved Samuel from the minute he was born and we wanted the best for him. We certainly didn't want him to be brought up in hospital. But once your child is born you take what comes and you try to make the very best life you can for them.

And, as one parent said to me on that ward, "If it means I'll spend my entire life on C2, I'll do it to keep my child alive."

To help with Samuel's breathing, Boo suggested I take him out for a short walk. I was grateful to get out and I tried to remain upbeat in front of him and my friends, but it was all an act. In reality, I felt worried, ill and exhausted. On top of that, I felt guilty, as I knew Samuel was going through far worse and yet I just wanted to sink into bed and sleep.

That evening, instead of Glenn and Nicola seeing me give my baby a bottle, they watched as I put five different syringes of medicine through his NG tube before hooking it into a container of milk and setting the machine to drip the feed through at thirty millilitres per hour. Our new routine was very different from our old one, but I still tried to make Samuel's life as normal as possible by incorporating aspects of our old routine to help him feel secure. So, we still attempted to put him to bed at seven and we still played his musical fish box first, but it was a long way from the life we wanted him to lead.

Every evening we were given Samuel's blood counts, which included his haemoglobin levels, his white blood count and his neutrophils. Whilst he was having chemotherapy the blood counts would fall. After that they would stay flat for a few days – or longer if he had an infection – and then, hopefully, they would rise again.

We'd been in hospital for almost four weeks and his neutrophils should have been rising, but they weren't. We might get a reading of 0.02 one day, but then by the next day they would be back at 0.00. They needed to be at six before the doctors could start the next round of chemotherapy, but they just weren't going up. If I'd known then what I know now I would have been worried, but at this stage I thought this was normal. Every time the nurses took his temperature it was above thirty-eight degrees, suggesting he still had an infection. He would then be given Calpol to bring his temperature down, but despite intravenous antibiotics the infection wasn't clearing.

This had been going on for several days with Stuart and me waiting expectantly each evening for his blood results.

"Why aren't they going up?" Stuart asked, looking over the numbers one evening.

I looked at his face and saw how the stress and tiredness had taken their toll.

"It must be this infection keeping them suppressed. I'll ask the doctors if they can do anything when they come round tomorrow," I said.

Samuel couldn't sleep that night. The croup lingered and his temperature remained high despite the regular administration of Calpol. By three in the morning, the nurses decided to get a doctor to see him. A lady doctor I'd not met before came to examine him.

"I'm really worried that Samuel's temperature isn't coming down, despite the antibiotics and Calpol," I said as she looked him over.

She checked his notes.

"I think I'll arrange a CT scan to ascertain where exactly the infection is," she said.

"How will that help fight the infection?" I asked, confused.

"It will determine if we're giving him the correct antibiotics," she said. "At the moment he's having good general antibiotics – think of them like Domestos. They're designed to kill all bugs, but they aren't specific and may not be the best ones for the infection he has."

I nodded.

"That makes sense. Will he have the CT scan tomorrow morning?"

"I'm going to try to get it done now. We need to get this infection under control and his temperature down."

I was shocked. I knew a serious infection could kill him, so the fact that this doctor wanted the CT scan done immediately indicated she thought Samuel was at risk. In the end, the scan wasn't done until morning as there were no slots available and, by then, Samuel and I were both absolutely shattered. Even more of a concern was that his temperature was still high.

As it's essential to be still whilst the CT scan is done, young children are usually anaesthetised. However, it was decided there wasn't enough time to wait for an anaesthetic, as he would need to be starved for six hours prior to it. As he continued to have his milk feed throughout the night, we would have had to wait until the afternoon. He was so tired I thought he would either lie completely still, or he would be anxious and cry and hold his arms up for me. Luckily he stayed still as the giant Polo-shaped machine passed over him, and we were able to get back to the ward quickly.

We'd just returned to our room when Stuart's parents arrived. Samuel was sitting on my lap and one of the nurses had put a pillow under my arm so he could lie back and fall asleep. I gave him his bottle of milk and watched him drink. He was desperately tired and his eyes kept closing, but he was unable to relax for long enough to sleep. I felt unbearable sorry for him. He was a charismatic, engaging little person, who should have been running around, playing with his friends, and living life to the full. Instead, he was in a hospital room, barred from seeing other children, and tethered to a machine most of the day. I truly appreciate the wonderful medicines and tests available to him but, at the same time, it's incredibly difficult to watch someone so vulnerable, someone you love so much, go through endless, invasive treatments. Right at that moment, watching him struggle and with both of us feeling so exhausted, I wondered how we would cope with another five months of it. I tried to hold back the tears, but they slipped down my face anyway.

"Oh, Amanda. How do you keep going?" Derek said.

He told me later he felt fearful seeing me upset, as I'd been so positive until then. But four weeks in hospital, with Samuel still seriously ill and countless sleepless nights, had drained me, and at that moment I was unable to hide it.

Mike came to see us when Stuart came back from work that evening.

"We've decided to give Samuel something called GCSF," he said.

"Sounds like something he should be doing at school!" Stuart said, trying to remain upbeat.

Mike smiled.

"We give it to patients to increase their neutrophil count. This will kick-start his immune system and he should then be able to fight off this infection."

"Will you be changing his antibiotics as well?" I asked.

Mike shook his head.

"He's on a really good mix already. I think we should just see how he is when his neutrophils start to rise."

Another sleepless night followed, and then another. Then, just when I wondered if we could go on any longer, the GCSF took effect and Samuel's neutrophils shot up. In an amazing turnaround, he began to pick up. The croup went and his breathing settled down. He slept more easily and he wanted to play again. At last Stuart and I began to feel more optimistic. Samuel's strong character had never left him, even when he must have felt worse than I can imagine, but now he had more energy and, better than that, he smiled again.

Then, before we'd even had time to ask, we had another huge boost to our spirits when Mike gave us more good news. It was early evening and the nurse had just left Samuel's medicines for me to give him. I washed my hands in preparation whilst Samuel sat on my bed and watched the telly. I was just drying my hands when Mike knocked on the door and walked in. His smile was the first thing I noticed, and this time it was a smile that reached his eyes and lit up his face.

"Is Stuart around?" he asked.

"He's not back from work yet. Is everything all right?"

"Yes," he said. He hesitated for a moment. "I just wanted to update you on how Samuel's treatment is progressing. Ask one of the nurses to give me a call when Stuart's back and I'll fill you both in."

I don't think I'd ever seen Mike look so happy, and I was cautiously excited about hearing his news.

"Okay," I said.

Mike put his hand on the door handle and went to go, but I suppose he was used to worrying people so he thoughtfully added, "It's good news," before leaving the room.

I couldn't wait for Stuart to return from work.

"Hello, little man," he said to Samuel as he walked in. He picked him up from my lap. "I've just seen a couple looking really upset in the corridor. I think she was crying. I wonder what news they've just had."

"Oh, no!" I'd been so excited about hearing Mike's good news but there was no getting away from the seriousness of the other children's conditions. This was a cancer ward and young lives were hanging in the balance.

"Mike came in a few minutes ago to tell us he's got good news for us, but I feel sorry for those people."

"What's the good news?" Stuart asked.

I could tell he was as desperate as I was to hear something positive regarding Samuel's condition.

"I don't know; he's going to come in and see us."

"Well, whatever it is, we'd better keep it to ourselves – or at least from the other parents."

I agreed. We asked Helen, the nurse, to let Mike know that Stuart had returned from work, and a few minutes later he was back in our room, still smiling.

"I wanted to tell you that we've just been looking under the microscope at the cells in Samuel's central nervous system." This was the area of Samuel's body that had also been found to have leukaemia cells and was the reason why he had chemotherapy injected directly into his lumbar spine twice a week. It had been a huge worry to all of us – including, I think, Mike – as no one knew how easy or difficult it would be to get rid of the leukaemia from there. We looked at Mike expectantly. "I'm pleased to say we can't see a single leukaemia cell!" he continued with a huge grin.

"Really? That's fantastic!" Stuart said.

"I can't believe it. That's wonderful!"

I was so happy I wanted to hug Mike, but he made a quick exit! Helen came in a minute later.

"Everything okay?" she asked.

"We've just had good news," I said.

"I thought you must have done," she said. "It's not often we see Mike smile like that."

All the nurses were really happy for us, but at the same time perhaps they were thinking of the parents who'd had the opposite news. Every child on that ward had a life-threatening illness and all of them were vulnerable. From experience they must have known that just because things were going our way now, it didn't mean they always would. But we quietly celebrated Samuel's good news and hoped that it would continue.

After almost five weeks of hospital treatment, Samuel suddenly seemed considerably better. As a result, he spent most of his time off his machine, as he didn't need the intravenous antibiotics, blood, platelets or TPN feed. Apart from a few trips out, he'd spent much of the past few weeks dressed in a Babygro, sitting on my lap. Now, however, he felt better and he wanted to play and behave like a normal child of fifteen months, so I dressed him in daytime clothes again.

Suddenly he appeared older, and the doctors and nurses began to see the full extent of his character. He began to bottom-shuffle around the room and would go right up to the door and try to get out. He would bang on the door and look at me with such sadness. It really broke my heart. I, too, wanted to get out. At least it was easier to entertain Samuel now he was feeling better; the play ladies brought in more toys, including some paper and paints, to keep him occupied. For a few days we remained barrier nursed, and then we were given our freedom. The door to our room was opened and allowed to stay that way. Samuel was able to leave his room and see what was going on in the rest of the ward.

It was so lovely to be able to take him into the playroom again. On that first day I carried him into the busy room and he couldn't stop smiling. A table had been set up with trays filled with lentils, some scoops and sieves, and what looked like water wheels to pour the lentils into. Samuel stood up at the table next to Oscar and looked so busy and important as he played his game. It was the first time he'd stood for weeks and yet he stayed there for at least twenty minutes, completely absorbed and uncomplaining. I sat with Sarah, Oscar's mum, to chat, and if it hadn't been for the nose tubes and lack of hair I could have convinced myself we were at a children's playgroup.

Samuel began to walk again, holding my hands, and would frequently lead me to the doors of C2 to let me know he wanted to get out. I took him out as often as his treatment allowed, carrying him if all the pushchairs were in use. This meant we couldn't go very far, but I felt it was important to get him out of the room he'd been imprisoned in for so long. One sunny morning I carried him to the trees at the front of the hospital and I got him to feel all the different barks and leaves. We stayed doing that until I could hold him no longer. On another afternoon we went to the café on the concourse, I sat him in his own chair and we shared a muffin. He was more interested in throwing bits of muffin on the floor and watching where they landed, rather than eating it, but at least he had fun!

By the weekend we heard murmurings amongst the doctors and nurses about allowing us to go home for a few days before starting the second round of chemotherapy. We had put all thoughts of going home out of our minds – it made it easier to get on with the treatment – but at the first mention of home I realised how desperate I was to get back there. Nothing concrete was mentioned, however, so we waited each day for news.

On the Sunday we were by ourselves and not expecting visitors. The day before, we'd taken Samuel to a little park just outside the grounds of the hospital. We were considering going back again. However, the weather was bad and we wondered if the wind and rain would do Samuel more harm than good.

"I'd love to go to that pub they told us about," Stuart said.

"Imagine asking the consultants that!" I laughed.

"Well, why not? Sarah and Nick have taken Oscar there."

"That's true. And they've been allowing us to take Samuel out for longer and longer."

"Samuel would love to go to the pub. Wouldn't you, little man?"

Samuel looked up at me and smiled.

"I think that was a yes. Wasn't it, poppet?"

When Matt, the consultant on call that weekend, came to see Samuel, we asked him.

"Apparently there's a lovely pub in Grantchester that does a nice Sunday lunch," Stuart said as Matt examined Samuel.

"Yes, I've heard that," Matt answered.

"We were wondering if we could take Samuel there. As long as he keeps off the beer, of course."

Matt laughed.

"Well, we were thinking of allowing you home this weekend, but I'm afraid Samuel's blood counts are not quite high enough. But Grantchester's only a ten-minute drive away, so I should think you could take him there as long as you're not back too late."

Just then, Samuel whipped his dummy out of his mouth and gave it to Matt to hold. It was as if he was saying, "There you are, my good man. You may have my dummy for being so nice!" Matt dutifully held it whilst he talked to us then, after a while, Samuel held out his hand to have it back.

I think neither Samuel nor I could believe it when we got in the car. It was our first time out in over five weeks. The furthest we'd been in all that time was to the park; a five-minute walk from the hospital. Our lives had become so centred on the hospital and his treatment that we'd both forgotten what normal life was like.

The Red Lion at Grantchester was old, large and beautiful. As we walked in and saw healthy children and their families, I felt very aware of how different our situation was, but then I shifted my focus back to Samuel and Stuart. I was lucky to have them both, and to have time away from the ward.

We ordered our drinks and food, including soup and a roll for Samuel, then found a table. Samuel kept giggling and holding his arms out to be passed back and forth between us; we slid him across the table to each other, which he loved. Luckily we were in a little booth, so nobody could see our terrible table manners! We had our meal and were pleased when Samuel ate some of his. We talked and laughed, slowly shaking off some of the stress we'd been under, the sadness we'd felt and the strangeness of being in and then out of hospital.

All too soon it was time to go and we were back on the ward and in our room. I could see the happiness leave Samuel's face as we came back, and I wished with all my heart he didn't have to go through all this. We put on the telly to distract us, but now we'd had a taste of freedom we were all desperate for some more.

On Thursday we finally got our wish and were told we could go home for the weekend. I phoned Stuart at work and told him our news, and he said he would try to leave a bit early to help me pack. I asked Jane at Acorn House if we could leave our things there, rather than packing them all up to take home. Unfortunately, they couldn't keep the room for us as someone else may need it over the weekend.

I packed our room at the hospital and then the room at Acorn House. It took more than two hours to do just the hospital room and I had to ask Judith, one of the play ladies, to look after Samuel whilst I carried everything from our room to Acorn House. It took about five trips and Samuel was slightly distressed at being left with Judith, as he'd become so used to only being cuddled by Stuart or me.

But when I said to him, "We're going home, poppet," he gave me the biggest smile; I knew he understood.

At Acorn House, Samuel sat on the bed whilst I packed all our clothes and toiletries into the suitcase. It then took several trips to carry the suitcase and bags downstairs to the front door. I had to carry Samuel in one arm whilst I did this, as well as trying to open the heavy fire doors. I remember thinking, *I can't wait for Samuel to walk; it will make life so much easier.*

Thankfully, I was able to leave him in the playroom downstairs, where he could see me in the kitchen, as I packed up our food cupboard. I'd bought a jar of baby food from one of the shops on the concourse on the way through, so I heated it up in the microwave and gave to him. He wasn't too keen, but it was getting late and I didn't know what food my sister would have got in for us at home.

Eventually Stuart arrived, and it took another hour to pack everything into the car. Then, at about half past seven, we were off. On the way home I phoned my sister to let her know we were coming, and then we stopped to get fish and chips. It was about half past eight when we finally walked into our house; six weeks to the day since we'd left it. Samuel should have been exhausted; it was way past his bedtime. Instead, his face lit up with happiness and excitement. He manoeuvred himself straight over to his little trike and took great pleasure in being wheeled around the living room. It was gone ten before we got him into bed that night, and that was after he'd helped himself to several of my chips. So much for my Gina Ford routine and organic diet – now my baby was eating chips and staying up all night! But I don't think we could have been happier that night. I only wished it could have been forever.

CHAPTER 12

Round Two

~~

OUR LIVES WEREN'T SUDDENLY NORMAL now we were back at home. We still had to give Samuel his medicines and set up his night feeds, but we did have our freedom back. Also, Samuel was able to relax with no doctors or nurses around who could potentially do something painful or frightening at any moment. We gave him his own toys to play with and pushed him in his own pushchair, but it all felt like a novelty – as if we were only playing at normal family life.

As we only had a few days before going back into hospital we didn't want to waste them doing things like shopping, washing and cleaning, but we did need to get some food in. So, on that first day at home we took Samuel into town. Our first stop had to be Bakers Oven. We joined the queue and were waiting our turn when suddenly one of the ladies behind the counter saw us.

"There's Samuel!" Kirsty exclaimed, grabbing Rachel's arm.

Rachel looked up and immediately burst into tears. We were so touched. It was amazing to think our little boy had such an impact on people, but – as Rachel herself had told me – he was very special.

Once we'd done our shopping, we walked back home through the Abbey Gardens. It was 4ᵗʰ November and a lovely sunny day. We walked past the huge horse chestnut trees and formal flowerbeds with their autumn displays until we reached the river at the end, where we stood and watched the ducks. Samuel was all tucked up in a pale-blue fleece snowsuit, so we didn't get him out of his pushchair, but he looked happy just to watch the wildlife.

We bumped into several neighbours on the way home and everyone was pleased to see him and eager to find out how he was getting on with his treatment. I heard how shocked everyone had been to hear of his diagnosis and how many people had cried when they'd heard the news. When we were in hospital, I had become so consumed by what the three of us were going through that I'd forgotten how much it had touched our family and friends as well.

Our neighbour Nancy came round as soon as she got the chance and we all sat in the living room, Samuel on Stuart's lap. He looked so content being back in his own home, and I'm sure he knew we were all talking about him. At one point he reached up and touched his nose tube. I wonder if he thought he shouldn't have it in as he was no longer in hospital.

"If you pull that out we'll have to go back to hospital," Stuart said. Samuel's little mouth turned down immediately and his lip started to wobble. "Don't cry, little man," Stuart said, hugging him. "Everything's going to be all right."

Stuart didn't realise Samuel would be so upset, but I think he'd become more sensitive since he'd been in hospital. He'd had several nose tubes put down now – he'd pulled two out and a nurse had blocked another one by not diluting a medicine – and it was always distressing for him. He obviously hated the thought of returning to hospital and I worried about taking him back on Tuesday, as we hadn't explained we'd only be home for a few days. He was only fifteen months, but I think we underestimated just how much he understood. Because his illness made him less active than a healthy child, he spent more time watching and listening, and he clearly took everything in.

"He's going to be such a good boy at school," Nancy said, seeing how easily Samuel did as he was told.

As a teacher, her thoughts always leapt forward to school years, even with her own children, but I didn't dare think that far ahead. I just hated to see him upset. He'd been through so much more than most other children and I wanted to protect him from every hurt.

The weekend was lovely. We were all far more relaxed and Samuel slept better, but we were aware the whole time that the clock was ticking and we'd soon be heading back to hospital. Then, on Monday morning, we had a call from the ward clerk. They only had one vacant bed and the admissions department was trying to fill it with a non-oncology patient as they were short of space elsewhere in the hospital. They asked if we could come back right away instead of waiting another day, as they were concerned Samuel wouldn't get a bed and they didn't want to delay his treatment. We knew we didn't have a lot of choice, but we didn't want to cut our stay at home short as it felt all too brief as it was. In the end, they agreed to us returning early that evening.

During the day I managed to buy Samuel a few Christmas presents and a replacement BB (Bedtime Blankie), as the original had been lost in hospital, most probably hiding in the laundry department somewhere. Stuart got some work done at home.

Late that afternoon we reluctantly began to pack. Samuel sat on our bed with the suitcase as we took clothes from our wardrobes and put them in the case. He was quite happy until he suddenly realised what this meant. His little mouth turned down and he looked from one of us to the other, then he bent his head as the tears rolled down his face. We rushed over to him.

"I'm sorry, Samuel," Stuart said, putting his arm around him.

We sat on the bed with Samuel between us and hugged and kissed him. We stayed there for some time, just holding each other whilst Samuel cried quietly.

After a while, Stuart explained, "We have to go back to hospital because you're still not well and the doctors and nurses are going to make you better."

"And then we'll come home again, poppet," I added.

Samuel stopped crying, but he also stopped smiling.

We packed the case quickly, grabbed some food to take back to Acorn House, and drove back to Addenbrooke's. We stopped at the front of the hospital so I could carry Samuel straight in, as it was dark and getting cold. I also took a carrier bag full of all the teddies he'd been bought since he'd been ill so I could make his cot feel cosy as soon as we got there. We'd only been away for four days, but it felt strange going back. During the six-week stay I'd begun to feel like I lived on the ward, but going home had shaken things up and the hospital now felt like an alien environment again.

Jo, the nurse, walked out from behind the nurse station as I struggled up the corridor with the bags and Samuel.

"Hello, Sam," she said. "I'll show you to your room."

I was expecting to go into J Bay, the isolation room we'd occupied before, so I was surprised when she led us to C Bay, the two-bedded room.

"I was thinking we'd be barrier nursed again," I said, "but, of course, he hasn't got an infection."

Jo laughed and said, "Make the most of it!"

"We will. We'll be spending all our time in the playroom, won't we, poppet?"

Samuel's cot was waiting for him and there was nobody in the other bed. Our room had been so packed with our things last time that it really did feel like we lived there. Returning to an empty room made it feel much more like a short stay in hospital. However, that feeling didn't last.

Stuart soon came in carrying lots of bags and then we got Samuel ready for bed. It didn't take long before we felt fully back in the thick of it all.

Samuel started his second round of treatment the next day and, like the last time, he was scheduled to have ten days of high-dose chemotherapy. This time, however, he wasn't immediately ill. Knowing that barrier nursing could be our fate at any moment, I made the most of every opportunity to get him out. We went to the playroom first thing every morning and then out for a walk as soon as the doctors had seen us for the ward round and he was off his pump. When he had chemotherapy or blood going into him, I would drag his pump around with me on castors, although we never left the ward. I would carry him in my free arm, but I had to be careful not to pull on his Hickman line. If the battery got low, I would need to plug the pump in. However, the playroom had plenty of sockets available for such an eventuality.

Hospital life was definitely easier second time round. Knowing how cooped up I felt on the ward, I took Samuel to Acorn House as often as possible and sometimes even gave him lunch there. Stuart and I also spent many evenings there, as it helped with the days if I knew I was going to get a couple of hours away later on. This was a dilemma, though, because I hated the thought of Samuel waking up and finding us not there. On one occasion, our roommate told us he had been left crying for some time the previous evening and no one had come to him. This put a stop to our trips away for a while, until we spoke to the parent about it some more. He was sharing C Bay with us whilst his little girl, Chloe, was an inpatient there. Unlike us, however, he didn't stay every night as he had another daughter at home, so he and his wife took it in turns.

We asked him if it had just been a one-off occasion or if he'd heard Samuel cry many times. He assured us it had only been the once, so we gave him our mobile number to call us if it happened again. As his daughter was older, he tended to stay by her bed until she fell asleep. We also stayed with Samuel until he fell asleep, but obviously that was much earlier than his daughter, who was eight years old. I found it essential to get a break in the evening, but I worried about Samuel. In the end, we went to Acorn House if he'd had a good day, but stayed on the ward if he hadn't.

It was amazing what a difference it made not being barrier nursed. There were many more activities arranged for the children who were well enough to do them, and I felt it was such a shame that Samuel had missed out on these before when he could have really done with some entertainment. Older children who can't get out of their rooms are given crafts to do and Mick, the chef, cooked with the children, but I suppose Samuel's age limited his options. However, Mick still entertained him, as did Maureen and Hazel, the cleaners.

"Cooee, Samuel!" they would say as they entered the room. Samuel would wave at them and hand them Woof Woof to hold. "Ahh! Isn't he lovely, Maureen?" Hazel would say, and Samuel would bask in their admiration.

The TV was still our constant companion, though, and we were watching it just after Samuel woke from his midday nap a few days into our second stay. He was sitting on my lap, as always, when suddenly his head whipped round and he looked towards the door. C Bay had double doors that were kept open as it wasn't a barrier-nursing room. I looked towards the door but could see nothing there.

"What can you see, darling?" I asked him. Samuel pointed towards the door and looked up at me. "Do you want to go out?" I asked.

He started to wiggle off my lap, but then gave a huge smile and sighed with happiness. I looked back at the door and saw a dog put its head round.

"Oh, a doggy!"

Samuel giggled as the dog then its owner, a gentleman of retirement age, came into our room.

"Hello there, young man," he said. "This is Jodie, and she's a PAT dog." He worked as a volunteer with the Pets As Therapy charity.

The rusty-coloured whippet sat obligingly in front of Samuel, who demonstrated that he knew what "pat" meant by doing just that to the top of her head.

"Oh, you like dogs, don't you?" Jodie's owner said.

Samuel smiled.

"He loves dogs," I answered for him.

Samuel continued to pat Jodie's head.

"Perhaps it would be better if you just tickle her under her chin," Jodie's owner said, somewhat nervously.

I noticed Jodie's head was dropping lower and lower with each enthusiastic pat that Samuel gave her.

"Stroke under her chin," I said, taking his hand and attempting to show him what to do.

He pursed his lips, frowned and yanked his small hand out of mine. He then resumed patting Jodie on the top of her head with his smile back. I attempted to show him again what to do, but he wasn't having any of it. Thankfully, Jodie was a very understanding dog who allowed him to give her all the love and fuss he wanted.

One afternoon, when we'd been back a week, some people came to the ward to do ceramic painting with the children. I took Samuel to the playroom and he sat at a long table with about eight other children, of all ages. I always thought it was good when he mixed with the other patients; not just for the obvious social benefits, but because he was able to see other children with nose tubes and bald heads and this, I hoped, would make him feel normal. I picked a plate for him to decorate and decided to have his hand print in the middle. Being a child who always liked to have his hands clean, he didn't take kindly to them being covered in red paint. The man who was organising the event pressed Samuel's hand firmly onto the plate. He quickly pulled his hand away with annoyance. I wondered if he felt he was having another medical procedure done, but a week later, when the plate was returned to us after being glazed, he surprised me by remembering what he'd done.

My mum had just come over to see us and was sitting on the bed next to me when Judith, one of the play ladies, returned the plate to us.

"Look what Samuel's done, Mum," I said as I peeled the tissue paper away from the plate.

I revealed Samuel's red handprint and he immediately leant over and, quick as a flash, put his hand on the plate. I was amazed. He looked up at his grandma with such a proud look on his face.

All these events helped us get through the days, but the person who helped the most was Claire, the music lady. In fact, she was a godsend during our stay in hospital, and no more so than when we were barrier nursed. During our time in C Bay, however, we would go to the playroom for music sessions, and sometimes other children would join us. She had a big trolley filled with all sorts of musical instruments that the children could play whilst she played her ukulele. During the course of Samuel's treatment, I think he tried all the instruments: the tambourine, the drum and the bells, but what he always wanted to play the most was Claire's ukulele. It made us both laugh as she would go through every instrument to see what Samuel wanted to play.

"How about the drum?" she would say. Samuel would patiently shake his head. "What about the bells?" she would say, getting out a colourful row of bells. Again, he would shake his head. Finally, after she'd been through just about every instrument she had and Samuel had patiently shaken his head at every one, she would say, "Do you want to play my ukulele?" to which Samuel would smile graciously and hold out his hands to accept the instrument.

Sharing the room with Chloe had been nice. Samuel had spent a lot of time playing with her, even though she wasn't able to get out of bed a lot of the time. But when she could, they would roll a ball to each other and she would give him a lot of attention. He really seemed to enjoy her company even though, at eight, she was much older than he was. But, predictably, after just over a week she went home. Most of the patients weren't in hospital as much as we were, and some of the parents joked that they could always rely on us to be there when they came back in. I have to say, it wasn't quite as comforting the other way round!

Chloe's replacement was a very young baby who was a surgical patient, not an oncology patient; there must have been a shortage of beds elsewhere in the hospital. Samuel often woke in the night, but I was quick to pick him up or feed him so we didn't disturb the other patients. It was bad enough that all the children had machines going through the night – many parents wore earplugs to help them sleep – but this young baby's mother also insisted on sleeping with her light on, so she could see to pick her baby up. The ward wasn't in darkness, anyway, so this was totally unnecessary and just meant I had more trouble sleeping than ever. Luckily, it didn't seem to disturb Samuel, but after three nights of this I'd had enough and spoke to Helen, the nurse, about it. Helen made me laugh, as she wore a headband with an LED light on it so she could see the children's machines at night.

Many of the nurses carried little torches, but I thought Helen's head-band was ingenious.

"Please can you turn off that lady's light?" I asked her at about two in the morning, when I was feeling really irritated at not getting any sleep.

"She wants it on so she can see to feed her baby," she said as she put a thermometer in Samuel's ear.

"Please turn it off, Helen. I can't sleep."

"You're too used to having a room of your own," she said with a laugh.

That was the trouble when the nurses worked nights: lovely as they were, they always seemed to forget you'd been up all day as well.

"We've got to be in here six months," I said, not feeling very amused.

"I know," she said, sensing my annoyance. "I'll say something to her."

The light was turned off and I managed to get some sleep. I think the ideal solution would have been a room to ourselves – but without being barrier nursed, so we could get out during the day – but that was just wishful thinking.

I was conscious that the time would come when Samuel would become ill again, but he had almost two weeks of good health before the effects of the chemotherapy really kicked in. I knew we'd been lucky, and every day I expected that to change, but I still dreaded the thought of being barrier nursed again.

A few days after the chemo finished, Samuel started to be sick. Nobody likes being sick, but Samuel must have been so tired of it. Often I would hold the grey cardboard bowl under his chin and he would push it away. It was almost as if he was annoyed with himself for being ill. It amazed us that he never cried and, in fact, one friend said she'd never seen someone be sick with so much dignity!

It was a Friday night and Stuart's turn to look after Samuel. I suggested that before taking over he should have a rest and a bath, and I would join him in the parents' room once Samuel had fallen asleep. It was seven o'clock – the time I usually tried to get him to sleep. However, his nurse had not brought round his anti-sickness drugs or his milk for his overnight feed.

"On your way out, would you remind the nurses that Samuel's medicines were due fifteen minutes ago?" I said to Stuart.

"Oh, that's not good," he said.

"I know, and I'm worried if he doesn't have his anti-sickness drugs soon he'll be sick again."

"Okay. I'll go straight round to the nurse station and let them know."

He did just that, and came back to tell me he had before going to Acorn House, but still no medicines arrived. I turned the lights off on our side of the room and got Samuel ready for bed, but I could tell he was feeling unwell. He clearly didn't know where to put himself and was starting to pant heavily. I gave him some water to try to calm him and make him feel better, but he was obviously feeling worse. By this time it was gone half past seven and his medicines were getting on for an hour late. I decided to press the call button. Nobody came and Samuel was violently sick. Not only was he sick, but the force brought up his nose tube as well. Eventually, after about ten minutes, a nurse called Stewart answered the call. He wasn't actually due to start his shift until eight o'clock, but as he was ready early he came to us.

"Samuel was due his medicines, including his anti-sickness drugs, an hour ago. He's not had them and now he's been sick and brought up his nose tube."

It wasn't Stewart's fault, but I didn't hold back in showing him how angry I was.

"Oh dear. I'm so sorry. I'll get his medicines now. He's due his milk feed as well, isn't he?"

"He is, but I don't want another nose tube put down now. Not when he's feeling so unwell."

"That's okay. He can have another one put down tomorrow. I'm sure it will be fine for him to miss his feed for one night."

"I'm furious! If his nurse hadn't been late with his medicines, he wouldn't need another nose tube put down. He hates having them put in and it's distressing for all of us."

"Who was his nurse?" Stewart asked.

"The one in charge!"

"Oh!"

"Yes, and I expect she was catching up with paperwork instead of thinking about her patients."

"I know they've been short staffed today."

"Well, I'm sure that's difficult, but this is the consequence. Samuel's been very ill and will now have to have another nose tube fitted. It's all so unnecessary."

What could I do? I could see how busy the nurses were, but Samuel was going through enough. He was fifteen months old. He was having high doses of chemotherapy and he felt very unwell. His life was bad enough. I was angry that his nurse hadn't just given him his medicines on time and prevented this, and I was angry with myself for not being firmer. I suppose over a period of six months it was to be expected that sometimes things would go wrong. But whilst we were lucky it wasn't something more serious, it still wasn't fair that a vulnerable, sick child should suffer.

That night, Stuart encountered further problems. As Samuel's father, he wanted to make sure he did everything he could to keep him comfortable and, after our earlier experience, he was keen for Samuel to get his medicines on time so he wouldn't be sick again. At about two in the morning he woke to see Samuel tossing and turning and panting heavily. He checked his watch and realised his medicines were due. Hoping to prevent a repeat of earlier, he immediately pressed the call button.

After fifteen minutes, and with no sign of a nurse, he decided to go to the nurse station to let a passing nurse know how important it was that Samuel got his anti-sickness medicines. This was a difficult decision to make because it meant leaving Samuel whilst he was awake, which always made him anxious. When Stuart got to the nurse station, he found two nurses sitting at the desk filling in paperwork. He explained the situation and asked why they hadn't answered the call button.

"We have to fill in the patients' notes whilst we remember exactly what happened," one of them told him.

"And, in the meantime, Samuel's feeling sick because he should have had his anti-sickness medicine," Stuart answered. As he walked away, he saw the nurses raise their eyebrows at each other. He later told me he'd wanted to say to them, "I'm sorry to be such a nuisance, but my son has leukaemia and you're meant to be helping him!"

It's easy to make excuses for the nurses when it's not your son lying there ill, but the truth is, some nurses are better than others. Some are exceptional, and we encountered a few who were, like Sophie, one of the ward sisters. But there are others who are less helpful, and when you are the parent of a seriously ill child it's hard to be tolerant.

The next day, Stuart spoke to the nurse in charge of that shift and told her how unhappy we were. She was less than sympathetic. What the medical staff sometimes seemed to forget was that being sick and having nose tubes fitted is not normal. These children have cancer but they are more than their illness. They have homes they once lived in, friends they once played with, and lives that were not dominated by hospital stays. Unfortunately, if you are seeing these symptoms every day the impact decreases and, though I hate to say it, I sometimes detected a blasé attitude towards the illness.

When I arrived on the ward the next morning, Samuel was quiet and obviously trying to manage his sickness by lying still and watching TV. I remember thinking how strange it was that it was a Saturday. I thought about what most people would be doing with their day: going to the shops, visiting relatives, snuggling up at home in the evening with a takeaway, or going to the pub or cinema. It seemed a million miles away from our life.

We kept the day as quiet as possible so Samuel could rest, but by the middle of the afternoon we were given the news he was to be barrier nursed again. Apparently, the cough that he'd now developed alongside the sickness was something called RSV (respiratory syncytial virus), which is like a chest infection. It is an infection that can hospitalise even healthy children, and can be extremely dangerous for a patient who has no immune system. Therefore, the doctors wanted Samuel to start on antibiotics straight away and, in order to protect the other patients, he was to be isolated. At about five o'clock we moved our bags, furniture and Samuel's cot across the corridor to B Bay.

B Bay was another large, single-bed room, but the window was too high to look out of and was facing a wall. It did, however, let in the sunlight in the morning, which made the room bearable. I was now well and truly obsessed with getting daylight, so in the mornings I turned off the overhead lighting and sat with Samuel in the stream of sunshine that came through the window for a few hours. If I craned my neck, I could even see some sky! It sounds like such a small thing to ask for, but that bit of light helped me cope, and I'm sure it helped Samuel as well.

That evening, along with Samuel's medicines, the nurses brought with them another nose tube. The nurse who was going to perform the procedure (I'll call her Lesley) was the one Stuart had spoken to about the treatment he and Samuel had had in the night. This particular nurse was always a little self-important, and after their earlier confrontation she was brusquer than ever. Samuel sat on Stuart's lap whilst Lesley measured the tube against Samuel's tummy.

"Mum, mum, mum, mum!" Samuel said with terror.

"Be brave, darling," I said, rubbing his knees.

I never told him something was going to be all right if I knew it would hurt or upset him. This way, I reasoned, he would trust me when I told him a procedure was going to be painless. Lesley pushed the tube up his nose and down the back of his throat. He gagged.

"Swallow!" she said to him.

"He's fifteen months old!" I wanted to say to her. "He doesn't understand your commands."

"Swallow!" she said again.

I gave him some milk out of his bottle, which of course made him swallow, and the tube went down. Lesley stuck the end of the tube to the side of his face then I picked him up and cuddled him.

"It's all done now, darling. Well done. All done." Samuel didn't cry, but I did. I didn't let him see, but I couldn't stop the tears. It was just so horrible. *My little boy shouldn't be going through all this*, I thought.

The evening was calmer. We watched some television and Samuel finished his bottle of milk. Stuart and I saved our anger for later, but Samuel never got used to having nose tubes fitted or having them in.

I often saw him touch it and, although he never tried to take one out again until he was in his last week, it was obvious he didn't want it in.

Monday 3ʳᵈ December (2008) was Stuart's birthday.

"Why don't we do something that night?" I said a few days beforehand.

"What – like a burger on the concourse?"

I laughed.

"We do live the high life, don't we? No, I was thinking that maybe my mum might babysit for the evening so we can go to the pub in Grantchester. Perhaps Angie and Len might be able to come with us."

"Do you think your mum would do that?"

"I can ask her."

When Samuel was first diagnosed, Mike had suggested it would be a good idea to ask family members to do the odd night at hospital in order for us to have a break once in a while. He'd said that most people find it difficult to keep going night after night as life on the ward wasn't easy. I never felt particularly comfortable with the idea. I reasoned that Samuel was the one suffering, not us, so the least we could do was be there for him. However, I thought just one night would be acceptable; Samuel was used to seeing a lot of my mum so I didn't think he would feel frightened being left with her.

Unfortunately, on the morning of Stuart's birthday the whole ward was barrier nursed due to the winter vomiting bug, norovirus. This meant every patient had to stay in their room and use a toilet allocated to them. No visitors were permitted and parents were only allowed short visits to the parents' room to get food and drink. Acorn House was also closed in case any of the parents staying there had already picked up the virus. Carol, the ward manager, came in to see us that morning.

"I'm afraid we can't let your mum in tonight, Amanda, as she might bring the infection in with her."

"Oh, you're joking!" Stuart said.

"No, sorry; we can't take any chances. You can still go out, though. But you'll have to go home afterwards, in case you bring the bug back with you."

"We can't do that," I said. "I'm not leaving Samuel here all night without one of us with him."

"Can't you make an exception?" Stuart asked. "Amanda's mum is perfectly healthy."

"No. Those are the rules. Sorry," Carol replied.

I'm afraid at that point Stuart erupted. Over two months in hospital had taken their toll. Life on the ward was stressful and highly restricting. This night out had given him something to look forward to. We could have relaxed for one night, in the knowledge that my mum was taking care of Samuel. We were even going to have a drink, as Len had volunteered to drive, and then we were going to stay the night at Acorn House.

"I'd like you to check with infection control if there is any way round this," Stuart said once he'd calmed down.

Carol agreed to this and didn't seem perturbed or offended by Stuart's outburst. After a while, she came back to us.

"Infection control has agreed to Amanda's mum coming here, but she will have to stay at Acorn House, instead of you, as you might have picked up something from the ward."

This didn't really make sense to me, as Mum would have been on the ward by the time she went to Acorn House, but we didn't argue as we were so happy to be going out for the night. I phoned Mum and explained the situation to her. She arrived just before it got dark. We all stayed together in the room for a while so Samuel wouldn't be upset by our sudden departure. Then, after he'd had some tea, we got changed and went to meet Angie and Len.

Samuel's nurse for the evening was a lovely lady, also called Amanda, who had explained to my mum every routine procedure she did on Samuel and what medicines she was giving him.

Apparently, Samuel had held up his arm when he heard the blood pressure machine go on, and gave ever such a proud smile when Amanda said, "Well done." I think he was showing off a little bit for his grandma, but sometimes I felt sad that he had become so knowledgeable about medical matters.

Samuel had been lent a projector by the play team, which threw an image like a lava lamp onto the ceiling. As it neared his bedtime I would put this on, together with the wave setting on his musical fish box. It was calm and relaxing and I hoped it would help to settle him. I had explained this to Mum, but instead of following my instructions, she let him sit up past his bedtime to watch a bit of television. Samuel was now a firm fan of the telly and had even worked out how to switch it on and off by himself and how to change channels. He sat in his cot and proceeded to show Mum how to do this.

"Yes, very good, Samuel," Mum said. "Now can I watch *Emmerdale*?"

Samuel just smiled at Mum and switched channels again… and again… and again! Once he was fed up with that game, he took the stethoscope from the back of his cot and demonstrated how the doctors listen to his chest. Speaking in his own little language, he told his grandma all about it whilst lifting up his pyjama top and placing the stethoscope on his tummy. When he started yawning, Mum laid him down and put his music and projector on, and within five minutes he was asleep. When she told me, I wondered if I made work for myself by rocking him to sleep. I never used to do this and I knew it went against all the advice the books gave, but I could never now just put

Samuel in his cot and expect him to sleep. He would always hold his arms up for a cuddle and I would end up rocking him until I heard his breathing deepen and I knew he'd drifted off.

Stuart and I had a wonderful night out, made all the more special by the rarity of the event. That night Mum slept at Acorn House whilst Stuart and I shared the pull-down bed next to Samuel. By the morning the ban on visitors was lifted, Mum was allowed back in the ward and we were allowed back in Acorn House. How typical that the ban should happen on our one night out in six months!

As December rolled on, plans for Christmas were on everyone's mind. We had been warned when we first arrived that it was highly likely we'd be in hospital for it. Our only chance of being home was if the gap between chemotherapy treatments fell over those few days. We began working out our dates. If Samuel was in hospital for six weeks, like last time, we could just be in with a chance. Stuart quizzed the doctors and consultants, but no predictions could be made.

"You might be in for only four or five weeks this time," Boo said. "Can I look in your mouth, Samuel?" He shook his head and she laughed. "Then again, you could be in for six – in which case you might be home over Christmas. How's that tummy?" she asked Samuel, giving it a little prod. Samuel watched her intently.

"I see you've got your Advent calendar up," she said. "Are you counting down to Christmas or just until you get out?"

I smiled.

"It's starting to feel like ages and it's only been just over three weeks."

"Well, it's nine weeks really, isn't it?" she said. "You can't really count the few days you had at home. But Samuel's doing well; his counts are starting to come back up. Hopefully, this infection will go soon and then, as long as he doesn't get something else, you might be able to get home again for a few days."

"But then we'll be back in again for Christmas," Stuart said.

"Oh yes, probably. But it's very nice in here at Christmas."

"Everybody says that," Stuart said, unconvinced.

She laughed.

"Sorry, Stuart, but you can have your family in and, you never know, you might get to go home."

That afternoon the play team and the children who were well enough began to decorate the Christmas tree. The tree (a fake one because of the risk of infection) was assembled next to the nurse station, which Samuel could see if he stuck his head out the door. We weren't supposed to even have our door open, let alone let Samuel poke his head out, but he could hear the other children and the Christmas songs being played and he wanted to join in. By now he was starting to feel a bit better and had begun bottom-shuffling around the room again, so he quickly made his way towards the door and through it.

"Stay here, poppet," I said, attempting to keep him behind the line.

But Samuel thought it was great fun to be dragged backwards on his bottom, so he wiggled out even more. To be honest, I was so pleased to hear him laughing that I let him. It seemed such a shame he wasn't allowed to join in, as he was clearly much better and I guessed his infection must have gone. In fact, the next day we got the news that the RSV had cleared. However, they'd detected a possible bug in his urine, which they wanted to retest; this meant we were still considered barrier nursed, even though it was highly unlikely he could pass on a urine infection.

We were really pleased with Samuel's progress, but I was starting to feel exhausted with it all. We had now spent almost ten weeks in hospital, plus two months of him gradually declining beforehand, and that was a lot of time to exist on little sleep and in an almost permanent state of fear. We still had no idea when we would be going home or, ultimately, if the treatment would be successful, and every day spent on the ward was wearing me out more and more. I was still only getting between two and four hours of broken sleep a night, and occasionally I went the whole night without sleep. It helped that Stuart did two nights a week on the ward so I could sleep right through, but I was so shattered by then I felt that I could sleep for a week.

From watching the nurses, I had learnt to press the orange button to silence Samuel's pump when it went off in the middle of the night. I'd also learnt "downstream pressure" could be sorted out by wiggling the lines, and "call nurse" meant the drugs had gone through. I gathered that only doctors and nurses were supposed to do anything to the pump, but I was tired of it waking Samuel up and then having to spend an hour or more getting him back off to sleep. Consequently, the pump only needed to make its first loud bleep before I automatically pushed the orange button. I would then press the call button so the nurses would have the bleep in their ears rather than in Samuel's and mine. One night when I did this, Stewart answered.

"Is it just this?" he whispered, indicating the pump.

"Yes, thanks," I said.

As he started fiddling with the buttons, I pulled the blankets up over my arm and closed my eyes. I was now used to nurses coming and going whilst I tried to sleep.

"I don't mean *just* this, because it must be annoying," Stewart said.

I opened my eyes.

"Yes, it is."

"It must be," he said. "I don't know how you stick it. I know you don't have a lot of choice, but it must drive you mad."

"Yes, it does."

"It must do. These bleeps drive *us* mad and we work here. They're so loud, aren't they? Piercing and right in your ear." He finished pushing buttons on the pump. "How are you, anyway?"

Some nurses, like Stewart, were very understanding and empathetic, and I was glad of their company – but I preferred it when our conversations took place during the day!

My mum's birthday was on 8th December. It was a Sunday, and technically we were still barrier nursed. However, we had been allowed out of the ward as the RSV had cleared and Samuel seemed so well. We decided we would all go to the pub in Grantchester, and Samuel was dressed in a very smart navy-and-white striped shirt and navy cords.

"Oh, don't you look smart, Samuel? I like your shirt," Angela, the nurse, said to him before we went.

Samuel looked down at himself, touched his shirt, and then up at her as if to say, "What – this old thing?"

Mr Darcy was very much in evidence!

The pub was packed, but we had a reserved table. Mum opened her presents whilst we waited for our order to arrive. Samuel sat very happily in a high chair and watched everyone around him.

"Do you think you should have ordered Samuel a meal?" Mum asked.

"No. He can have some of ours. He generally only has a few mouthfuls of anything, and I don't think he'd like the food on the children's menu."

The meals were all brought out and Samuel watched as Grandma, Aunty Nancy, Uncle Richie, Mummy and Daddy received their food. His mouth turned down and he lowered his head.

"You can have some of Mummy's," I said, holding up a spoonful of my lasagne.

Samuel continued to look down. He had the saddest expression on his face.

"Excuse me," I said to a passing waiter. "I didn't order for my son as I didn't think he'd eat anything off the menu, but do you think the chef could make him a little portion of mashed potato and some baked beans?"

The waiter said he was sure he could, and five minutes later he brought a small bowl of potato and baked beans over to Samuel. He cheered up immediately. I think he just wanted to feel the same as everyone else and was upset at being left out. Stuart and I took it in turns to offer some of his food to him but, although he had a few mouthfuls, he wasn't very bothered about eating. However, he had a nice time, so it was worth it!

The next morning I was standing at our door talking to Helen and her daughter, Rosie, in C Bay opposite us. Samuel was balanced on my hip nibbling on a cream cracker when Mick walked up the corridor with a packet of three Bourbon biscuits in his hand. Samuel looked at the biscuits, then at the cracker in own his hand, then back at the biscuits. Quick as a flash, he handed Mick his cream cracker and made the exchange!

"Good work, Samuel!" I said, and we all laughed.

"I see you're not barrier nursed any more," Mick said.

"Aren't we?"

I was surprised. I felt a little bit of hope rise within me.

"Well, the sign on your door's been turned round. Haven't the doctors said anything to you?"

"No. I'll ask them when they come in."

It looked like things were on the up. I could now take Samuel into the playroom, and to look at the Christmas tree. We'd been in hospital for exactly four weeks. Our stay this time had had its ups and downs but had been far more tolerable than the first six weeks. I should have been coping well, but inside I felt like I was only just getting by. I was so tired I could barely concentrate, and I felt tearful and jittery. I wanted to be a source of infinite comfort to Samuel twenty-four hours a day, but I worried that exhaustion was making me fall short.

Samuel struggled to sleep that night. He shouldn't have been in pain and his breathing had returned to normal now the RSV had cleared up. As he was having his milk feed go through his nose tube he shouldn't have been hungry, so I couldn't think why he wasn't dropping off. Feeling shattered, I desperately tried to rock him to sleep so I could get some myself. At about two in the morning, after rocking him for two hours, he fell asleep. I carefully put him in his cot and climbed into bed.

After what seemed like five minutes, but was actually about an hour, a nurse came in to take his blood pressure and temperature. He woke up, and although I tried to soothe him in his cot, he still cried and held his arms up to me to be cuddled. I picked him up and sat on the edge of my bed and began to rock him again. He cuddled into me. After about half an hour I attempted to return him to his cot, but he immediately cried. I put the wave setting on his fish box and went back to rocking him. About another half an hour went by and I again tried to return him to his cot. Again, he cried. I put the fish box on again and went back to rocking him. My back was aching and I could feel my heart racing.

The nurse then came in to turn off his night feed as he was due in theatre the next morning to have more chemotherapy put into his lumbar spine. Samuel watched as she disconnected his nose tube from the feeding tube. After she left I returned to rocking him. It was now five in the morning. Samuel wasn't asleep but he was calm, so I attempted to lay him back in his cot. He cried.

"Samuel, please go to sleep now. Mummy's tired," I said, my voice full of agitation. He cried some more and held his arms up for a cuddle. I picked him up, but more roughly than usual, and he cried even more. "Samuel, I'm tired!" I snapped. Not surprisingly, he cried even harder. "Samuel, stop it!" He continued to cry. "I mean it, Samuel. Mummy is tired. You're being very naughty."

I had never said anything like that to him before and the words sounded alien to me. Still he cried. I smacked his legs. Shocked, he stopped crying for a moment. And then he really cried. I laid him in his cot, put his waves on and walked out the door and down the corridor to the parents' room. I got myself a cup of water and tried to calm down. I couldn't believe what I'd just done. My sixteen-month-old, seriously ill son was having trouble sleeping and instead of comforting him, I had hit him. I felt disgusted with myself. I walked back down the corridor. My heart was racing and every part of my body ached with tiredness. As I got closer to my room I could hear Samuel's cries.

"I'm sorry, darling," I said, picking him up. He cuddled into me. *How can he not hate me?* I thought.

But I knew he needed me. He needed his mummy to be good, kind and loving. Samuel hadn't been naughty. Hadn't I learnt, in all this time, that if he could sleep he would? There was obviously something wrong, either physical or emotional and, with hindsight, he'd probably picked up on my agitation from the beginning.

Surprisingly, he fell asleep. He must have been exhausted. I laid him down in his cot and then got into bed. It was now six in the morning. At seven o'clock the light went on and a relief nurse, whom I'd not met before, walked in.

"Good morning," she said.

She switched on the blood pressure machine.

"No, please don't do that," I said. "We've had a bad night. I've just got Samuel to sleep. Please come back later."

"Oh, I don't know," she said.

"Please," I said. "Please go. And switch the light off behind you."

Thankfully, she went, but I couldn't get back to sleep. I lay in bed for a bit longer, and then at eight o'clock I put on my dressing gown and walked down the corridor. Stuart was walking up the corridor in the opposite direction, dressed for work.

"I'm so glad to see you," I said.

I told him about my night and he was shocked by my behaviour.

"Go and have a drink in the parents' room and I'll see to Samuel," he said.

When I returned to our room, he'd got Samuel up.

"Please take today off," I said. "I need to sleep."

"I can't," he said. "I've got Wednesday off, so I can do tomorrow night but I've got work to do today."

I felt utterly desperate, but I knew I had no choice. For Samuel's sake, I had to keep going. Samuel went into theatre early. The procedure went well and he slept off the anaesthetic back in his room. I looked at his beautiful, sleeping face and felt so ashamed for not treating him with the love, empathy and respect he deserved. Children are so precious, but also so vulnerable. I loved him with all my heart and hated the fact that I'd caused him even more distress. I made a silent promise to never treat him like that again. I looked up from his cot and saw Boo at the door. I walked over.

"Is he asleep?" she asked.

"Yes."

"Okay, I'll come back later. Is he all right?"

"He is now. We had a bad night; he couldn't sleep."

"Oh, why was that?"

"I don't know, but I wasn't much good at comforting him."

"Oh, Amanda!" She pulled a sad face. "Never mind. He looks fine now. Are you all right? A bit tired, I expect."

"Yes, and fed up of being in here."

"Well, you can go home today if you like – which I'm sure you would!" she added with a laugh.

I was completely taken aback.

"Can we? Nobody's mentioned to us we might be going home today!"

"Well, we've just had his blood results back from this morning." She looked down at a small piece of paper in her hand with numbers scribbled on it. "He's doing really well. His neutrophils are up... white blood count... everything. So, yes, pack up your things and when he's awake I'll come and have a look at him and then you can go."

"Okay!"

I smiled. Relief flooded through me. Suddenly, everything felt bearable.

We're going to be all right, I thought. *This has been hard but, one day, when Samuel's better, it will seem like just a short moment in time.*

I did just as she said, and when Samuel had been given the once over, I began to take everything over to Acorn House, just as I had four and a half weeks ago when we were discharged last time. Angela, the play lady, wheeled Samuel round the ward in a pushchair to keep him entertained whilst I made endless trips with a sack barrow, then I took him to Acorn House. He was such a good boy, sitting on the bed in our room whilst I packed everything from the wardrobe into the suitcase. I remembered the last time when Stuart and I had done this at home to come back into hospital, and Samuel had realised and cried.

"We're going home, poppet," I said.

He looked up at me. Despite everything he'd been through, his big blue eyes were filled with love and warmth. He smiled. I picked him up and hugged him.

"I love you," I said.

CHAPTER 13

Christmas

~⌐

IN THE END, WE WERE home for twelve days. I'm so glad we were given that time because, after ten weeks in hospital, I think we were all desperately in need of a break.

The day after we arrived home, Samuel went back to bed at half past ten in the morning and slept solidly for two hours. Previously when he'd had a nap I would get on with housework or preparing food, but that day I knew I needed sleep more. I went back to bed, too, and that sleep couldn't have been more welcome.

Gradually, we got our strength back. Like before, Samuel slept better at home. In the evening we returned to our old routine of tea, dance, bath, milk and bed, and he seemed happy to fall back into our old ways. In hospital, we'd tried on a few occasions to give him a bath in a large baby bath, but for some reason he'd found it upsetting, so we'd had to just wash him instead. Back at home, he didn't seem to have any problems in the big bath and was soon back to throwing the sponge over the side to get Mummy wet!

Because we could be returning to hospital at any time, we didn't bother buying a Christmas tree or putting up decorations, but it was nice to just be back in our own home, and we soon had it looking cosy again.

One afternoon Angie came round and we sat in front of the fire with our cups of tea and a big box of biscuits. She'd bought a gorgeous little cardigan for Samuel, which we dressed him in and then took photos. Samuel was happy to pose for the camera before returning to his toys and biscuits.

It was possible for us to be home for so long thanks to the help of a wonderful nurse called Audrey. She was a community nurse linked to both Addenbrooke's Hospital and our local West Suffolk Hospital. Every few days she came to our house to take blood and to check on Samuel. I thought the sight of a nurse in uniform would unsettle him, but he was perfectly relaxed with her. In fact, as she drew blood from his Hickman line for testing, he would happily remove the pens from her breast pocket and then pop them back in again! She would phone me with his results just before teatime and I would diligently write them in his notes, which I'd been given by the hospital when we left.

We even had an evening out. On Thursday 18th December, Stuart's work held their Christmas party at a hotel in Cambridge. Had we been in hospital, we wouldn't have been able to go, but with my sister still staying at our house we had a babysitter on hand. Now Nancy has very fond memories of dressing Samuel for bed in his pyjamas and Christmas socks to keep his feet warm!

She then got herself ready for bed and he must have been thinking he was about to go in his cot when she said to him, "Let's go and watch some telly!"

Apparently, he gave her a big grin, as if he knew it was a little bit naughty, and they had a lovely time cuddled up on the sofa. He stayed there with her until his eyes began to droop. Then she put him in his cot and he went straight to sleep.

Two days later we got the call asking us to return to hospital for his third round of chemotherapy. We spent the day packing and loading up the car for what we thought would be another four- to six-week stay.

"I can't believe we're going back to hospital just five days before Christmas," Stuart said as we drove along the A14.

"I know; it does seem a shame," I agreed.

"It means Samuel will be having chemotherapy on Christmas Day! What kind of Christmas is that for him?"

"We just have to be grateful he's here at all. If he hadn't been diagnosed, he probably would have died in October."

Stuart looked over at me and smiled.

"You're right. That's the best way of looking at it."

"Mum, Nancy and Richie will come over Christmas afternoon and we'll make it nice."

"I just hope Samuel doesn't get too ill. Last time he was fine whilst he was having the chemotherapy, but got the RSV infection a few days after it finished."

"But each time he starts his chemotherapy he's in a better position than the previous time, so maybe he won't be so ill with this session."

"What do you mean?" Stuart asked.

"Well, when we first came in 100 per cent of Samuel's blood cells were leukaemia cells. Now the leukaemia has gone and he seems much better. I think this break has done him good, too, so maybe he won't get so ill this time round."

"Let's hope not," Stuart said. "Are you all right, little man?" he asked Samuel in his rear-view mirror.

When we arrived at the ward, we were shown into G Bay, which is the largest of the bays. It had four beds and was the first bay we'd occupied when Samuel was admitted in September. This bay is furthest from the nurse station and usually given to the patients who are the least ill. It had to be a good sign. We were told to pick a bed as there was no one else in the room when we arrived and, true to form,

I chose one next to a window. It wasn't long before Martin, one of the doctors, came to see us.

"As you know, Samuel goes into the clinical trial for his next round of chemotherapy," he said, "so his next dose will be shorter than the last two, as the randomised choice made for him was the American route rather than the traditional British route."

"So how many days of chemotherapy will he have this time?" Stuart asked.

"Just five days… which will take us to Chr—"

"Christmas Day," Stuart cut in.

"Yes, Christmas Day. So, I'm afraid you'll have to be in for the morning whilst Samuel has his last dose of chemotherapy, but then you can go home."

Stuart and I looked at each other.

"Go home?" Stuart repeated.

"Yes – as long as he doesn't have an infection, of course."

We both thought there had been some mistake.

"He has *all* his treatment in hospital," I said, just to clarify, "as he has A*M*L, not A*L*L."

"Yes. Usually the chemotherapy is too toxic and the chance of infection too high to allow the patient to go home, but, as he'll be following the American route for the next two doses, he shouldn't get so ill and, therefore, can go home."

"So, let me get this straight," Stuart said. "This chemotherapy is not so intense and that's the reason why we can go home."

"That's right – and, of course, the fact that you know what you're doing now. You can administer all his medicines and the night feed from home, and if you have a problem you're only ten minutes away from your local hospital."

"We weren't told this before," I said.

In the back of my mind I still thought he'd made a mistake.

"Well, to be honest, Samuel is only the second AML patient that we're allowing home, but experience has shown us patients don't become so ill with this chemotherapy and, as long as the parents are happy to do all the nursing, we think it's in everyone's interest for the patient to be at home."

I was starting to feel excited but I wanted to be sure of one last thing before allowing myself to be happy.

"You say the chemotherapy Samuel will have this time isn't as toxic. Is it just as effective?"

"The clinical trial has been going for over six years now and no difference has been found in the outcome of the patients."

Stuart and I looked at each other.

"So we're going home Christmas Day," Stuart said.

"All being well," Martin said. "I'll ask Samuel's nurse to put his chemotherapy up straight away. The quicker it starts, the quicker it will finish."

He walked away holding Samuel's notes.

"I can't believe it!" I said with a massive smile.

Stuart picked Samuel up out of his cot.

"Not long to go this time, little man."

Samuel smiled.

We were soon joined in G Bay by three other patients. Opposite us was a young boy who also had leukaemia. He came in with his little sister as his mum, a Lithuanian lady, was a single mother and had no family here to help look after her.

How difficult! I thought to myself when she told us.

I found it hard enough to cope, and I had Stuart and our families to help me and no other children to think about. The lady was also a great help to us one evening after we'd been back in a couple of nights. Unusually, Samuel had fallen asleep before his seven o'clock bedtime, which told me he felt a bit better with this round of chemotherapy.

He'd just finished a bowl of chicken soup and had enjoyed dunking his bread in it. I always felt happy when he ate proper food, rather than just relying on his overnight milk feeds, as it seemed more normal and healthy. After he'd finished I took him out of his high chair, got him changed for bed, then put him on my lap to watch *In the Night Garden*. My usual routine was to give him his medicines and a bottle of milk once his programme had finished but, on this occasion, he fell asleep during the programme.

I gently put him in his cot and placed Woof Woof and BB beside him, before covering him with a blanket. I drew the blue paper curtain partially around our bay and then turned off the light above his cot. Stuart couldn't believe it when he came back from the parents' room with a freshly made bottle of milk for him.

"What shall we do now?" he asked.

We were used to it taking until at least eight o'clock to get Samuel to sleep; it felt odd having free time.

"Perhaps we should have dinner now, whilst he's asleep?" I suggested.

"Okay. Shall we go to Acorn House and have a bit of a break, then?"

We left the bottle of milk on the table at the foot of Samuel's cot and told the mother opposite us where we were going, in case Samuel woke up. We also informed his nurse.

Stuart was due to sleep on the ward with Samuel that night. When he came back from Acorn House, just before ten o'clock, the Lithuanian mother came over to him.

"Samuel woke at about eight o'clock," she told him. "I knew he'd fallen asleep before he'd had his milk, so I said to him, 'Do you want your milk?' and he quickly pulled out his dummy and opened his mouth." She demonstrated Samuel's actions, which made Stuart laugh, as he could just see him doing it. "After he had his milk, I said to him, 'Do you want a cuddle?' but he shook his head and put his dummy back in his mouth. Then he closed his eyes and fell asleep."

It was so kind of her to see to him as it meant we were able to have a break, and I was impressed that Samuel got himself back off to sleep without either of us there with him. It makes me realise just how ill he must have felt before, and that he would have been quite a confident, self-sufficient child if he'd been well.

The days went quickly with Stuart there to keep me company. Samuel had to have eye drops put in every two hours with this round of chemotherapy as the drugs used could make his eyes very sore, but after a while he got used to this and coped well with it. He felt far better this time round and even started walking up and down the long corridor of the ward with his wooden baby walker for support and me walking behind pushing his pump. On one such occasion, he spotted his daddy coming through the double doors of the ward, along with his nanny and grandad.

"Da da!" he shouted from one end of the ward to the other. He was definitely feeling better!

On Christmas Eve, Martin, Amos and Boo did the ward round.

"Home tomorrow, guys," Boo said.

"Yes. Christmas Day at home," Stuart said.

"You got your wish," Boo said with a smile.

"Do you celebrate Christmas, Boo?" I asked her.

"Well, I don't because I'm Muslim, but my husband does as he was brought up a Christian."

"So how does that work?" I asked.

"Well, it just means my children get twice as many presents because they join in with the Christian festivals and the Muslim ones."

"They've got it sussed!" Stuart said.

Boo laughed.

"Now, remember," Amos said, "as soon as Samuel gets a temperature, it's straight back into hospital. You'll need to be in within the hour so we can get some antibiotics in him."

"And if he doesn't get a temperature, when will we see you again?" I asked.

"Come in Monday morning to the day-patient unit for an appointment with Mike," he said.

"But we'll probably see you Boxing Day," Martin said with a laugh.

"I hope not!" Stuart said.

Amos looked at us seriously.

"I'm afraid it's not *if* he gets an infection; it's *when* he gets an infection."

It was a sobering thought.

That afternoon Claire, the music lady, gathered all the children round the Christmas tree to sing songs. Samuel took his place amongst them, sitting on a little red chair. He was the youngest child there by at least a year, but he seemed happy and confident with the other children so Stuart and I stood back so he could mix with them on his own. Each of the children was given a musical instrument and Samuel had to be content with the tambourine, as Claire needed her ukulele!

"Rudolf the red-nosed reindeer," they all sang, and Samuel joined in with the tambourine. "You'll go down in history!" they finished, at which point Samuel threw his hands in the air and shouted, "Hooray!"

Everyone burst out laughing.

"Well done, Samuel!" Claire said.

Everyone clapped and Samuel joined in, not knowing what all the fuss was about.

Surely that's how every song should finish? he probably thought to himself – typical Leo!

He had such a good time that afternoon, listening to the children singing, playing his tambourine, and cheering and clapping. It's how we like to remember him best: happy and confident, and enjoying the moment.

Once the singing had finished, we took him to Acorn House where we watched a Christmas film with the tree lights on, and Samuel played happily with a wooden doll's house. Apart from the fact that we weren't in our own home, we could have been a normal family relaxing in front of the telly before Christmas.

At teatime we returned to the ward. There was a definite air of Christmas about the place. At the nurse station several nurses and children were gathered around a computer.

"I wonder what they're doing," Stuart said.

We walked over to them.

"Hello, Samuel," said Angela, one of the nurses. "Do you want to see where Father Christmas is?"

Stuart carried Samuel over. At just under seventeen months, I'm not sure he understood who Father Christmas was, but he was happy to be shown his whereabouts on the computer.

"Look, here he is." Angela pointed to a map of the world on the computer. "Just over Norway. He'll be here in a few hours!"

The children's faces were a picture. Samuel looked at them all and smiled.

When we got back to G Bay, one of the beds was empty and the other two patients were packing to go home.

"Oh, are we going to be the only ones left?" I asked the Lithuanian mother.

Her daughter came skipping across to us. Samuel and I had spent quite a lot of time with her in the playroom during the week, as her mother had to look after her little boy.

"We're going home," she said.

I bent down to her.

"Well, you have a lovely Christmas."

She held her arms open and I gave her a hug.

"Bye-bye, Samuel," she said, giving him a kiss.

Her brother then came over and gave us all a cuddle as well.

A wonderful consequence of being in hospital was feeling part of a strong community. Everyone in there was going through the same thing and everyone helped each other out. Talking to the other parents normalised the situation, and watching other people cope made us feel we could cope, too. In fact, Stuart and I often commented on how rational everyone seemed when you would have thought they would be falling apart.

During those five days, Stuart and I stayed alternate nights on the ward. On Christmas Eve it was Stuart's turn, so I returned to Acorn House. Once there, I packed all our belongings and left them by the door ready to take to the car the next day, then went to bed. It felt strange waking up alone in Acorn House on Christmas Day. I felt unsettled for a moment. I was also slightly upset that we weren't experiencing a normal Christmas but, I reasoned, everyone in Acorn House and the hospital must be feeling the same thing, including the staff.

I got washed and changed and walked across the grounds to the hospital, even though it was still very early. The concourse was empty and everywhere felt eerily quiet. Stuart and Samuel were just waking up when I arrived.

"Happy Christmas," I whispered to them, giving them both a kiss.

I noticed Samuel's Hickman line was attached to a drip. I looked at the clear liquid in the bag: it was chemotherapy. From what I could tell, it looked like there were still several hours' worth to go, but I was pleased it was already up, as once it was finished we would be able to go home. A full dose of this particular type of chemotherapy took five hours to drip into Samuel's blood. If we'd been randomised to take the traditional British route then he would have been having this drug alongside two other chemotherapy drugs.

"You're early," Stuart said.

"I didn't want to miss Samuel opening his presents." At the end of Samuel's cot, I could see a pillowcase bulky with toys and covered in Christmas stickers. "Oh, look – Father Christmas has been."

"Oh, yes. The nurses must have done that in the night," Stuart said.

"Shh!" I said, glaring at him then looking at Samuel.

"Sorry! I'm not fully awake yet."

"I'll get us a cup of tea and a bottle for Samuel," I said, leaving Stuart and Samuel to wake up properly.

We all sat on the pull-down bed and I gave Samuel his bottle before letting him investigate the contents of the pillowcase. I'd also placed several presents from us on the bed. First out of the bag was a cuddly Tigger. Samuel gave a big smile, kissed him on the nose, then dropped him on the floor as he returned to the pillowcase. Next out was a bright-red deflated balloon. Samuel held it up and frowned.

"It's a balloon," Stuart said, taking it from him and blowing into it.

Samuel smiled as he recognised his new toy. Stuart let it go and it whizzed round the room, just as Scary Mary walked through the door. Samuel giggled.

"Time for Samuel's eye drops," she said sternly.

"Happy Christmas, Mary," I said. She picked up his eye drops from the table at the foot of Samuel's cot. "It's okay, Mary; I'll do them," I said.

"Are you sure?" she asked.

"Yes, that's fine. So you drew the short straw – working Christmas Day."

"Oh, I don't mind," she said. "My family live a long way away so it would be difficult to see them."

"That's a shame. Still, I expect everyone's grateful to have you here."

She smiled awkwardly.

"You won't forget those eye drops, will you?"

I promised her I wouldn't and she left the room.

"Can you believe her?" Stuart said. "You'd think she'd at least let Samuel open his presents first."

"I don't think she knows how else to be," I said.

"Well I don't think we should put his drops in until he's opened his presents."

"I agree. It can wait ten minutes."

Afterwards, I began to get him dressed. I'd spent too much money on a lovely pale-blue shirt from a designer children's shop for him to wear on Christmas Day, but as I tried to put it on him he shook his head.

"No?" I said.

He shook his head again. I tried to put that shirt on him several times over the next few hours but he wouldn't let me, so in every picture we have of him on Christmas morning he's just wearing his vest and trousers. Later that day he allowed me to dress him in a jumper, but he never did wear that shirt!

Once Samuel had looked at all his presents, he was keen to get off the bed and start walking, so Stuart decided to get everything from Acorn House packed away in the car so we could go as soon as the chemotherapy had finished and the doctors had given us the all clear. As Stuart walked down the corridor, Samuel followed with his wooden baby walker and I followed him with his pump. Halfway down a photographer stopped him. I later found out the charity COPARS (Childhood Cancer Organisation for Parents and Relatives Support) had organised for the photographer to be on the ward that day.

"Can I take your photo, Samuel?" she asked. Samuel stopped walking. "He looks very grand," she said to me.

As she stepped aside, he continued on his way. When I look at those photos now, I'm struck by just how brave he was. He was on his fifth day of chemotherapy; his third session in total. He must have felt weak and ill, but he determinedly kept going.

It wasn't long before Father Christmas arrived. Angela came and got us and the three of us queued up in the playroom to meet him. The playroom can be divided into two separate rooms and in the second, darkened room we could just see fairy lights twinkling and hear the sound of Christmas music. When our turn came, we walked through the door and saw Father Christmas sitting in a big chair with his elves each side and his sleigh filled with toys. It had been done beautifully. I hoped that even though Samuel had to go in with his pump he would forget he was in hospital for a while and could instead be filled with the wonder of Christmas.

We left the hospital just as Christmas dinner was being served. I was so pleased to be going, but I felt sorry for every child and parent left behind. I could just imagine how they were feeling, watching us go and not knowing how much longer they had to endure hospital life for. It reminded me of how envious I felt when I took Samuel to theatre in the day unit and saw the patients who would be going home after their procedures, instead of back to the ward, like us. The hospital staff and volunteers had worked hard to make the day special for everyone, but there's no getting around the fact that it's just not pleasant living in hospital. And that's from my perspective – it's un-doubtedly far worse for the child who has cancer and is undergoing chemotherapy.

We arrived home in time for dinner. My mum, sister and her husband were all there waiting for us and had even put up Christmas decorations. We could smell the turkey cooking as we walked through the door, and the table had been decorated with candles and crackers. Beautifully wrapped presents and unopened cards were piled high in the living room. It was wonderful to be there and I didn't take it for granted for one minute.

We sat Samuel up at the table with us in the dining room and gave him a small bowl of Christmas dinner, but he wouldn't eat any of it. Chemotherapy has the nasty side effect of making food taste metallic so, even if the sickness subsides for a while, the food still tastes awful. No wonder Samuel preferred to stick to his milk feeds. But he enjoyed being at home with his family and was so cheerful you would hardly have known he'd been having chemotherapy just a few hours earlier. Later, when I looked back at the photographs of Christmas Day, I noticed he wasn't smiling in any of the photos taken in hospital, but he was in all the ones taken at home. You can never underestimate how much a child is aware of their environment; even a child as young as Samuel knows where they're happiest.

He was spoilt rotten by all his family, of course. His grandma had bought him a garage. Although not quite as big as the one he played with in hospital, he still enjoyed it – even if Daddy didn't enjoy putting it together! Aunty Nancy bought him a talking and singing bear, which he found hugely funny, and Richie's mother gave him a toy dog that wagged its tail and woofed if you woofed at him first. Samuel loved it almost as much as he loved real dogs. It was so funny hearing him attempt to talk to his precious puppy.

"Oof!" he would say. "Oof, oof!"

That evening, once my family had gone home, we put Samuel to bed in his cot, which we'd dragged into our bedroom last time we'd been home; I felt happier having him nearby in case he was sick in the night. He'd also become so accustomed to having us close by in hospital that I thought it might be less unsettling for him. Again, I wondered if I was setting myself up for trouble in the future but decided that that moment was all that counted. I'm so glad now that I took that approach because, as it turned out, we didn't have a future together. I think it's a lesson that everyone should learn; none of us can be sure what tomorrow has in store for us.

Boxing Day was spent at Debbie's with her two grown-up daughters, Hannah and Ellen, as well as Cynthia and Derek. Everyone made a huge fuss of Samuel and showered him with presents, including a xylophone and organ from his grandparents and a ukulele of his own from Debbie and the girls. Samuel impressed his grandad by knowing exactly how to play his musical instruments.

"How did he know how to do that?" Derek asked, surprised as Samuel delicately placed his hands on the electric organ as if he were about to perform a recital. He'd seen Claire play many times and had taken it all in.

It was only at the end of the day, when we were back in our own home, that Stuart said, "We've managed to be at home for most of Christmas Day and all of Boxing Day! We didn't expect that when we drove to hospital six days ago."

"Better not speak too soon," I said, fearful we'd been negligent and not noticed Samuel having a temperature. "Let's take his temperature before he goes to bed." I put the temperature gun in Samuel's ear. "It's thirty-six point five. It looks like we're home for another few hours, at least."

During the day we checked Samuel's temperature roughly every four hours, but we decided not to do it once we'd gone to bed unless he woke up. I figured we'd had enough broken nights and Samuel needed sleep if he was to stand a chance of getting better. The last temperature reading would be at about eleven o'clock, just before I went to bed, when I would also feed his medicines down his nose tube using a syringe. Usually, Samuel would wake at least once in the night so I would quickly check his temperature then, but I wasn't regimented about it.

Amazingly, Samuel didn't get a temperature for the next few days. On Monday morning we turned up for our outpatient appointment with Mike in the day clinic. A nurse took his temperature and blood pressure then weighed him. Everything was fine.

"I'm going to need some more medicines," I said to the nurse, "if we're going to be home for a few more days."

"I'll ask Mike to write a prescription," she said, probably not believing we would be going back home again.

After a while, Mike called us into his consulting room.

"How has he been?" he asked as he felt Samuel's stomach.

"Fine," I said.

"No sniffles? Coughs? Sickness?"

"No, nothing. In fact, he's been really well. Much better than when he was in hospital."

At the end of his examination, Mike seemed genuinely impressed.

"Well, if he's not ill beforehand, bring him in on Thursday – New Year's Eve. He'll probably need some platelets by then as well, so be prepared to stay a couple of hours."

Stuart and I smiled, hardly able to believe we were being allowed to return home again.

"But, remember, if he gets a temperature between then and now bring him straight back in."

"Yes. Amos said it's not *if* he gets an infection but *when*," Stuart said.

Mike nodded.

"It's highly likely," he said, "but he looks okay at the moment, so go home and enjoy the rest of your Christmas break."

And so, with that, Stuart picked Samuel up.

"Right, little man, we're off!"

We went to the door and Samuel gave Mike a little wave. He had a very contented smile on his face.

CHAPTER 14

Five Wonderful Weeks

~

STUART AND I WERE IN the kitchen, and I was packing Samuel's baby bag ready for hospital. Neither of us could quite believe we'd got to New Year's Eve without him getting an infection. I put in a freshly made bottle of milk, a beaker of water, some organic crisps that looked suspiciously like cheesy Wotsits, and a small box of raisins. Mick cooked for the children visiting the day unit as well as the ones on the ward, so I could get Samuel a meal if he wanted one, but I always liked to have some basics with me. I don't know why, as he hardly ever wanted food when I offered it to him, and he certainly never initiated it. I suppose it was a way of feeling normal.

"If Samuel could just stay well for one more night, we can have New Year's Eve in our own home," Stuart said.

"I think we've been really lucky to have a whole week at home," I said.

"I know we have, but it would be good not to have to spend New Year's Eve in hospital. Can you imagine drinking champagne in the parents' room?"

I laughed.

"I'm afraid I can. That place has become all too familiar."

"I'm really looking forward to Angie and Len coming over tonight. Just one more night and then I don't mind after that."

"I do. I'm dreading being back in that hospital whilst you're at work. It doesn't sound long when you tell people you're going back in for four weeks, but it feels like an eternity when you're in there."

"You do really well. I wish I could be with you more but I should be getting back to work now – now that Samuel's doing so well and we're getting used to things."

"I can't believe you've decided to go back another day a week and they've not even asked you to."

"It just looks better if it's my idea, rather than them asking me. You'll be fine. You cope really well and my mum and dad will visit, and your mum and sister."

"Well, let's hope they say we can go home again," I said, picking up my overflowing pram bag, "then they won't have to."

We arrived at the day unit for our nine o'clock appointment. We had to be in early as we knew it was highly likely Samuel would need a platelet transfusion. A sample of his blood was taken and his temperature and blood pressure were checked. He was also weighed. In the week that we'd been at home he'd put on weight. Mike wasn't working that day so Martin examined him.

"He seems fine," he said. "How are you finding it, being at home?"

"We love it, and Samuel seems happier. We're just hoping we can go back again after this appointment today," I replied.

"It would be nice to have New Year's Eve at home," Stuart added.

"I don't see why you shouldn't go home. Samuel seems well, although he does need some platelets. His temperature was slightly raised…"

"Oh no!" I said.

"Only slightly. It could just be because he needs more platelets. We'll get that sorted out and then I'll assess him once he's had the transfusion. But if his temperature is still under thirty-seven point five, you can take him home."

We followed a nurse to the six-bedded bay that Samuel usually recovered in when he'd had chemotherapy injected into his lumbar spine. She set up the platelets to run through the machine and then attached the line to the end of his Hickman line. Samuel was very pleased to see his old friend, the telly, again, and soon had it switched on to CBeebies.

Stuart went off to get us both a coffee and a Danish pastry. Being in hospital seemed to give us an insatiable need for treats! We'd just finished our snack when the nurse came to see Samuel again.

"I'm just going to take your temperature, Samuel," she said.

His eyes flicked to the side to check what she was doing before returning his attention to the characters on *Balamory*.

"It was a little high earlier, wasn't it, Samuel?" she said.

He frowned. Obviously not in the mood for conversation, he stared even harder at the television.

"Thirty-seven point five, I'm afraid."

"Oh, no!" I said.

I looked at Stuart and he sighed.

"Typical!"

"Don't upset Samuel."

But Samuel wasn't listening. He was watching television and wasn't going to have his attention diverted for anything.

"Don't worry," the nurse said. "It may just be because he's having his platelets. Let's wait until they've gone through and then see what's happening. I'd better let Martin know, though, just in case."

After the platelets had gone through, Martin came over with a temperature gun and Stuart and I crossed our fingers as he put it in Samuel's ear.

"Still thirty-seven point five."

"So we have to stay in, then." I said.

It was a statement rather than a question. I suddenly remembered the feeling of walking back to the ward from this room and I really wished we could walk out the front door instead.

"Well, he looks well enough." He paused and looked at Samuel. "I think you can go home. We don't start antibiotics unless he has a temperature of thirty-eight, anyway."

"Oh, thank you!" I said with a big grin.

"If it goes up, let us know. And if it hits thirty-eight, come straight back in."

All day we vigilantly checked his temperature. It hovered around the thirty-seven point five mark until about teatime.

"Let's give him dinner then check it again," I said to Stuart as I lifted Samuel into his high chair.

"What do you think we should do? Cancel Angie and Len?"

"I don't know. Let's see which way it's gone then make a decision."

We tried to carry on as normal, but neither of us could settle knowing we might be returning to Cambridge at any moment. We took his temperature with great trepidation.

"Thirty-six point nine!"

"Hooray!" Stuart shouted, and I suddenly realised where Samuel got it from!

Angie and Len came round for the evening and I continued to take Samuel's temperature every couple of hours, just to make sure he remained well. Luckily, it went back down to normal and stayed that way. He even made an appearance at midnight, just like the previous year, and Angie and Len were very pleased to see him. So, not only did we spend Christmas at home, but also New Year. We felt like life was on the up and, for a while, it was.

In the New Year Stuart went back to work four days a week and worked from home on the remaining day. Samuel had to go into

Addenbrooke's twice a week to see Mike, or one of the other doctors if he wasn't there. On the days in between, Audrey, the community nurse, would visit. As we only had one car, which Stuart needed to get to work, I worried about how I was going to get Samuel to hospital for his appointments or if his temperature went up. Our families were really helpful with lifts for the appointments, but it was more difficult to know who to turn to in an emergency as both our families lived out of town. In the end, different friends offered to help and the hospital let us know about volunteer drivers.

At home Samuel seemed to go from strength to strength. In fact, it was only when I saw him with healthy children I remembered how ill he was. The extensive treatment he'd undergone over the last three months had zapped him of energy, but a blood transfusion would perk him up again and he always maintained his enthusiasm for life.

One Thursday morning Derek took us to the day unit. Snow lay on the ground but it was a beautiful sunny day. I remember thinking how the day unit was much lighter and airier than the ward, and I desperately hoped we wouldn't be returning there any time soon. I looked across the waiting area at Samuel. He was sitting on a little plastic aeroplane and Derek was energetically pushing him up and down the corridor. Samuel happily lifted his feet up and held onto the steering wheel as the propellers went round and round. He seemed so well (which was more than I could say for Derek, whose face was turning red from the exertion) but I knew things could turn around at any moment.

In contrast to when we were on the ward, Samuel didn't seem to mind going to the day unit and would sit quite happily with the other children whilst they waited for their appointments. I don't know if it was because he felt better or if he knew he wouldn't be staying long, but he often had a smile on his face in there.

I remember one particular occasion when my mum had driven us in. As we walked through the door, Samuel pointed to the toy garage, which a couple of older children were already playing with.

"Do you want to play with the garage?" I asked him.

He smiled. I carried him over and sat him on the floor next to it. I went to sit down with him, thinking he would be upset if I went to the waiting area, which was about ten feet away.

He fervently shook his head and gave me such a look as if to say, "Don't embarrass me, Mummy. Can't you see I'm with the bigger boys?"

I couldn't believe it.

I remember thinking, *You're seventeen months old; not seventeen years old!*

A volunteer driver took us in on another occasion. Samuel was due to have chemotherapy injected into his spine. The driver was really kind and helped me in with the car seat and bags so I could carry Samuel, but after the procedure he was sick and I was concerned about the same thing happening on the way home in the driver's car. I think it was just because he had a lot of milk when he came round and it didn't sit well with the anaesthetic, but it bothered me more being in someone else's car.

I also worried how much Samuel should mix with other people and, in particular, children. He would be neutropenic – have no immunity – for quite a few weeks, and I wanted to do all I could to prevent him from getting an infection. Shops would be a big problem due to the mixture of heat and people. As it was January, many people had colds and other viruses, so I was anxious to keep him away from anyone who showed the slightest sign of being ill. For a while Stuart and I took it in turns to do the shopping, the other staying at home with Samuel. But as the weeks went on and he remained well, I gradually became more relaxed about short trips to the shops, although I always kept to quiet times and never ventured in on a Saturday.

We were approaching the middle of the month. Samuel was still well and we were still at home. I kept him occupied with trips to the park and visits from friends and family, but I knew what he wanted more than anything was interaction with other children. Occasionally I took him next door to see Nina and Esther whilst I chatted to Nancy, and I could see just how much he enjoyed being with them.

One afternoon Nancy said to me, "I'm doing an extra session of Tadpole Tunes next Tuesday. If Samuel's well enough, why don't you bring him along? There won't be many children there as I haven't advertised it yet."

I looked at Samuel. Could I risk it? I wasn't sure. But when it got to Tuesday morning and I saw the other mums and children walking past our house on their way to Nancy's, I instantly decided to take him along. He had a big smile on his face as I walked him into her large lounge. We joined the other mums and children sitting on the floor in a circle. Nancy put the music on. Everyone sang "Tadpole Tunes" and the children clapped along. Samuel joined in with the clapping and even bounced up and down to the music. I sang along too, pleased that I'd taken him. I looked across the room and saw a lady called Tracy and her son, who I'd met through the NCT, but who I hadn't seen in a long time.

"What's wrong with Samuel?" she mouthed across to me whilst everyone carried on singing.

She indicated his nose tube and suddenly I became conscious of how different he looked.

"I'll tell you later," I mouthed back.

I'd become so used to his condition that it no longer shocked me, but I realised then how it might shock someone else. Cancer in a baby is, after all, very rare. She looked across at us several times. I could see concern in her eyes as she tried to weigh up whether he had something really serious or not, but Samuel didn't notice any curious glances; he was too busy enjoying himself.

"Right. Could all the children come to the front?" Nancy said at one point and, before anyone had a chance to move, Samuel bottom-shuffled over to her.

He looked back at me just to check I'd noticed he was at the front, and I thought I detected an ever so slightly self-important expression on his face.

How did he know what she'd said? I thought to myself.

He never ceased to amaze me.

Tracy and her son came over and sat with us when the session finished.

"So, what's wrong with Samuel?" she asked.

"He's got leukaemia," I answered.

The words sounded strange, like I was talking about someone else. Samuel was perfect to me and I couldn't match up this terrible disease with the happy, confident, funny, clever, kind person who I had the privilege of calling my son. I told her all about it, but I still couldn't believe it was Samuel's story I was telling.

"I'm going to pray for you," Tracy said to Samuel.

She held his face and kissed the top of his head. I could see she was upset.

"He'll be fine," I said automatically. "He's doing really well – aren't you, poppet?"

Samuel looked up at me and smiled. Just then, Nancy opened the doors to her conservatory, which doubled up as a playroom. Samuel gave me a little wave and bottom-shuffled off to play with the toys. Again, I marvelled at his independence in the face of all adversity. I was incredibly proud of him. A little while later he was back, holding a balloon. I was expecting him to come straight over to me but, again, he just gave me a little wave and bottom-shuffled over to Nancy at the other end of the room. They batted the balloon back and forth to each other a few times and then eventually he returned to me, quite satisfied with his morning.

We went to Tadpole Tunes one more time, the following week. Again, Samuel enjoyed himself enormously, but I have one memory that always upsets me. After the session had ended, Nancy went round to everyone and offered them a homemade biscuit from a tin. Samuel happily helped himself and sat contentedly nibbling on his biscuit whilst he watched the other children playing. After a while, a baby of about nine or ten months crawled over to him. Samuel always shared everything, which amazed me as it came totally from him; I'd never asked him to share with anyone. With this baby sitting opposite, looking longingly at the biscuit, Samuel did what came naturally – he offered the baby a bite. The baby took the biscuit and sank his teeth into it. Samuel smiled and then held out his hand to have his biscuit returned to him, but the baby, oblivious to anything other than the biscuit, just kept on eating. Samuel looked at me and made a little worried noise. He did this several times, but I didn't take the biscuit off the other child. What I should have done was get him another biscuit and explain that this baby was too small to understand about sharing. I've been over it in my head so many times since he died, and I really regret how I handled it.

I think I said to Samuel at the time, "I'll get you a biscuit when we get home," but it wasn't good enough. I just have to hope that he forgot it quickly and focused instead on all the happy times we enjoyed together.

On Wednesday 14th January, Samuel and I were taking one of our walks in the park before lunch. For the first time since he'd been diagnosed I took him to the children's playground at the bottom of the Abbey Gardens.

"Do you want to go on the swing?" I asked. He smiled. I lifted him up, put him in the baby swing and gave him a gentle push. "Do you remember the swings?" I asked.

I saw a lovely, contented look in his eyes that seemed to say, "At last – back to normal!"

It was such a special moment, like the aftermath of war. I took a picture of him on my phone and sent it to Stuart with the title *Normality Returns!* And, at that moment, I really thought we'd got there. I thought he would be all right and I would get to keep my precious baby, whom I loved more than anything in the world. We continued to be fooled for a few more days. On Monday we played around together and I filmed it on my mobile. Afterwards, Samuel held my phone and watched it.

On it I say, "There's Mummy – look."

He blew little kisses as he watched me on the screen. My heart filled with love for him.

The next day, Tuesday 20th January, was President Barack Obama's inauguration day. Samuel surprised me by coming to find me when I'd gone to the toilet.

I'd left him happily playing in the living room with his garage and was just washing my hands when I heard, "Ehyo! Ehyo!"

I came out of the bathroom and saw him standing in the archway between the dining room and the kitchen.

"How did you get there?" I exclaimed. He giggled. "Did you walk by yourself? Clever boy!"

I could only think he'd gone round the furniture and the walls until he'd got to the archway. Later on, he was playing in the dining room whilst I made him some soup when I heard him giggle again. I looked round and he had moved from the dining-room chair to his high chair, which meant he must have taken a few steps by himself. I laughed with him.

"You are so clever," I said. 'Next time you walk, I want to see you do it!"

That evening, when Samuel was bathed and ready for bed, Stuart's friend Jon came round. We all sat in the living room chatting and Samuel stood at the footstool doing some drawing. I was sitting on the floor behind him. I grabbed hold of him and dragged him a few steps away from the stool, then let go. He took a couple of steps and got himself to the stool.

"Clever boy!" I whispered in his ear whilst his daddy and Jon talked, oblivious to anything.

Samuel giggled. I did the same thing again and this time took him a bit further back. With lots of giggles, he walked by himself again.

When Jon had gone I said, "You sit near the wall and hold Samuel." Samuel stood in front of his daddy, who put his arms around him. I sat a few feet in front of him. Barack Obama was delivering his speech on the TV. "Now, let go," I said.

Samuel walked towards me.

"Hooray!" Stuart said. "Well done, little man!"

Samuel performed his party trick a few more times before bed that evening.

"What an important day for him to choose to take his first steps!" I said.

"He's a very important baby," Stuart replied. "A *VIB*," he added with a laugh.

Thursday was my birthday and we were due to go to Addenbrooke's for an outpatient appointment. Samuel sat in front of us on a little chair at a table in the waiting area. There was some drawing paper and a pot filled with pencils, and he had a little box of raisins. He sat happily taking one pencil out of the pot, doing a little squiggle on his paper, then replacing the pencil and choosing another one.

The day unit was quiet that morning and no other children were sitting at the table, but then a little girl walked over. Samuel immediately picked up his box of raisins and offered her one. The little girl hesitated but then sat down. Samuel wasn't bothered. He just gave her a smile and returned the box to the table before carrying on with his drawing.

After a while, Archana, one of the doctors, called us through. She smiled at Samuel.

"We've missed Samuel. It's been a very long time since I last saw him." She flicked through his notes and I saw her frown. "When was he an inpatient last?" she asked.

"We went home Christmas Day," Stuart said.

"Yes. That was his last chemotherapy, but he must have been in since then."

We shook our heads.

"No; not as an inpatient," I said.

"He's not had an infection?"

"No."

"Not even a cold?"

We laughed.

"No, he's been really well," I said.

"His only temperature was on New Year's Eve," Stuart added. "But even then it didn't go up high enough for him to go on antibiotics."

"Well, I'm amazed. I don't think I've ever heard of anyone not having an infection between chemotherapy sessions." She shook her head in disbelief and laughed. "Well, I'd better check him." She was pleased that he seemed perfectly well. "We just need his blood counts to come up now and then we can start his final session of chemotherapy."

We left the hospital feeling very happy.

The next day I bought Samuel a new Grobag to wear in bed. I remember my sister and Stuart laughing at it as it was huge – it was for children aged eighteen months to three years. I was obviously desperate for Samuel's good health to continue, and looking towards a positive future helped me to think it would. There were always times, though, when I feared I would lose him. I also bought him an educational DVD from the Early Learning Centre to teach him about colours, which I played before I got him ready for bed in the enormous Grobag.

We'd arranged to go to Angie and Len's house that evening, for the first time in five months. I sat upstairs with Samuel and cuddled him whilst I gave him his milk. He seemed slightly restless and then, all of a sudden, he was sick. Stuart was in the bath and my sister was downstairs watching television in the living room. I called down to her and she helped me clean him up before getting him changed.

"I think I'd better ring Angie and let her know we won't be coming," I said.

"You don't have to," Nancy said. "I don't mind looking after him."

"Thanks, but I don't think we'd better leave him in case this is the start of an infection."

We stayed in for the evening and Samuel continued to be unwell, although his temperature never went up. By the morning the sickness had subsided, but overnight he'd developed a cold. He was also quieter and more lethargic and seemed to just want to sit on my lap. In the afternoon I decided to take him out to see if it would make any difference. I phoned Angie and asked her if she would like to meet me in the Marks and Spencer's café.

"He doesn't seem himself, does he?" she said.

"No…" I hesitated. "I'm quite concerned about him, actually."

"It's just a cold, though, isn't it?"

"I don't know." I cuddled Samuel into me and kissed the top of his head. "I'm worried though." Again, I hesitated. "It reminds me of when he was ill in September; before we got him diagnosed."

Angie told me much later that a cold chill went through her when I said those words, but at the time she just said, "When are you seeing the nurse again?"

"Audrey will be round on Monday. We only have to go into Addenbrooke's once a week now as he's been so well. They're just waiting for his blood counts to rise again and then he can have the final dose of chemotherapy."

"Won't that be a blessing!" Angie said. "Then you can all get on with your lives and put this behind you."

Audrey came just after lunch on Monday.

"I'm worried about him, Audrey," I said as she walked in. "He doesn't seem right to me."

"Okay, I'll just lay my things out and then take a look at him." She washed her hands. I always left kitchen roll out for her to dry her hands on as I knew she was fastidious about hygiene and wouldn't dry her hands on a normal towel when she was examining Samuel. She laid her tray out on the dining room table and got everything ready to take his blood. "I'm just going to take some blood from your line, Samuel," she said, attaching a syringe to the end of his Hickman line. He sat still on my lap.

"He's very pale, Amanda. He might need a blood transfusion."

"Maybe, but I think it's more than that. I don't think he's well at all."

She worked quickly and efficiently, changing over the plastic tubes until she had three separate blood samples.

"Has his temperature remained stable? Is it still thirty-six point five or thereabouts?"

"Yes. That's what's confusing."

"But you really feel something's wrong?"

"Yes, I do. At Addenbrooke's last week we bumped into another oncology patient and she was just getting over chickenpox. I've noticed Samuel has a couple of tiny spots on his head and a few on his body. I wonder if he could have it as well."

"I'll just put these blood specimens away and then I'll examine him." She labelled her blood samples and wrote in Samuel's medical notes before checking his skin. "They don't look like classic chickenpox spots. However, I have seen a patient who was neutropenic with chickenpox and the spots *were* a bit like these. I think it would be worth taking him up to the West Suffolk Hospital and getting one of the doctors to check him over."

I nodded.

"Thanks, Audrey. I've really been concerned."

"I'll drive you up there then I can get his blood checked at the same time."

I always really appreciated how Audrey listened to me and took my thoughts into account as part of her examination of Samuel. In fact, Mike was the same, and I began to understand that the medical staff who did this were the most effective. I always regretted listening to doctors who dismissed me without checking out my concerns.

I realised straight away that Samuel was quite the celebrity on Rainbow ward at the West Suffolk Hospital. It seemed that in the four months we'd been in Addenbrooke's all the doctors and nurses had heard about him and had been following his progress.

"He looks much better than the last time I saw him," said Lorraine, the nurse who'd kindly travelled to Addenbrooke's in the ambulance with us on the day of his diagnosis.

"Yes. He's been doing really well. I'm just a bit worried about him at the moment, though."

"I'll get one of the doctors to see him," she said, leaving the room. "Oh, thanks for the card, by the way."

"No problem. Thanks for everything you did."

For some unknown reason, Samuel perked up whilst he was there. For a while he was content to sit on my lap and look at books, but then he wiggled off and stood up. He'd not walked independently since his little spell of activity six days before, so I held his hands as he investigated his surroundings. After a while, a doctor called Lucy came in and examined him.

"His blood results are all normal," she said. "In fact, they're just starting to creep up."

"That's good news!" I felt extremely relieved.

At that point in time I hadn't acknowledged, even to myself, the extent of my fears. I looked at Samuel. He was edging his way around the bed. He looked back at us and smiled.

"He looks really well," Lucy said.

"He does at the moment, but he's not been himself all weekend. I wondered if he had chickenpox," I said, returning to the original reason we'd come to the hospital.

"No, they're not chickenpox spots," she said. "I really think he's fine. He's not had a temperature and his blood test results are normal. After seeing him, I'm happy that he's okay. Take him home and see how he is. If you're worried again, give us a call."

I didn't have a car with me so I had no way of getting home; Audrey had had to leave the hospital to see her next patient.

"Would it be all right for us to sit in the waiting area for an hour or so until my husband can pick us up after work?"

"Of course. It will give us a bit longer to observe Samuel, as well."

We sat in the waiting room and Samuel played with all the toys and was absolutely fine. Whilst we were there, a little boy of about the same age came in with suspected tonsillitis. His mother was very anxious and kept asking the nurses questions. One of the nurses tried to take the little boy's blood pressure, but he cried so hard and made such a fuss that they weren't able to do it. Samuel watched intently, taking it all in, before turning to me with pursed lips. Then he raised his eyebrows!

If he could talk I'm sure he would have said, "What a fuss about nothing, Mummy!"

We returned home and I tried to feel reassured by the doctor's assessment, but a nagging doubt lingered. Samuel just didn't seem himself. I was vigilant about taking his temperature and it remained stable. However, I couldn't shake off the fear that something was wrong. Samuel didn't seem happy and he didn't want to walk or stand. His sleeping had also worsened and we were back to being up for long periods in the night. His preference was to sit quietly on my lap and watch TV or look at books. This seemed such a contrast to the little boy who'd wanted to play independently a week or two back. I dreaded to think what these changes meant.

Early Wednesday afternoon, 28th January, my dad and his girlfriend came round for a visit, together with my mum. Audrey arrived at about the same time.

"I'm still worried, Audrey," I said. "I know he's not right."

I explained my concerns and Audrey listened, then examined Samuel.

"I agree; he does seem quieter than normal." She considered him. "But his temperature has remained the same?"

"It was slightly higher last time I took it, actually."

"Do you think we should take him to Addenbrooke's?" my dad asked.

"No. If anything, the West Suffolk Hospital would be the first port of call," Audrey replied. She took his blood and wrote in his notes. "I'll get these samples straight to haematology then give you a call with the results. In the meantime, if his temperature goes up give me a call on my mobile number."

"Okay. Thanks, Audrey."

"If you're not happy, Mandy, I think we should get him into Addenbrooke's," my dad said after she'd gone. "I don't mind driving you."

I hesitated. A big part of me wanted to take him straight there, but I felt we should be following the protocol.

"I'm not sure what to do," I said. We talked for a bit longer and then I took Samuel's temperature again: "Thirty-eight point one!" I exclaimed. "We should get him straight to the West Suffolk Hospital and let the doctors examine him. Perhaps he's just had an infection brewing and it's taken this long to come out."

I phoned Audrey and quickly packed some things for Samuel.

"I'll let the hospital know you're on your way," she said.

Having spent so long in Addenbrooke's, I really noticed the difference in the doctors' knowledge at the West Suffolk Hospital. At Addenbrooke's, the doctors were specialists in their subjects and spent all their time with children with cancer, but at the WSH the doctors were paediatricians and their knowledge was far more general. Rather disconcertingly, I felt my own knowledge on Samuel's condition was more current than the doctors', and this made me feel less confident in their abilities and diagnostic skills.

The nurses settled us into the same room we'd had the night we'd found out about Samuel's condition. They checked his temperature and blood pressure and then brought us all cups of tea. After a while, the doctor who'd called us originally with the news in September came in to see us.

"We'll start Samuel on some general intravenous antibiotics tonight," she said.

"Are you going to do any tests to see what the infection is?" I asked her.

"Not at the moment. We'll see how he gets on with the antibiotics first."

"Have you let Addenbrooke's know we're here?"

"Yes, we have informed them."

"And what about his blood test results?"

"They're fine. We'll take more blood in the morning and the consultant will visit Samuel. His knowledge is a bit more specialised, so he'll know more."

My family stayed with me until Stuart arrived.

"Samuel will be having antibiotics for the next forty-eight hours," I told him.

"Okay. Do you have everything you need? What about all his medicines?"

When I look back now, I can see how far we'd travelled from the fresh-faced, naive parents we were in September to the knowledgeable, efficient ones we had become.

"The nurses said they would get a fresh batch from the pharmacy, but they haven't got it yet and he's almost due them."

In the end, Stuart returned home for our medicines as the pharmacy at the WSH couldn't get hold of them.

After Stuart left for the night, I settled down on my bed with Samuel and quietly watched TV. Samuel was calm, but he took a long time to drop off. I thought back to the times when he'd had an infection before and reasoned his behaviour was similar to then. I told myself how lucky we'd been to be at home for five weeks, and that it was inevitable he would get an infection at some point. I didn't feel trapped or anxious about being an inpatient, like I had done before at Addenbrooke's, and I was just glad Samuel was getting some treatment. If all went well, he would need a couple of days on antibiotics and then he would be fit enough to have his final session of chemotherapy. He fell asleep eventually and I put him in his cot.

That evening I was surprised when Helen, one of the nurses from Addenbrooke's, came to see us.

"What are you doing here?" I asked her when she walked through the door dressed in her uniform and wearing her familiar headband with the LED lamp.

"I used to work here and I'm still on bank, so they asked me to come in to look after Samuel as I have some experience of working with children with leukaemia."

"That's great! It's really good to see someone who knows what they're doing."

"Oh, no! Has it been bad?"

"No, I can't say that, but I just get the impression they're not used to nursing a patient who's so seriously ill."

"I think you're right. They don't get to see many oncology patients here as Addenbrooke's generally takes care of them. And, of course, childhood cancer is rare."

Helen stayed and chatted for a while. She was very efficient at changing Samuel's drugs and seeing to his pump as soon as it bleeped. One positive I did find with being in our local hospital was that the staff were more anxious about Samuel's health and well-being, as they hadn't become used to childhood cancer in the way that I felt some of the medical staff had at Addenbrooke's.

Samuel woke a few times during the night but was, in general, quite relaxed. I realised being in hospital had become normal for him, and as long as he had Stuart or me with him he was fine.

By morning he appeared slightly better and was anxious to walk about and not be confined to one room. Unlike in Addenbrooke's when he had an infection, at the WSH he was not barrier nursed or expected to stay in his room. Barrier nursing is really for the protection of the other vulnerable patients and, as the other patients in this ward were not nearly as ill as those in Addenbrooke's, they didn't need to take the same precautions.

A sample of Samuel's blood was taken first thing and then he was allowed out of his room. I held his hands whilst he walked down the corridor, stopping every now and then for a passing nurse or doctor to admire him! Later that morning the consultant came to see us with the doctor we'd seen the day before. He was a distinguished gentleman, whom I'm sure many parents found reassuring. However, with all the experience I now had of doctors, I no longer trusted them on face value. He asked me many questions about Samuel's condition and treatment.

"I think I'm going to have to brush up on my knowledge of leukaemia," he said very honestly.

I just smiled but wondered to myself if Samuel would be better off in Addenbrooke's.

"Do you have the results of the blood tests done this morning?" I asked.

"Yes, we do."

The other doctor handed him a printed sheet of paper.

"Are his counts still going up?" I asked.

"They're about the same as yesterday," he said, "with the exception of the platelets, which have gone down slightly."

"Gone down?" I was immediately concerned. Samuel's particular type of leukaemia was in his platelet precursors. The fact that his platelet count had gone down made me worry that he wasn't producing proper platelets. I didn't want to think any further than that. My heart thumped in my chest. "Please will you ring Addenbrooke's and see what they have to say about that?" I asked.

"Yes, of course," the consultant said. "But I shouldn't think it's anything to worry about." I'm sure he believed that, but I didn't. "Now, Samuel doesn't need any more intravenous antibiotics until this evening, so you're free to take him home or out until then."

I was very surprised. At Addenbrooke's I always had to fight to take him out. I didn't have a car to take us home but I rang my mum and she kindly drove the twenty miles to come and get us. We went into town, but Samuel was clearly not himself. He whimpered a few times as if he was uncomfortable or in pain. In the end, we took him home and let him have a sleep in his cot for a couple of hours. At about half past five we took him back in.

We were just walking down the corridor towards the nurse station when the doctor called out, "Samuel's mum!"

We walked towards her.

"I've just spoken to Martin, one of the doctors at Addenbrooke's, about Samuel's platelet count. He said, 'Reassure Mum his platelets have just gone down as a reaction to his infection.' Okay?"

I hesitated. We hadn't spent as much time with Martin as we had with the other doctors and consultants at Addenbrooke's. I would have preferred to have had Mike's opinion. However, I had always found Martin to be knowledgeable when he spoke to us.

"Okay. I'll be reassured by that." As we walked back to our room I said to my mum, "I do hate it when they call me Mum; it's so patronising."

My mum agreed.

The next morning Samuel seemed much better than he had the previous afternoon. I was baffled, but reasoned that the antibiotics must have taken effect and any infection had gone. In fact, he'd not had a temperature again after the night we'd brought him in. A lady came into the room with breakfast for both of us. This was another area where life was a bit easier in this hospital than Addenbrooke's. There, I'd had to go to the parents' room at the other end of the ward to get myself something to eat, leaving Samuel in the process. But here they delivered my meals and drinks alongside Samuel's, which made looking after him much easier.

After I'd eaten I felt slightly queasy, but I put it to the back of my mind and took Samuel to the playroom. He was attached to the pump for the morning for the last lot of antibiotics, and then we would be allowed home. I still hadn't worked out how we would get home, but I did have his car seat with me, so in a worst-case scenario we could get a taxi.

I pushed the pump with one hand and carried Samuel in my other arm down the corridor to the playroom. Once in there, I took him to a table and gave him some things to play with. Pretty soon two other young children and their mums joined us. I noticed one of the other children also had a nose tube in. The mother and I started to talk and I found out her daughter also had leukaemia, although a different type from Samuel's. I should think at that point the third mother at our table thanked her lucky stars her child didn't have a serious condition, and probably resolved never to complain again!

I was still feeling slightly sick but kept trying to focus on Samuel and the other children and parents at the table to take my mind off it. After a while, a young lady joined us at the table and told us she was on work experience. She had only been sitting with us for about ten minutes when I knew I was going to be sick.

I quickly handed Samuel to her and said, "I'm going to be sick," before rushing off.

Luckily, the sister on the ward spotted the situation immediately and showed me to a bathroom. After I'd been sick, she got me a glass of water and a chair.

"I must get back to Samuel," I said.

"No, you don't. You look dreadful. Samuel's fine and we didn't know what job to give that work experience girl, anyway. Go and have a lie down," she ordered.

I must admit, I was secretly grateful for her bossiness as I felt awful. I lay down for a while but then needed to be sick again. I rushed to the bathroom.

"Sam—" I said to Sister as I came out again.

"... is sleeping in the arms of the work experience girl. Now go and get some sleep yourself."

I lay down for another half hour. There was a huge part of me that wanted to stay there forever, but I felt I had to sort things out and I knew it wasn't hygienic being sick in a hospital. I wondered if I had the norovirus, which had been so prevalent at Addenbrooke's, and then wondered if that was what Samuel had had when he was sick the previous Friday. After a while, I called Stuart and asked him to come and get us.

"You're going to have to look after Samuel, I'm afraid," I said. "I'm really not up to it."

"I can't. I can't leave work. I've already had one day off this week."

"Well, I'm afraid you're going to have to. There's no one else to do it."

Stuart took some convincing, but as soon as he turned up and saw me being sick, he regretted his earlier allegiance to work.

"I'm sorry. You look really ill."

I was too glad of him being there to say anything. Instead, I let him look after Samuel whilst, between bouts of sickness, I packed our belongings. We were ready to leave just after midday. As we walked down the corridor we passed Lucy, one of the doctors.

"I hope you feel better soon," she said.

"Thank you."

"Are you happy with everything now, Amanda?" she asked. "I know yesterday you were concerned because Samuel's platelet count had gone down."

I hadn't given it any conscious thought that morning as I'd been preoccupied with feeling ill myself, but I suddenly realised I still had concerns about Samuel.

"Actually, I know his temperature has been stable so any infection he had has gone, but he still isn't himself."

"Okay, I'll look into it," she said. "You need to be sick again, don't you?"

I nodded and rushed off. If I hadn't been so ill, I might have focused more on what she'd said and asked her to explain what she was going to do. Instead, I just concentrated on getting home without being ill. Once we got there I went straight to bed, leaving Samuel sitting on Stuart's lap watching telly. A couple of hours later I got up and went downstairs. Stuart was sitting at the dining-room table, working at his computer.

"Where's Samuel?" I asked.

"In bed; he fell asleep on me. He's been up there about an hour."

"That's good. He needs his sleep. Perhaps that will make him feel a bit better."

I wandered into the living room, sat down on the sofa and flicked through a magazine. The nausea had subsided but I still felt weak and ill; I hated thinking of my own health when Samuel had already suffered so much at only eighteen months. Just then, the phone rang. I picked it up.

"Hello. Is that Mrs Murray – Samuel's mum?"

"Yes?"

It was a consultant paediatric haematologist from Addenbrooke's Hospital whom we'd not met before. He said he was Mike's replacement while he was on holiday.

"I'm sorry to have to do this to you when you've never even met me."

"What is it?" I asked.

"The haematologist at the West Suffolk Hospital has just looked at a slide of Samuel's blood under the microscope and we're concerned with what they've seen."

My breathing quickened and my voice caught in my throat.

"I-I w-was just thinking," I said shakily. "I knew he wasn't right. What have they seen?"

I already knew the answer.

Slowly, with a kind voice, he said the words I most dreaded hearing: "I'm afraid they think they've found more leukaemia cells."

I tried not to cry but couldn't hold it back.

"It's come back, hasn't it?"

"We're not certain. We need to do more tests, but..." he paused. "It does look like it has. I'm so sorry."

CHAPTER 15

Relapse

~

IN AN INSTANT, I WAS back in September, hearing the news for the first time that Samuel had leukaemia. Everything that had gone before – the endless hours of chemotherapy that Samuel had endured, the blood transfusions, the X-rays, the operations, the time spent locked away in one room – all meant nothing. They had only temporarily rid his body of leukaemia. Now it was back and the treatment would be much worse. It was almost impossible to imagine.

"Would you like me to give you some time to take this in?" the haematologist asked. "I could call you back in fifteen minutes."

I could hear Stuart tapping on the computer in the dining room.

"Just tell me what happens now," I said, "and then I can let my husband know."

"Well, we'd like you to bring Samuel in tomorrow and we can take some more blood. By looking at his blood under a microscope, I should be able to tell you more."

"What will the treatment be, if it has come back?"

"We'll do two more rounds of chemotherapy to get him back into remission. Then he will either go to Bristol or Great Ormond Street for a bone marrow transplant."

"What does that involve?"

"We can talk more about that tomorrow but, basically, we'll need to find a donor whose bone marrow is a match for Samuel's and put that into his system. He'll be in hospital for about three months during this process but he'll be in very good hands. They're experts in doing this procedure."

I took in what he said. *I knew Samuel wasn't right*, I kept thinking. My body was shaking. I now had to tell Stuart.

"I'll tell my husband, but would be grateful if you could call back in fifteen minutes to speak to him, as I know he will want to know more."

He agreed. I put the phone down and walked into the dining room to break the awful news to Stuart. I hated having to do it. We'd been through too much already as a family. I didn't want us to suffer any more.

For the rest of the day and that night we talked about the possibility of a relapse whilst trying not to show Samuel our distress. We existed on two levels: playing with him, feeding him, bathing him and pretending everything was normal, all whilst feeling we were about to be robbed of the most precious thing in our lives. It's almost impossible to express the level of anxiety we felt, yet if anyone had come round that day they would have guessed nothing from our demeanour.

First thing the next morning we set off for Addenbrooke's Hospital. We were shown into a room opposite the nurse station. Julie, one of the sisters who was older and probably more experienced in these matters, came to see us. She knelt down beside us as she took Samuel's blood.

"We won't know anything for sure until the haematologist looks at his blood under a microscope," she said.

We nodded, but it was impossible not to leap ahead.

"How difficult is it to get a bone marrow donor?" Stuart asked.

"It depends, but there are two large databases in Britain: one run by the Anthony Nolan Trust and the other by Blood Donors (British Bone Marrow Registry). Samuel's details will be cross-matched to find a suitable donor. They can look worldwide, if necessary." I noticed she'd not actually said if it was easy or difficult. "Try not to worry until we know more," she added.

Around eleven o'clock we found out the haematologist had been delayed by a puncture and had had to go to a garage to get his tyre changed. It felt as if we were being tested. How much could we take before we cracked up altogether? "Try not to worry" was the general message from nurses and doctors alike, but it was impossible not to. Eventually, just after twelve o'clock, the haematologist came to see us.

"I'm sorry," he said. I noticed the pained look on his face; he clearly felt awful about delaying the conversation we'd been dreading since yesterday. "I looked at Samuel's blood cells under the microscope expecting to see leukaemia cells but, in truth, the cells are too immature for me to be able to distinguish exactly what they are."

"So they might not be leukaemia cells?" I asked.

A feeling of hope rose within me.

"Possibly not. I really can't tell at this stage. The haematologist at the West Suffolk Hospital looked at his cells under the microscope because you'd expressed a concern that he still seemed unwell…"

"Don't they normally look at them, then?" I asked.

"No. The blood counts are done, but if they're going up it's generally assumed the leukaemia is still in remission. Samuel's counts were going up until two days ago, so there seemed no reason to think anything was wrong."

"So why did his platelet count drop?"

"It could be that the leukaemia has returned,' he replied gently, "or it could just be a reaction to the infection."

Although I'd never been totally convinced he'd had an infection in the first place – and despite all the other signs that told me Samuel was unwell in the same way he'd been in September – I clung on to the little bit of hope that the haematologist was offering.

"I suggest we bring Samuel into the day unit on Tuesday and do a lumbar puncture to extract some of his bone marrow. We'll be able to tell from that whether or not the leukaemia has returned."

Tuesday was three days away. How would we cope in the meantime?

When we got home, our sixteen-year-old niece, Ellen, rang.

"Is it still okay for me to get changed round yours?"

"Sorry – changed for what?"

"My concert." She paused. "At the cathedral."

I'd forgotten all about it. Ellen was due to sing in the cathedral that night and as she lived twelve miles away I'd told her she could get ready at our house.

"I'm sorry. Yes, of course," I said.

With hindsight, perhaps it was a mistake, but I didn't want to let her down.

When she arrived later, she asked, "Is it okay for Mum, Nan and Grandad to come round and wait for the concert to start?"

I hesitated.

"Ellen, we've actually had some rather worrying news," I said. "There's a possibility that Samuel has relapsed."

"Oh!" she said, rather shocked. "I'm sorry. I'll put them off."

"No. It's all right. Maybe it would be nice to have some support."

I asked Stuart what he wanted to do, and he agreed that seeing his mum, dad and sister might be just what he needed. Unfortunately, this wasn't the case. They didn't seem to know how to cope with the possibility of Samuel relapsing – or our feelings – and thought the best thing to do would be to act like nothing had happened. Ellen had told them our news when she'd phoned them, but perhaps they'd not grasped just how serious the situation was. I understand that everyone reacts to things in different ways – and we found out afterwards that they thought putting a brave face on matters would be the right thing to do – but we really needed to talk, or at least acknowledge what was going on. Stuart and I always found talking to be the best antidote to our stress, but I know not everyone feels the same way.

The next morning Stuart told them how we felt, and they apologised and explained their reaction. I know only too well that conversations like that are difficult; it's sad to think that later they would get so much practice.

A little later that day Stuart and I were sitting in the dining room having lunch, whilst Samuel had a nap, when I had an idea.

"Why don't we ask the lady who did reiki on Debbie and David's son if she would do some on Samuel?"

Debbie and David were a couple we'd met in hospital, whose four-year-old son had been given a terminal prognosis. However, he'd gone on to have experimental chemotherapy treatment, together with reiki healing, and had been cured.

"She works in the Floatation Centre in town. We could put a card through the door and ask her if she'll help us."

"That's a good idea. It's got to be worth a shot, hasn't it? It worked for that little boy. And wasn't there another boy in hospital with tumours that went after he had reiki?"

"Yes, there was. I think he had chemo at the same time, but maybe the two things together will have an effect."

Stuart wrote a card to Linda Graham (who we only knew then as "the reiki lady") and put it through the door of the shop in town where she worked.

We woke on Monday morning to several inches of snow. Our road – usually busy with traffic at that time of day – was blocked off due to roadworks. As a result, snow covered the ground, completely obscuring the division between road and path. Linda called first thing that morning.

"I can come to see you today," she said. She asked me where we lived. "Just one other thing: precisely when and where were you all born?"

"Samuel was born 2nd August 2007, at 7.27 p.m. in Bury St Edmunds."

"A Leo," Linda said.

"Yes."

"Lovely star sign. And you?"

I gave her Stuart's and my times and dates. She said she would see us that afternoon.

"It's strange," she said just as she was about to put down the phone. "I never work on Mondays. Normally, I wouldn't have seen your note until you'd already gone back into hospital, but I felt compelled to come in this morning. Very interesting."

I looked forward to meeting her.

The phone was busy that morning. Shortly afterwards, my friend Angela asked if she could visit us that afternoon, so I arranged for her to come over at lunchtime before Linda's visit. I had just spoken to her when the West Suffolk Hospital called and asked me to bring Samuel into the ward to have some bloods taken, as Audrey had been unable to get in due to the snow. I hesitated. I could walk, but it would take me half an hour; probably longer with the snow. Getting a taxi might prove difficult as I would have to ask them to wait, and if the nurses kept us waiting any length of time it would be expensive. I phoned Angela back, but she wasn't able to help as she was at work all morning and her husband was busy. In the end, I phoned Stuart.

"What do you think I should do?" I asked. I knew I shouldn't be bothering him at work, but I was completely at a loss. It felt like one stress too many. "I've told them I can't do this afternoon as Samuel has an appointment with an alternative therapist, so they've said we have to be in within the next hour."

"You're not taking Samuel anywhere," Stuart said. "It's freezing cold, he has no immunity, and he's possibly got leukaemia again. I can't believe they're even asking you to bring him in. I'll phone them."

Five minutes later he phoned back. "It's all sorted. Someone will be with you within the hour."

I was so grateful, especially when half an hour later the sister who'd looked after me when I'd been sick turned up. She'd no sooner walked through the door than she put her arms around me and gave me a hug.

"We want you to know we're so sorry that you're all going through this. He's such a lovely little boy. We can all see how special he is and it's really not fair."

I swallowed back my tears.

"Thank you. There's still a chance he might be okay. The haematologist couldn't tell when he looked at Samuel's blood on Saturday."

She nodded and patted my arm. I noticed she had one of those sad smiles on her face. How I hated seeing them! "He's actually asleep. He's in his cot in our room."

"Then let's not wake him. I'll come up and try to do it gently."

I led her upstairs and carefully undid the side zip on Samuel's Grobag. I unpopped the poppers on his sleepsuit then undid the little fabric wallet that concealed the end of his Hickman line. She put on her rubber gloves and delicately took blood without waking Samuel. I put the end of his line away, did up his poppers, and was just zipping up his Grobag when he suddenly opened his eyes. He looked straight at me, then whipped his head round to look at the nurse. His mouth turned down and I recognised the three-second warning.

"It's okay, poppet," I said quickly.

But it was no good. He started to cry.

"Oh, I'm sorry!" the sister said.

"I think it was me that woke him, actually. Don't worry."

I comforted him and the sister let herself out. I gave him some milk, then cuddled and rocked him until, half an hour later, he fell back to sleep in my arms. I was gently lifting him into his cot just as Angela knocked on the door.

We chatted for about an hour until Samuel woke up again. I tried to keep my mind off my worries, but every so often they sneaked through.

"I hope it's just an infection," I would say, but I knew I was ignoring my intuition, which had been telling me for over a week that Samuel wasn't okay; it wasn't an infection and the leukaemia had returned.

Angela and her daughter, Teresa, had bought Samuel lots of new toys, including some colouring pens and a beautiful book to draw in. They'd also got him a pretend telephone. When Samuel woke I brought him down and he played with the toys, but it was an effort and I could tell he felt ill. I kept my voice upbeat and light, but he kept putting his hand to his head, which told me had a headache. He must have felt so ill; more ill than I can imagine. Were my actions more annoying than reassuring? I wonder now if we should just have sat together quietly.

After a while, Linda rang saying she was unable to find us. I directed her to where she could park as the road was closed. Angela went out to find her and brought her to our house, then she left.

Linda wore a grey fur coat that went down to her ankles. A hat added inches to her already tall frame and a colourful walking stick contributed to her stately stature. Pulling myself together, I welcomed her in and, with as much dignity as I could muster, told her our story. I made her a cup of tea and then we sat together in the living room with Samuel on my lap. Her features softened as she smiled at him. I noticed she had a little diamanté in the middle of her forehead. She took a sip of her tea then picked up the toy telephone that Angela had brought round earlier.

"Hello?" she said. "Do you want to speak to Samuel?" She smiled at him. "Yes. Who's calling?" She handed the phone to Samuel. "It's Nancy."

"What made you say the name Nancy?" I asked.

"The name came to me as I sat in this seat," she said. "Why do you ask?"

"It's a name that Samuel hears a lot; my sister's called Nancy and so is my next-door neighbour. My sister lives with us and she was sitting where you're sitting now. It's quite an unusual name so I wondered why you thought of it."

"That sort of thing always happens to me," she said. "It's because I'm psychic," she added, with a directness that I gradually became used to.

As she drank tea she told me in great detail – and with alarming accuracy – about my character and Samuel's. It was as if she'd known us all our lives. She then proceeded to do the same about Stuart, whom she'd never even met.

"On first impression, you're friendly and calm. This is because your ascendant is in Libra and your star sign is Aquarius, but that hides a much stronger character. The moon in Aries makes you much more determined than people first assume. You're not afraid to stick up for what you believe in and you can be fiery. This can lead to arguments with your husband as he is a fire sign with his ascendant in Scorpio. This is a very intelligent combination, but at times quite a nasty one, and you should both try hard to control your tempers as I suspect, when stressed, they can get the better of you. I sense that you like to be outdoors and gardening would be a very good way to calm you."

I laughed.

"That's spot on. And I do garden."

"This combination doesn't always work well for Samuel," she continued. "He's a Leo, with Leo ascendant, so he needs a lot of positive attention and would hate to feel ignored whilst you and your husband argue."

"Can I just point out that we don't argue much? Well, not any more," I conceded. "We used to when we were younger."

Linda looked at me as if she could see inside me.

"That's good, because Samuel has the moon in Pisces, which makes him extremely intuitive and conscious of the moods and atmospheres around him. He hates it when you argue and when you're upset, but he's also very forgiving. I'm sensing from him that his favourite thing is when you show him how things work and I'm getting from him telepathically that this is something you do a lot. At the moment his relationship with you is his strongest bond, but that will change as he desires closeness with his father."

As she finished, Samuel began to wiggle on my lap and make whimpering noises.

"I think he's in pain," I said.

She held out her hands and placed them in front of Samuel, who promptly started to cry.

"It's okay, darling," I said. "Nothing's happening."

"You can't say nothing's happening; he can feel the energy coming from my hands. He may even be able to see it. Ooommmm," she chanted.

I watched, feeling like we had landed on a different planet. What a difference from the purely medical conversations that usually dominated our lives! As she continued to chant and hold her hands up in front of Samuel's body, I became aware that he had gone silent. After just a few minutes, he turned and cuddled into me and instantly fell into a deep sleep. I was amazed. It usually took me ages to get him to sleep, and he wouldn't sleep in front of other people unless it was very late or he was highly medicated, but he'd not had any painkillers and he'd already had his midday nap. Whilst he slept, Linda continued to do reiki healing on him, and at the same time amazed me with revelations about Stuart, Samuel and myself. At some point during our conversation the phone rang.

"Hello. This is Lorraine from the West Suffolk Hospital."

"Oh, hello," I said, surprised.

I wasn't expecting a call from the hospital; we were due to go into Addenbrooke's first thing the next morning.

"The doctors have asked me to let you know that Samuel's platelets are very low, so they would like you to bring him in tonight to give him a platelet transfusion."

I went cold. If Samuel's platelets had dropped that much there had to be a problem with his platelet precursors – the part of his bone marrow that produced the platelets. I knew this could only mean one thing: the leukaemia had returned.

"My husband's at work," I managed to say. "We'll bring him in when he gets home."

I hung up. Fear permeated every part of my body. My heart thumped, my face tingled and my mouth was dry. I felt like I might faint.

"Samuel needs a platelet transfusion," was all I could say before the tears fell down my face.

Linda hugged me tight.

"And what conclusion are you jumping to with that?"

"That it's come back!" I sobbed.

"Well, if that's his journey, it's meant to be. And you're meant to be there with him. He chose you and Stuart as his parents to help him and give him the courage to cope with this amazing journey he is on. Your horoscope charts have shown me that you and Stuart were both incarnated this time to learn how to be parents, and what a brilliant lesson Samuel is giving you in that!"

"He's been through enough. I don't want him to keep going through this pain. He's just a baby."

"Actually, he's not just a baby – he's an old soul. You all chose this before you came to earth this time. This is for the spiritual growth of all of you. If he wasn't ill, you wouldn't have had the opportunity to be such a dedicated mother. This is meant to be, and wherever this illness takes him is right. It's your job to give him all the comfort and reassurance he needs."

She hugged me tighter.

"You're doing a brilliant job at looking after him, and your strong characters mean you will always make sure he's given the best treatment by the medical staff."

I tried to smile. I kissed the top of Samuel's warm head.

"Okay, so he needs these platelets," Linda continued, "but isn't it wonderful that the medical knowledge exists to give him them and that we have an NHS to provide them free of charge? Go to Addenbrooke's tomorrow with an open mind, but if it has come back then you're in the best place. Remember, wherever this journey takes him, it's meant to be. I sense angels and higher spirits with him. He's being looked after."

We talked some more until Samuel opened his eyes. The child who woke up was different from the one who'd fallen asleep. He was bright, alert and perky. His eyes were full of love and he had a smile on his face. Linda played with him and tickled his feet.

"Is this your sock?" she asked him.

Samuel looked up at me and smiled. I cuddled and kissed him.

"It is, isn't it, poppet?"

Linda pulled the sock off his foot and held it in front of her.

"Pooh!" she said, pretending to smell it.

Samuel leaned forward and gave a little sniff. Linda and I fell about laughing and Samuel, suddenly embarrassed, cuddled into me and hid his face like a little Orville the Duck.

"It's okay, darling," I said, wrapping my arms around him.

I couldn't believe how well he suddenly seemed. Despite my earlier convictions, I suddenly felt hopeful that perhaps the leukaemia hadn't returned. I didn't associate this change in him with the reiki healing, as I so desperately wanted to believe that he hadn't relapsed. At that moment I heard the key turn in the lock and Stuart walked in.

"Hello. You must be Linda," he said with a smile. I could tell from his expression he wasn't as worried as I was about Samuel's chances the next day. Either that or, like me, he hid his feelings well.

"That's right," she said, "and I know all about you."

Stuart laughed.

"That sounds rather worrying!"

"Linda's done our astrological charts," I said, "and it's uncanny how close they come to us."

"Really? Like what?" Stuart asked.

"How interesting," Linda said. "Your aura is firing off bright yellow. You're very interested in this conversation and your mind is thinking of numerous questions all at once."

Stuart smiled at me.

"Actually, can you just say hello to your son and make a fuss of him? He's sitting here thinking you've not acknowledged him. He should be the first person you go to. He shouldn't be ignored just because he's a baby. In fact, I'm picking up that he was in a position of authority over you in a previous life." Stuart laughed. "I'm serious. He could have been your boss. You need to show him some respect."

Stuart went over to Samuel and gave him a kiss.

"Hello, little man. Actually, I do usually go straight over to him, but I was sidetracked with you here." As much as I could tell he was enjoying the conversation, I thought we should be getting to the hospital; I told him about the telephone call from the hospital. He looked worried. "That sounds rather concerning," he said.

Linda repeated her calming words, but I could tell Stuart was anxious and he just wanted to get Samuel to the hospital. We said our goodbyes and promised Linda we would call her whatever the outcome. She told us she would happily come to Addenbrooke's to give Samuel more healing, if needed.

There seemed to be some confusion at the West Suffolk Hospital. They were under the impression we were going to stay the night so Samuel could be hydrated with a saline drip after his overnight milk feed was switched off at 4 a.m. Normally the milk feed runs all night, but as he was due to be anaesthetised in the morning it would need to be turned off early, and they felt it was too long for a baby to go without fluids of any kind. I actually thought it sounded like a good idea, and wondered why it had never been done all the times he'd had procedures at Addenbrooke's Hospital. But that night I wasn't prepared for it. I hadn't packed for an overnight stay and I wanted Samuel in his own home in case it was his last opportunity for a while. Samuel had his platelets and then Lucy, the doctor, came to talk to us.

"I don't mind you going home," she said. "I think you're practised enough at looking after him. Will you give him water once you've turned off his overnight feed?"

"Yes, I'll set the alarm for four and turn off his feed, then get up at six to give him water."

She nodded and sat on the bed opposite us.

"I'm afraid there's something you've not been told," she said gently.

I felt panic rise within me.

"When the haematologist looked at Samuel's blood sample, they found something they didn't like."

"We know there's a possibility that he's relapsed," Stuart said.

"Oh, you do? I didn't know." I felt split in two: part of me knew without doubt that it had come back, but after hearing Linda's reassuring words, I was also managing to stay optimistic.

"I think you both cope brilliantly," Lucy said.

"Thank you."

"I really admire you. It's a lot for you all to go through."

She wasn't tearful, but I could see she was upset. I was struck by her compassion. At Addenbrooke's we'd become used to an attitude of quiet stoicism, and seemed to have unconsciously copied this model of conduct ourselves.

I couldn't help thinking, *Even the doctor thinks this is bad.*

As we left the hospital, Stuart pointed out the moon to Samuel, bright in the night sky. He looked up and appeared to take it in. A month later he found the moon again by himself, even though that time the sky was still light.

"Ah!" he said, pointing to the pale, round glow in the sky.

What an amazing little boy he was, remembering the moon all that time later – and when he was so ill!

The next morning, Tuesday 3rd February, we drove to Addenbrooke's. It was still early and snow, as yet untouched by traffic, covered the ground. I didn't even change Samuel out of his Babygro; just pulled his snowsuit on over the top, hoping he would get more sleep in the car. Stuart and I maintained a level of calm that seemed impossible under the circumstances. When we arrived at the hospital Boo was the first to greet us, taking us into one of the consulting rooms in the day unit.

"We'll get Samuel's lumbar puncture done straight away," she said, "so you can have the results."

"We're being optimistic," Stuart said.

"I know you don't want to believe he's relapsed, but his white blood cell count is very high, which would suggest it *has* come back."

"We don't want to hear that, Boo," Stuart said with a smile. "Let's just be positive and see what happens."

Stuart and I had convinced ourselves that if we thought positively enough we could will the leukaemia not to have come back. We couldn't have been more positive. We were so positive we were deluded. We saw Sarah and Nick with Oscar but played down our reason for being there, just so we didn't release negative vibrations into the air. It sounds like madness now, but I'm still glad we behaved in this way because, at the very least, it stopped us from panicking Samuel. Had we been uptight we would have shown our anxiety, which he would no doubt have picked up on.

We took Samuel into theatre and held him tight whilst they injected anaesthetic into his Hickman line. "You're going to be all right, aren't you, little man? You're a rufty-tufty!" Stuart said.

Samuel fell asleep quickly and we left the doctors and nurses to their jobs. We waited just outside the door. "Keep thinking positively," Stuart said. "Imagine the cells as healthy."

I tried hard to focus on positive images and even imagined Mike giving us good news. But an hour or so later, when Samuel had woken up, Mike called us through to his consulting room. If it had been good news he would have told us there and then. He would have had a smile on his face. And he wouldn't have had a lady in the room with him whom he introduced as a CLIC Sargent volunteer.

But all these things I doggedly ignored as I followed Mike to his room and took a seat.

"I'm sorry," Mike began, "I know you were hoping to hear good news, but the leukaemia *has* come back."

For a few moments we tried to fight against it.

"But, but… There must be a mistake. Could it not just be…? What about…?"

But slowly we began to accept what our hearts had known all along. There was no mistake. I cuddled Samuel even tighter, as if protecting him from a predator – *If I love him enough, he won't die.*

"What now?" we managed eventually. "Stronger chemotherapy?"

"Yes. We have another chemotherapy we can try called FLAG." Mike paused. "This chemotherapy is more aggressive than what he's had before."

He spoke slowly, with that sad look in his eyes. I knew this was something I was supposed to take in. What Samuel went through before had been bad, but this was going to be even worse.

"It's very likely Samuel will become very ill with infections."

I nodded. We'd been through that before.

"The chemotherapy may even affect his organs. He'll have to have regular heart scans."

Were we being given a choice? In my mind, there was no choice. But did some parents say no at this point?

"Fine," I said. "Well, he has to have it, doesn't he?" Mike gave me one of his sad smiles.

"So, he has two lots of chemotherapy and then when he's in re-mission he has a bone marrow transplant?" I asked.

Mike spoke gently: "That's *if* he goes into remission."

I was shocked.

"Don't…" was all I could say.

"It will be harder this time. The leukaemia cells that have survived are very strong. It will be more difficult to get him into remission this time."

Stuart and I held hands. I could feel my heart beating in every part of my body.

"But you'll do it?" Stuart said with a trembling voice.

"We will try, but you need to be aware of the risks."

We nodded. Samuel could not die. We could not let that happen. We thought we could control it by the strength of our will, but perhaps Linda was right – perhaps some things are predestined. Mike left us to ourselves in the room for a while.

"We have to get him better," Stuart said.

I nodded. *Yes, he has to get better. There is no alternative.*

Stuart telephoned his parents to let them know.

"We're going to stay positive," he told them; silently giving them the instruction they must do the same.

I called my dad. I couldn't bear to give my mum the bad news over the phone when I knew she was by herself.

"Whatever happens," my dad said calmly, and with a wisdom that I'd not heard in him before, "no life is ever a waste."

"Will you tell Mum?" I asked through my tears.

"I'll go to Mum. Don't worry; she won't be on her own."

Eventually we went to the recovery room. Sarah was opposite, sitting by an empty bed.

"Oscar's gone down to the main theatre," she said as she wandered over. "Nick's with him." She smiled at Samuel. "How did it go?" I shook my head. "What?" she asked with concern.

"It's come back," I told her.

She hesitated.

"What have they said? More chemotherapy?"

"Yes, and a bone marrow transplant."

"He'll get there!"

She had such optimism in her voice that I almost believed her.

"I hope so."

"He will! It's a rocky road we're all on but we're going to get there; he'll get through it."

I think there was a part of us, and in all those parents on the ward, that didn't think it would be our child who died. It was just too unlikely. Which children die? From our limited experience, it was either starving children in Africa or those born seriously handicapped. It couldn't happen to *our* child. It couldn't happen to *us*.

Sarah put her arm around me and said, "He's crying."

I looked in surprise at Samuel. He had a tear running down his face.

"Oh, poppet!" I said, and he turned his head away from me, as if he didn't want me to see his tears. He was eighteen months old. It hadn't occurred to me that he would understand what I was saying or, more shockingly, that he'd learnt to hide his feelings.

A nurse eventually came to get us.

"We have a room ready for you now," she said.

Stuart had gone to the car to get our overnight bag, which I'd packed just in case, so it was just me and Samuel that followed her round. She took us through the double doors onto ward C2 and B Bay, the single room with a window overlooking a brick wall.

Back again, I thought as I sat down. "Do you want to watch TV, poppet?" I asked with my fake, happy voice.

Samuel just stared straight ahead as I put the TV on and pretended that this life we were living was bearable.

CHAPTER 16
And So It Begins Again

THERE WAS NOTHING FOR IT but to carry on. The chemotherapy was started as soon as the consent form had been signed.

On the form was a question: "What is the aim of treatment?" There are two options underneath: "cure" or "palliative". I kept looking at those boxes, checking that "cure" had been ticked, but the word "palliative" wouldn't leave my mind. It was like an un-resolved argument, determined to be examined, but the word was so frightening that I kept pushing it away, only for it to come back with more force. Was I bringing it into existence by thinking about it? Nothing made sense to me any more. I wanted to know why this was happening to Samuel, but the medical response was *it's just one of those things*.

"Is it hereditary?" I would ask, because my mother had had leukaemia.

"No, leukaemia isn't hereditary," came the reply.

"Is it the electricity pylons at the back of our house?"

"Not disproved, but unlikely."

"Was it something I did in pregnancy? Is it because I'm a vegetar-ian? What about when I lost my tempter once when I was carrying him?"

"No, no, and no."

"But why Samuel?"

"Why not?"

With no answers forthcoming from the medical front, we turned to Linda for an explanation.

"The planetary activity when Samuel was born suggests he would have difficulties with health, which could be life-threatening," she said when Stuart phoned her to tell her Samuel had relapsed. "But this doesn't mean he will die," she continued. "You need to think positively. The atmosphere in hospital is actually very difficult for healing. It will help Samuel if you both stay optimistic. Focus on a future with Samuel in it as a healthy little boy."

It helped. We are naturally optimistic people and staying worried and upset was not a state that suited us. Samuel was being given a chance. The consent form said "cure" and we had to think he would be cured; otherwise what were we putting him through all this for?

"Pink is the colour of healing," Linda told us, "and yellow will give him determination."

We tied pink and yellow helium balloons to his cot and tried to make the room look less clinical and more homely. But Samuel struggled to sleep in hospital. After a few nights, as I sat on the edge of the bed attempting to comfort him by cuddling and rocking him, Kelly, the nurse, suggested he might be in pain. I don't know why I hadn't thought of it, but as he was already on two different painkillers I think I just assumed they would be doing their job. But as Kelly watched Samuel squirm and whimper in my arms, she volunteered Oramorph.

"It's a form of morphine," she said, "but he won't get addicted to it. I just think he's suffering and it would help him."

Morphine. He'd never been offered that before. It sounded like something that was given to a terminally ill patient, not one who was getting better. However, if Samuel's unsettled behaviour was due to pain, then I knew he had to have it. And he *would* get better – the form said "cure".

Kelly checked with the doctor on call and then came back with a small syringe of Oramorph. She put it directly into his stomach via his NG tube, and ten minutes later he was asleep. I thought of all the sleepless nights we'd had. Were they due to pain? I felt so awful thinking his discomfort could have been brought to an end so quickly and effectively, and yet I'd not thought to ask for stronger painkillers. I had been the mother of a seriously ill child for six months now, but it seemed I was still learning. Oramorph was added to his list of drugs from then on.

One evening, a couple of days into the new treatment, Mike came to speak with us.

"We'd like Samuel to have a new Hickman line," he said.

That meant another big operation, so we weren't keen.

"Why?" Stuart asked.

"At the moment, he has a single-lumen Hickman line. We can work with this whilst he's just having chemotherapy and the blood and platelet transfusions, but if he should need TPN, like last time, it will compromise how much we can give him."

"Perhaps he won't need TPN," I said. "He hasn't needed it since his first session of chemotherapy."

"He's been lucky, but now the leukaemia has returned, he might need this extra level of care. I really think it would be wise."

We talked some more about the pros and cons of a new Hickman line until we heard a knock on the door. Sophie, one of the nurses, put her head round.

"Your reiki lady just called to say she's running late. She'll be here in an hour."

"It's not that we don't trust you or anything!" Stuart said to Mike. Mike shrugged and smiled.

"No problem; whatever helps."

We heard the theme tune to *In the Night Garden*. Samuel was sitting on my lap, facing his favourite programme. He turned to Mike and waved, then looked back at the television.

"Oh, I get it," Mike said. "I'm being told to leave." Samuel frowned and concentrated on the television. We all laughed. Samuel gave Mike another wave. This time it was very obviously a dismissal! "Okay, I'm going," Mike said. "I'll talk to you some more tomorrow."

It was lovely that the doctors and nurses did as Samuel wanted at times. In a world where he had very little control, it must have strengthened his self-belief when people took notice of his feelings. Watching *In the Night Garden* was usually a cosy time when he cuddled with his mummy and daddy before bed, and he didn't want it spoilt! We watched his programme for half an hour; Samuel was able to do something *he* wanted for a change.

Mike spoke to us again the next morning about the Hickman line. It was obviously something they were very keen to do, so it felt as if we had little choice. Eventually it was agreed that the operation would be performed the following Tuesday, by the consultant who'd put Samuel's original Hickman line in. Coincidentally, his name was Mr Samuel. He was considered the best surgeon at performing such delicate operations on small children, so we were glad he'd been chosen, but we still weren't keen on the idea.

Debbie visited us on the Sunday before the operation. Samuel had already been through a lot that day. Before she arrived, he'd been to the X-ray department to have a chest X-ray (which always frightened him) and he'd had another NG tube put down. Because of this, we wondered if he would feel much like company. However, his aunty proved to be a distraction, and he enjoyed playing with the new toys she'd bought him. She stayed with us for a couple of hours and then, when it was time for her to leave, she gave Samuel a kiss and waved bye-bye to him.

Samuel sat on my lap and watched her walk out the door, followed by his daddy. I could see he was thinking about something, as he continued looking at the door for a few seconds after they'd walked out. He suddenly grabbed my hands and launched himself off my lap. I couldn't believe it; he'd not done that in about two weeks, since he'd started to feel ill again. He marched with determination to the door and out of the room. He walked, without stopping, the entire length of the corridor, more quickly than I had ever known him to walk.

"Wait for me!" I called out on his behalf as we got nearer to his aunty and daddy.

They both turned round in surprise and made a huge fuss, congratulating him for his efforts.

The next morning, Debbie sent us the following text: "Sam is such an amazing child. I couldn't get over the look of determination on his face as he powered up the corridor yesterday. Coming to say goodbye to me was the most touching thing I have ever witnessed. What an inspiration!"

We couldn't agree more. He always was, and he always will be, our inspiration.

On Tuesday we were told Samuel was down on the list to have the operation at about eleven o'clock. This is late enough in the morning to keep a seriously ill eighteen-month-old entertained when all they really want is some milk, but as eleven and then twelve o'clock came and went, our agitation rose in line with Samuel's.

Stuart carried him up and down the ward in an effort to distract him, but it didn't work. He cried almost constantly for his milk. Every time we went back into our room, he pointed to the table where I usually kept it, even though I'd put his bottles and box of formula in a cupboard out of sight the night before. We put the television on, but even this didn't distract him. We tried taking him to the playroom to see the other children, but he was hungry and obviously this was all that occupied his mind. It got to one o'clock and I started to get angry. Samuel was a young child with leukaemia. It just wasn't right that he was being made to wait for so long. I went to the nurse station.

"Can you find out how much longer we'll have to wait?" I asked, barely concealing my frustration. The answer came back that they still had a couple of patients left to do before him. "This is ridiculous!" I said. "He's not had anything to eat for nine hours! He's eighteen months old. I'd like you to ask if he can be seen sooner."

We were told it wasn't possible to swap the list around, so we waited and waited whilst Samuel cried until he could cry no more. Eventually, he became lethargic in my arms. It was almost four o'clock. He'd not had anything to eat or drink for twelve hours. This was a child who usually had an overnight feed to keep his calorie intake up, in addition to as much food as we could get into him during the day. By now I was furious. Linda was right: this part of my nature was usually hidden, but when it came to Samuel's welfare I didn't care what anyone thought of me. I went to the nurse station again.

"If Samuel isn't taken to theatre now, I'll give him a bottle and he won't have the operation."

"They're just coming for him," I was assured.

Mick came over.

"Are you all right?" he asked.

"No, I'm angry."

"I know; I can see. I did say to the ward clerk a couple of hours ago that it wasn't fair to keep you waiting. But you're not the first. I've seen other parents walk out with their children in this situation. Although, of course, they have to come back."

I knew he was being kind, trying to distract me, but I was so agitated that all I could think about was Samuel. Luckily, at that moment the porters arrived to take him down.

"They're here!" I called out.

Stuart rushed from our room, carrying Samuel, who now had his head resting on his daddy's shoulder. He looked white and drained of energy. My heart raced with the combination of fear and anger. We followed the porters to theatre, where we were greeted by an Australian anaesthetist.

"This is not good enough," I said as soon as we walked in. "Samuel's been waiting five hours for this operation."

The anaesthetist smirked. "That's the way it goes sometimes."

"That's not an explanation!" I replied.

"Well, we'd thought he was a day patient who hadn't arrived. Nobody realised he was an inpatient."

"So there was a mistake, then?"

He shrugged.

"That's not good enough!"

"You can put in a complaint if you like, but I don't think it will do you any good."

He turned away from me.

"That's very arrogant!"

He turned back, surprised. I glared at him.

"I'm not at all happy about this. Samuel is eighteen months old, he has leukaemia, he's been left without food for twelve hours and that's all the explanation you can give us!"

The anaesthetist looked sheepish.

"I'm sorry," he muttered.

"Right. Well, I suggest you now get on with the operation and do the very best you can for him."

He nodded.

"Yes, right."

Samuel was lying in his cot. I wondered if we were upsetting him, but he just lay still and looked at us. I should have waited to say my piece. We kissed him while the anaesthetic was given, and then he went to sleep. We were given a bleeper to carry with us so they could contact us as soon as the operation was complete. Then we were left on our own.

"Come on," Stuart said. "Let's get some fresh air." As we walked around the grounds, he remarked, "Well done, by the way. I think it's wonderful the way you stick up for Samuel." I gave him one of the sad smiles that I was so used to seeing on the faces of medical staff. He hugged me. "Actually, I was quite scared!" he said, and we both laughed.

As we walked, we talked about Samuel's illness and the situation we were now in. We both agreed we had to stay positive in order to get Samuel through it. We knew we were on a long road and that even when we'd got him into remission he would still have a bone marrow transplant to contend with. All we could do was stay focused on his recovery, but fear permeated every cell in my body.

We had been given books from Leukaemia Research with information on what happens when a patient relapses, and about bone marrow transplants. We'd started to look at them, but they made for grim reading, so I'd put them away. I didn't want any negative information to infiltrate my mind.

We'd also been deliberately scant with information when it came to telling our families and friends. I suspect they now think we were protecting them, but as much as anything, we were protecting ourselves. We needed to focus on Samuel getting better and we just couldn't bear to think, or talk, about the alternative.

Some of our family knew how bad the situation was but chose to respect our wishes. Stuart's brother and sister-in-law had looked Samuel's condition up on the Internet and had found out just how serious it was. This was something we'd stopped ourselves from doing, deciding instead to trust the consultants. We have since looked for more information, and learned that not only is acute myeloid leukaemia M7 extremely rare, we couldn't actually find anyone who'd survived it. However, there must have been survivors, otherwise there wouldn't have been a treatment plan for Samuel to follow.

My sister had a practical and realistic viewpoint, as she'd watched her husband's nan die from cancer and knew how quickly it could take over. When a friend had said to her, "He'll get over it," she'd replied, "Well, it'll go one way or the other; it's a life-threatening illness."

However, Stuart's parents and mine believed without doubt that Samuel would get better. At times this helped us to stay optimistic, but at others it made life difficult, as they didn't realise how worried we were. I think the fact that my mother had survived acute myeloid leukaemia made her assume that Samuel would, too. But the truth is that AML is a far worse diagnosis for a child than an adult.

After our walk, we went back to the ward so I could make up a fresh bottle of milk for Samuel. Just after I'd done this, the bleeper went off to tell us he was out of theatre. He was already awake when we rushed back in. He was sitting up in his cot and one of the recovery nurses was trying to give him a bottle, but he kept batting it away as it wasn't like the one he was used to. As soon as he saw us, he held out his arms and gave a little cry. I picked him up very carefully, conscious that he would feel sore as he'd just had a big operation. I sat him on my lap and gave him his bottle.

"There you go, poppet. That's better, isn't it?"

He watched me as he drank from his bottle. He must have needed that food so badly. I thought he would be content after he'd had his milk, but he was unsettled and whimpering.

"Is he in pain?" I asked the recovery nurse.

"He shouldn't feel too bad," she said. "He's had painkillers, but we could give him some more if you feel he needs them."

I deliberated. I didn't want to give him too many painkillers if he didn't need them. Then I saw a television set in the corner.

"Could we put the telly on?" I asked. 'He won't need the painkillers if it distracts him."

The nurse wheeled it over and put a in a *Balamory* DVD. As soon as it came on, Samuel went quiet. He could barely take his eyes off the screen.

"I think he's all right," I said with a smile.

He was given a certificate for his bravery, signed by the recovery nurses, and then Mr Samuel came out of theatre to see us. He was very polite and went to great lengths to explain how well the surgery had gone. The cynical part of me wondered if this was because he was aware how angry I'd been at the delay, but then I remembered he'd also come out to speak to us after the first Hickman line had been put in, so I gave him the benefit of the doubt.

We carried Samuel back to the ward and were amazed to see how well he seemed, considering he'd just had five days of chemotherapy followed by an operation. We tried to take him back to his room, thinking he would need a rest, but he shook his head. Stuart carried him around the ward instead. We'd got as far as the playroom when Samuel pointed to the double doors that lead out of C2.

"Do you want to go out, little man?" Stuart asked.

Samuel smiled, so he carried him out of the ward and around the concourse. As we were walking around, going in and out of shops and showing Samuel things, he saw one of the doctors from C2 and gave her a little wave before she'd even seen him. How lovely, I thought, that he should be so confident and happy after everything he's been through. It was another proud moment.

Linda continued to visit two or three times a week, even though for several days running she had to battle with the snow. I think both Stuart and I found it really useful to talk to someone about Samuel and his illness who didn't just give the standard medical responses, which always sounded so negative. Instead, she encouraged us to be positive and grateful that Samuel was being given treatment which could save his life. She gave us a different view on the situation we were in: instead of feeling life was being unfair to us, we saw it as a chance to learn and grow in both a practical and spiritual sense.

After Linda's first visit to Addenbrooke's, Stuart walked her back to the multistorey car park where she'd parked and where Stuart also parked every night after work.

"Which floor are you on?" Stuart asked as they entered the lift.

"Third," Linda replied.

"Same as me," Stuart said.

They got out of the lift and walked to Linda's car. Stuart couldn't believe it when they discovered she was parked next to him. Linda had no idea what car we had, so was it pure coincidence that she had parked right next to Stuart in an eight-storey car park?

"It's because you're psychic," Stuart said with a laugh.

"That's right," Linda replied.

After a while, Linda began bringing a young man named Damien with her. He was training with her to become a reiki healing practitioner.

Stuart would talk to them in the parents' room about all sorts of interesting things whilst I tried to get Samuel off to sleep. Then Linda and Damien would come through and give Samuel healing whilst he slept in his cot. I wondered if it was having an effect on him, but it was hard to tell how he would have been without it. He certainly seemed to be coping with the strong chemotherapy better than expected. Every chest X-ray showed his heart still completely without problems and he never needed to go on TPN, even though he now had the double-lumen Hickman line.

"Reiki alone won't cure cancer," Linda told us, "but it'll help him cope with it and the harsh treatment."

So that was how we viewed it: not as a cure, but as an additional treatment. In my less rational moments part of me pinned all my hopes on it, whilst at other times I doubted whether it was doing anything at all. That's the human mind, I suppose, and it's normal to want proof. However, on a couple of occasions Linda laid her hands on me, and I definitely felt a heat coming from them, so who knows? Nothing surprises me any more.

Oramorph continued to help Samuel sleep better, but I never expected him to start having lie-ins. This seemed to be something that happened only when Stuart did the night shift. With me, he always woke at about seven, which coincided with when the nurses checked his blood pressure. He would then hold out his arms and I would pick him up and put him in bed with me to have his milk. Sometimes he would fall asleep again and, as he was in my pull-down bed, I would lie squeezed up against the cold wall, whilst Samuel did an impression of a starfish. I would then watch him, pleased he was getting the sleep he needed so badly, but feeling utterly exhausted myself. Sometimes I would try to wiggle down the bed so I could lie flat, but I had to be careful, as the slightest movement would wake Samuel, and then I'd be back to caring for him with no chance for a rest.

One morning, after staying the night at Acorn House, I rushed over to the ward, worrying I'd left Stuart alone too long and thinking he would be desperate for a cup of tea and breakfast. I'd got up late myself and then had a shower and put some washing on, so by the time I walked past the nurse station it was gone ten o'clock.

"They're still asleep," Sophie said.

"Really? It's gone ten!"

The ward round was usually about this time, so I was surprised Stuart wasn't up and ready.

"I know." She laughed. "You won't believe what Samuel did this morning."

"What did he do?"

"I went in to take his blood pressure, as usual." I nodded. "I switched on the machine, but as it bleeped Samuel opened one eye and shook his head."

I laughed and said, "That told you!"

"I know, but the funniest thing is I whispered, 'Sorry, Samuel,' then backed out of the room. It wasn't until I'd got outside that I thought, *I've just been told what to do by a baby!*"

We both laughed.

"He's always had a commanding presence," I said.

Sophie agreed. "I've never met a baby with such a strong personality."

We had to wake them up in the end; Sophie really had to get a blood pressure reading and the doctors were due any time. I gave Stuart a cup of tea and Samuel a fresh bottle of milk, then watched them yawn and stretch as they woke up. In the middle of the floor was a great big cardboard box.

"What's that?" Stuart asked, still bleary-eyed.

"It was delivered this morning for Samuel," Sophie said. "Me and one of the other nurses brought it in just over an hour ago, but neither of you woke up."

Even Stuart was amazed they'd both managed to sleep for so long, but secretly I was glad. Sleep had been in short supply for all of us for many months now. It's incredibly difficult to continue on so little sleep for such a prolonged length of time. It impairs your decision-making, it makes you more emotional, and it impedes your ability to do the simplest things, let alone look after a seriously ill child. And, as always, I knew it had to be worse for Samuel.

Stuart got Samuel up and sat him on his lap whilst I opened the box. A beautiful helium balloon of a pink-and-yellow flower with a blue butterfly floated out of it.

"It's from Lizzie," I said, reading the card.

Samuel smiled and watched it float up towards the ceiling.

"How lovely! Hey, little man, look what Lizzie got for you," Stuart said, squeezing Samuel's tummy and making him giggle.

It was such a thoughtful present. At a time when Samuel wasn't really capable of playing, he enjoyed looking at those balloons. In fact we were very lucky, as we were frequently sent parcels from family and friends. Lizzie, in particular, was very thoughtful, often including books and magazines for me.

I don't know how we would have got through our days in hospital if it weren't for our family and friends; Angela, Anita, Lizzie and Nikki saved my sanity on many occasions.

After a week of being back in hospital, I could see a definite improvement in Samuel. He was walking about again and playing in the playroom. He no longer appeared to be suffering, and his eyes were alert instead of shadowed by pain. I began to feel hopeful about the future, telling myself this was just a year out of our lives and then we would be a normal family again. But these things change you, of course, and we would have always worried about Samuel's health. In reality, I think it would have taken us a very long time to get over it, even if Samuel had lived, and I wonder how a year in hospital at such a young age would have altered Samuel's personality.

Periodically I saw one of the CLIC Sargent volunteers, who had also studied child psychiatry, and asked her if she thought the time in hospital was having an adverse effect. She always assured me it wasn't, saying if Samuel had become withdrawn then she would have worried, but as he was attentive and interactive she could see no problem.

On another occasion, two young doctors gave Samuel tasks to do to determine his age. They correctly placed him at around eighteen months, but said they thought his speech had slowed down. This was a shame, as he had initially been advanced with his speech, but I think the treatment wore him out so he conserved his energy.

One of the tasks they got him to do was point to parts of his body. It was so sweet when they asked him where his tummy was and he lifted up his T-shirt to show them. They then confused matters by asking him to point to mummy's mouth and daddy's nose. Stuart and I had never asked him to do this and we wondered how he would get on with it. However, he seemed to love the game and, after that, regularly pointed to parts of our bodies so we could identify them for him.

At around this time, I told Mike the leukaemia had gone.

"Your mother's instinct again," he said.

"Yes. It's just instinct, but I really think it has."

"I believe you," he said. "He's definitely improved, but we have to see what happens when his counts come back up."

"In case leukaemia cells grow back instead of healthy cells."

"That's right."

"Well, how can we stop them?" I asked.

Mike shook his head. "We just have to hope the chemotherapy has done its job."

"Could we start the second round of chemotherapy now, before the cells grow back?"

"No, that wouldn't work."

"What about if he goes straight for the bone marrow transplant?"

"That's been tried before, but the leukaemia always comes back after the transplant if the patient isn't properly in remission in the first place."

"So we just have to wait and hope that it's only healthy cells that grow back?"

Mike nodded. "Yes, I'm afraid that's all we can do."

The hospital pressed on with finding a bone marrow match and at least here we had good news: ten potential matches were found world-wide, with the closest donor living in Germany. Stuart and I also gave blood samples to see how we matched. However, we could only ever be a 50 per cent match as it was the combination of both of our genes that made Samuel's bone marrow. But, in a worst-case scenario, one of us would be used.

On Saturday 14th February, Graham and Wendy visited. We all went for a walk, taking Samuel in his pushchair. I noticed he was quieter than usual. However, he'd had a temperature that morning so I wasn't too worried; it seemed likely he had an infection. When we returned, he still had a temperature so was started on antibiotics both orally and intravenously. However, his temperature remained above thirty-eight degrees. He was monitored every four hours, but it still didn't come down. A fan was put in his room to cool him. Eventually, it was decided they needed to find out where the infection was so they could administer antibiotics specific to the illness.

The infection dominated our thoughts for most of the week. A serious infection could kill him, so it was essential the cause be found and the infection cleared up. For a while, it was speculated whether the new Hickman line could be to blame, and Stuart and I were annoyed that Samuel had gone through a big operation only for it to add another risk to his life. There was even talk of having the line removed but then, suddenly, the infection went. The antibiotics had finally taken hold and Samuel's temperature went back down to normal.

We were hugely relieved that this additional threat to his life had disappeared. With the infection gone, we looked forward to hearing that Samuel's counts were rising, indicating that the leukaemia was back in remission, and that this threat to his life had also disappeared. However, every time his blood results came back the neutrophil count was missing. We asked Boo why this was.

"Sometimes, if they run out of time in the lab, they just process the bloods by machine. The neutrophils have to be counted individually, so perhaps they're really busy at the moment," she said.

I thought it was strange that in the five months since Samuel had been diagnosed this had never happened before, but as she didn't give me any reason to worry, I accepted it. However, by the Saturday, after three days of not hearing his neutrophils results, I was starting to get annoyed. I felt as if we were on edge until we knew they'd started to rise. So, as I walked past the nurse station on Saturday evening whilst Samuel slept and Stuart had a shower back at Acorn House, I stopped and asked if Samuel's blood results were in. Stewart, the nurse, told me his platelet count was normal, as was his haemoglobin level.

"Still no neutrophil count?" I asked.

"No, sorry. I don't know why they've not given that," Stewart said, frowning at the computer screen.

"What about the white cell count? If that's gone up, then the neutrophils should follow."

Stewart continued scanning the computer.

"Twelve," he said, satisfied that he'd been able to give me that reading.

"Twelve? That's too high."

"A bit, but it's not that high."

"It's much higher than it should be. I can't understand why it's gone up that much in just a few days."

Stewart shrugged.

"It could just be something to do with the infection. It does strange things to the body."

I left the conversation there and returned to our room. Samuel was sound asleep in his cot, Woof Woof and BB either side of his head and, as usual, his covers kicked off. I gently placed his blanket over the lower half of his body so he wouldn't get cold, but also not too hot, then sat down on the bed.

Stewart hadn't seemed concerned, but a white cell count of twelve was definitely higher than I'd ever heard Samuel have before, apart from when the leukaemia had returned. Samuel didn't seem ill like last time, so perhaps it was just something to do with the infection. I decided to let it go. Mike hadn't raised any concerns with us so, hopefully, it was nothing to worry about. For some reason, I didn't mention it to Stuart when he came back over for dinner; perhaps because we were talking to the other mums and dads in the parents' room or because I was trying to convince myself there was nothing wrong. However, by the next morning I was worried enough to mention it to the young doctor who did the ward round.

"A white cell count of twelve is too high, isn't it?"

"I'm not sure," he said. "Would you like me to ask Mike about it?"

I hesitated, not wanting to bother Mike on a Sunday, but my need for reassurance overrode my politeness.

"Yes. If you could just call him and check, I would be grateful."

When Stuart came over from Acorn House later that morning, I told him what had happened. He wasn't particularly concerned; I suppose because Samuel didn't seem any different and, perhaps, because the doctors hadn't indicated there was a problem. However, a bit later, when the young doctor returned and told us Mike was coming in to see us, we both began to feel nervous. At the same time as Mike arrived, Stuart's parents and sister turned up to see us. Stuart showed them to the parents' room whilst Mike came to our room to speak to us.

"I've been keeping an eye on Samuel's counts," Mike said, "as I've been slightly concerned these past couple of days."

"Could it be anything to do with him being on GCSF?" Stuart asked.

This was a good point, and one I hadn't considered. Samuel had not been on GCSF since his first session of chemotherapy back in September, but it had been used again this time to bring his counts back up quickly so he could race through the chemotherapy stage and get on with the bone marrow transplant.

"Possibly," Mike said, "but I think it would be wise to do another lumbar puncture to check his bone marrow so we can see exactly what's going on."

Mike decided this should be done the next day so we all knew what we were dealing with and decisions could be made about how to proceed. Although I knew it was worrying, I didn't feel as concerned as I had when Samuel had relapsed three weeks earlier. Mike obviously wanted to check what was going on, but I didn't feel the same sense of doom that had prevailed last time.

When Stuart's parents and sister came into the room after Mike had left, we told them what had happened. They listened but didn't say much. As I wasn't sure if they'd grasped the seriousness of the situation, I pressed the matter home a bit.

"You know if he has relapsed it's very serious," I said.

"Oh," Cynthia said, looking down.

Perhaps she was wondering how serious "serious" was, or perhaps she was just struggling to know what to say.

"It would mean our options are extremely limited," I continued. Although, at that point, even I hadn't grasped just how limited our options were.

Samuel was sitting next to Stuart on our pull-down bed. When his nanny, grandad and aunty had arrived he'd smiled, pleased to see them. But now we suddenly realised he was crying and, just like before, he turned his face away so that we couldn't see his tears.

"I'm sorry, little man," Stuart said, pulling him onto his lap and hugging him. "It will be all right. Don't worry."

We dropped the subject then. It was obvious Stuart's family didn't want to hear more and we had no desire to frighten them or Samuel further, so it just became another wait and see, with Stuart and me practising more positive thinking. Stuart went to work as normal the next day. It seems like madness to us now, that we were so relaxed about it, but perhaps we didn't want to face the truth either. Even so, I asked my mum to come to the hospital, so there must have been a part of me that was anticipating bad news.

The lumbar puncture was done and then, at about three o'clock in the afternoon, the bad news came. Christine, the nurse, was already in the room with us. I liked Christine; she was my age with a child the same age as Samuel, so she showed a great deal of empathy for what we were going through. As with Sophie, I always found I could really talk to Christine about my fears and she didn't just give me the standard medical response, but took time to listen and understand. Mike walked through the door; he looked serious and solemn.

"Would you stay?" he said quietly to Christine.

I saw her hesitate. She looked at Mike and I saw the fear I felt reflected in her face. She took a seat on the bed next to me and my mum sat the other side. I held Samuel tightly and watched Mike pull a chair over and sit down in front of us.

"The lumbar puncture shows the leukaemia's returned," he said.

My mum put her hand to her mouth.

"Oh," she said.

She started to cry. I looked at Mike.

"I'm sorry," he said quietly.

"What can we do?" I asked.

My heart was beating fast; my brain frantically trying to think of answers.

"There's nothing we can do now," he said gently.

Christine started to cry. She and my mum put their arms around me.

"You *must* be able to," I said. Mike shook his head. "There must be something you can do. Mike, please. I can't lose him. Please, *please* do something."

"We've reached the end of the line as far as conventional chemotherapy goes."

"What does that mean? Is there something else you can try? An experimental chemotherapy?"

"Do you really want him to have more chemotherapy?" Mike asked quietly.

"Yes. I can't live without him. I don't want to live without him. Please try and find something, Mike. *Please.*"

"I'll speak to Great Ormond Street and a lady I know who manages all the clinical trials. She's aware of all the latest treatments. But if they know of nothing, then there is nothing."

I nodded. I felt that at least he wasn't giving up.

"I'll come and get you when I know more. I'll try to contact them now."

"Okay."

"Would you like me to ring Stuart and let him know?"

I shook my head. "No, I'll ring him."

"Are you sure?"

"Yes," I said.

I knew it would sound terrible coming from Mike and, as far as I was concerned, we weren't giving up. As Mum and Christine continued to cry, I became more determined this wasn't the end. I couldn't even think of the idea of Samuel dying. To me, at that moment, it wasn't even an option. So I didn't cry. Instead, I cuddled Samuel even closer to me.

"We'll get you better, won't we, poppet? We won't give up!" I said.

CHAPTER 17

Last Chance

~⁓

I WAITED A WHILE BEFORE phoning Stuart to let him know the outcome of Samuel's lumbar puncture, but when I did I stressed that I'd asked Mike to look into alternative treatments. I worried about him driving back to the hospital after hearing such terrible news, so I emphasised that we'd not come to the end of the line. My mum left soon after so Stuart and I could be together, but it must have been equally hard for her to drive away from us all.

Stuart had not been back long when he decided to see Mike to hear for himself our options and to press home the point that we weren't giving up. I decided not to go with him. I'd heard enough bad news for one day and didn't feel I could hear any more and still stay strong and positive, so Stuart went by himself and I tried to turn all my attention to the television and pretend none of this was happening. It seemed like forever before Stuart returned, but eventually I heard him walk up the corridor. My heart raced as I waited to hear what Mike had said.

"They've found a chemotherapy they can use."

"Oh, thank God!" I said, leaping on this news as if it was the answer to all our prayers. "This one will work; it has to."

Stuart sat on the bed beside me.

"It's been used on adults and had some effect, but they've only tried it on three children and none of them survived."

"You mean they didn't go into remission?"

"One of them didn't go into remission. The other two died from multiple organ failure." We both went quiet while I digested this news. "Mike said this could be Samuel's fate as well, and to think about if we really want to do this," Stuart continued. "This chemotherapy is very harsh. He said Samuel could end his days in intensive care with all his organs gradually shutting down. He actually said it could be a horrible death."

I closed my eyes and rested my head on top of Samuel's.

"That's awful."

Stuart nodded. I tried to take this information in, but it didn't seem real – not when Samuel was sitting on my lap, watching television and breathing.

"What choice do we have?"

"They've looked into everything; not just Mike but Great Ormond Street and Glasgow, too. There's nothing else. It's this or we take him home."

Without chemotherapy, Samuel would definitely die. How could I give my beautiful boy a death sentence? This chemotherapy sounded awful, but it was our only chance and I wanted to take it.

"What did you say to him?"

"I said he won't get organ failure; he's a strong little boy."

"Oh, thank you!" I hugged Samuel tightly. "We've got to try, haven't we? What else can we do?"

Stuart put his arms around us both.

"But, Amanda, Mike says if this doesn't work then Samuel only has two or three weeks left."

"Oh, God! It's got to work," I said. "Please let it work!"

"Mike's going to call my boss. He doesn't think I should go back to work until we know the chemotherapy's worked. I've told him he can be honest and say what Samuel's chances are."

"Well, I'll be very grateful to have you here."

"I want to be here. I don't want to miss anything."

I was relieved. We hadn't come to the end of the line. There was another option, another chance. I prayed it would work.

We needed to get away from the ward. I wanted privacy. I didn't want to be near the doctors, nurses and other parents who weren't in our position. I felt alienated from the people who'd supported us and whom we'd supported in return. Their children were still following a recognised treatment plan; they still had a strong chance of success. Our options had dwindled to experimental chemotherapy, which could cause multiple organ failure, or take our son home to die. Suddenly, I didn't feel I had anything in common with even the other parents. The situation we now found ourselves in was extreme, even by the standards of a children's cancer ward.

"What shall we tell our families?" Stuart asked as we walked across the hospital grounds to Acorn House.

"We tell them the chemotherapy hasn't worked so we are now trying an experimental type."

"Shall we tell them what Mike said about Samuel's chances and how long he's got if it doesn't work?"

"No. The doctors don't know everything and they don't know that this won't work. Have they ever tried it with Samuel's particular type of leukaemia before?"

"No. The other children all had ALL."

"So maybe this chemotherapy will be the one that works for AML M7. They don't know and I don't want anyone thinking negative thoughts. We'll continue like we did before: we'll stay positive. And we'll ask Linda to come and do more reiki to help Samuel cope with this strong treatment."

"Okay," Stuart said, "I agree. I don't want to have that phone call with my parents, anyway. They're too old to keep going through all this."

At Acorn House we took video footage of Samuel. In the backs of our minds, although neither of us acknowledged it, I think we were both aware we might not have many more chances. At that moment Samuel seemed relatively healthy and normal. However, when we watch the film back now, it feels so sad. Stuart and I are falsely up-beat and Samuel is hardly capable of interacting with us. He does the odd thing like holding up his Woof Woof, and Stuart and I pounce on these moments as proof that he's going to be okay. But it's obvious he's far from well.

We were both desperately worried. We could keep each other going with positive statements but, inside, the fear we felt was immense. However, we kept our feelings hidden for Samuel's sake. More than ever we felt the responsibility of parenthood and that we had to do all we could to protect and look after our precious son.

Samuel stayed at Acorn House with us that night. We'd never done this before, but I felt strongly that we needed time away from the ward and, as he wasn't attached to the pump for any drugs or transfusions, I thought it would be a good opportunity. Unfortunately, none of us slept well. Samuel was sick several times in the night; a result of the leukaemia taking over his body. It just convinced me more than ever that he needed chemotherapy. The drugs had a terrible effect on his body, but by the looks of things, the leukaemia would be worse. However, I needed everyone to be on our side. I knew Mike would respect whatever decision we made, but I wanted more than that: I wanted him to be hopeful.

So that night, whilst Stuart and Samuel slept, I went to the window and, by the light of the streetlight, wrote to Mike. I told him we needed to treat this course of chemotherapy as an experiment and to think how wonderful it would be if this new drug turned out to be the one that cured AML M7. I asked him to go into this treatment with hope and to allow Stuart and me to have hope. I said we wanted Samuel to be away from the ward as much as possible, so he could have some enjoyment in his life, as I felt this would give him a boost. And I said I would know if he was really ill and it hadn't worked, just as I always had before.

The next morning Samuel had to be back in his hospital room for half past seven, as he had to have some intravenous antibiotics put through his Hickman line. Stuart took him, as he knew I'd hardly slept all night, and I had an extra hour in bed. You don't think you're going to be able to sleep when you are that worried, but there comes a point where exhaustion takes over and you give in to it. When I joined them later, I gave my letter to a nurse and asked her to give it to Mike.

The first indication I had that the doctors and nurses were going to listen to my request was when Archana, one of Mike's registrars, came to see us.

The morning had been difficult. Stuart returned to Acorn House for a shower and, left on my own with Samuel, I tried my hardest to present a calm and positive demeanour to him. Despite our terrible situation, I was just about managing it, but everyone who entered the room struggled to stay composed. I remember Claire, the music lady, coming in and asking if Samuel would like to do some music with her, but as she spoke the tears ran down her face. It was the same with everyone. It was as if we were pretending everything was normal but we all knew it wasn't. By the time Archana arrived to check on Samuel, I was struggling to hold back the tears myself.

"He *has* to get better," I said to her. "He just has to." Archana knelt beside me and put her hand on mine. "I love him so much."

And then I could no longer hold back the tears. Samuel turned to face me and made a little whimper. He looked into my eyes then put his little arms around my neck and tried to cuddle me. It was so lovely, as if he was trying to comfort me, but I never wanted him to be in that position.

"We're going to give him this treatment," Archana said slowly, "and we *are* going to have hope."

"Really?"

I hardly dared believe what I was hearing.

"*Hope*," she said. There was a warning in her voice. She wasn't telling me it would work, but that there was hope.

"Thank you!"

Mike came to see us a bit later.

"Before you go out today," he said, "we'd like Samuel to have a portable pump attached to him to give him a continuous supply of morphine."

I was shocked. Despite what we'd already gone through, the terrible end results of leukaemia were becoming known to me more rapidly than I was prepared for. Although every stage of Samuel's illness had been distressing and difficult to cope with, I suddenly felt we were being pushed deeper into the reality of living not just with a seriously sick child, but a dying child.

"When can Samuel start the experimental chemo?" I asked, desperate for him to return to the status of "seriously sick" and not "dying".

"All being well, tomorrow," Mike said.

This wasn't as easy as we had assumed. In fact, Mike had to go to the Patient Care Trust (a board which governs how NHS money is spent) and put our case forward so this new chemotherapy would be funded for us. We felt extremely grateful to Mike for his dedication in treating Samuel.

"I know this is difficult for you, Amanda, but Samuel must have this pump. It will help him cope with his pain, and if he starts to show an improvement he can be weaned off it."

I nodded. I wanted Samuel to be pain-free, so I knew this pump was something we would have to get used to. Soon after, Sophie and another nurse came to our room to attach the pump.

"Do you think we're doing the right thing, trying this new chemotherapy?" I asked her.

I trusted Sophie more than any of the other nurses, and although her opinion wouldn't have changed my mind, I wanted to know what it was.

She rubbed a small patch at the top of Samuel's thigh with an antiseptic wipe and said, "If he was my baby, I would want to know I'd done all I could to save him."

I was relieved. I valued her opinion, which had now taken away the small amount of doubt I had that I was putting Samuel through unnecessary suffering. I smiled.

"That's what I think."

"Things don't always go the way you expect," she said. "I've seen children die who were doing really well, but I've seen other children, who we thought we could do no more for, make a complete recovery. I wouldn't have believed it before I started working on this ward, but sometimes it seems like miracles really do happen."

She carefully pushed the needle into Samuel's thigh and then removed it, leaving a thin plastic tube in its place. She taped it down.

The curled tube was attached to a portable pump measuring about twenty centimetres by ten. The pump was actually a syringe drive that gradually pushed morphine into him.

"He'll feel a bit better soon," she said, "and then you can take him out."

"We're going home for the afternoon. I know it's a bit of a way just for a few hours, but we feel we need to."

Again, our unspoken thoughts were that this might be the last time Samuel saw his home.

"I don't blame you. It's important to think about the quality of his life now."

She didn't add, "not the quantity," but I knew that's what she meant.

Samuel perked up within an hour. We took him to the playroom whilst the last lot of antibiotics went through his main pump. He now had three lines coming out of him: one from his nose, one from his chest, and one from his leg. It was difficult to hold him and not pull on his lines. Changing his nappy was even harder, and Stuart found it particularly stressful as Samuel often had diarrhoea and we had to be careful to keep all the tubes clean. But, as usual, Samuel coped brilliantly with this additional invasion of his body. That's not to say he didn't notice the pump. Several times he looked at it and frowned in annoyance, his lips pursed. But then it was as if he chose to ignore its presence, and would turn to occupy himself with something else. In the playroom he concentrated on putting toy cars down the spiral track of the garage.

"Un, oo, ee!" he said as he let go of each car.

Lizzie had sent Samuel a box of tiny chocolate bunnies for Easter. We had the box with us in the playroom to offer to everyone. Even though Samuel hadn't touched any food other than milk in over twenty-four hours, he reached across us and popped a chocolate in his mouth. Stuart and I laughed. If this was the effect of the morphine pump, then we were all for it!

Eventually, we were allowed to take Samuel home for the day. We strapped him into his car seat and, with relief, drove out of Addenbrooke's Hospital. At one point, Stuart looked in his mirror at Samuel and said, "I hope this isn't the last time." I turned away and screwed up my eyes to stop the tears. Stuart put his hand on my leg. "But it won't be," he said. "We're going to do everything we can."

I wanted to take Samuel to the Abbey Gardens again. We'd spent so many happy days there and I wanted to remind him of better times and feeling well. I thought if I could just do this, it would pick him up and stop him from feeling swamped by the illness. But despite his earlier burst of energy, he was quiet and withdrawn, barely tolerating his trip out. It was becoming terrifyingly obvious that the leukaemia was taking over. We turned back for home sooner than I had intended.

We had dinner and then Samuel fell asleep on me. Whilst he slept, Stuart sent a text to all our friends. He told them the last lot of chemotherapy hadn't worked and that Samuel was just about to begin experimental chemo. He attached the photograph that I'd taken of Samuel on the swing in the Abbey Gardens in January; the one I'd entitled *Normality Returns*. He asked our friends to focus on Samuel then, looking well and happy, and to imagine him in the future, enjoying his life again. We made one concession in revealing Samuel's chances; we told everyone that this chemotherapy was our last chance.

That evening the texts flooded in from our lovely friends, each one telling us Samuel was constantly in their thoughts. Several of them described happy scenarios in the future that they imagined Samuel taking part in, and many said they were praying for us. We were so grateful for their kindness and compassion. We knew they'd all have done anything to change the situation if they could. I hoped their prayers and loving thoughts would do some good, but my mind toggled between the two different views of the world being presented to us then: one purely medical and the other, Linda's magical version. But I just didn't know which one to believe.

Stuart filmed Samuel sleeping on my shoulder. He looked so beautiful. Without his dummy, his rosebud lips looked full and pink. I couldn't imagine him not being here.

"I don't think we should stay out too late," Stuart said, once he'd packed away the video camera. "Samuel has to have more antibiotics tonight and we don't want to keep everyone hanging around."

I agreed, but was reluctant to leave our home for the shut-in feeling of living on the ward. In the end, it was gone nine before we left. As we closed our front door behind us and stepped out into the night, I imagined all Samuel's little friends tucked up safely in their own beds. It seemed so terribly sad that our precious boy was returning to hospital and more chemotherapy. Boo was waiting for us when we arrived back on C2.

"Hi, guys," she whispered. The ward was in darkness and the nurses were working efficiently but quietly. I had the strange feeling that I'd left one of my lives and entered the other. "Ready for some more chemo?"

"Have you got it?" Stuart asked.

"Yes. Mike's been to the PCT and they've agreed funding. We're getting it tomorrow."

We followed her into Samuel's room.

"So, have you had a nice time at home?"

A nurse arrived and hung a bag of antibiotics on Samuel's pump, then attached it to his Hickman line. In contrast to the past few days, I felt very aware of how upbeat Boo and the nurses were. It no longer felt like it was all over. It felt like there was an alternative and we were going to take it.

Linda arrived the next morning to do something called a reiki attunement with us. This was a ceremony and set of instructions to follow that would mean we could perform reiki on Samuel ourselves. We went to the quiet room at Acorn House to do this, and Stuart's parents came over to be with Samuel.

The attunement took a few hours, but I think much of this time was really Linda trying to make us feel positive about what we were doing and Samuel's future. Again, we talked about life plans and how this was all meant to be, and somehow that made it seem better. It helped to think there was a purpose to everyone's existence, no matter what their age, and that it wasn't just a case of good and bad luck.

"What's the matter, Stuart?" Linda asked at one point.

"Oh, nothing," Stuart replied. "Carry on."

"No. There's something on your mind. What's worrying you?"

"That's very perceptive of you. Actually, I was thinking Samuel's new chemotherapy is due to go up at two o'clock and I would like to be there when it does."

"Give them a call," Linda said, "but I think they're running late and we'll be fine for another half an hour."

He went through to the kitchen to use the phone.

When he came back, he said, "They're running late. It's going to be another half an hour."

Linda just laughed as Stuart shook his head in amazement.

I don't know if the reiki attunement actually did anything. I never felt heat coming from my hands, like I did with Linda, but our session with her helped to make me feel better about the decision we'd made.

I think, perhaps, I was too near complete exhaustion to actually make a difference to Samuel in this way. Instead, I decided to concentrate on my role as his mummy and to try to be as much comfort to him as possible. Stuart, however, was extremely dedicated in practising reiki on Samuel, and would stand above him in the middle of the night, holding his hands over him and imagining the leukaemia cells disappearing. He did this even when Samuel was sound asleep and he should have been getting sleep himself. He was just as exhausted as I was, but such was his dedication to Samuel that he carried on when every bone in his body must have been crying out for sleep. I am so very proud of him for his determination, strength of spirit and love of our son.

When we returned to the ward, Samuel was sitting on our fold-down bed feeding chocolate buttons to his nanny and grandad.

"Is he eating them?" I asked Cynthia.

"No, but he's enjoying feeding them to us!"

Two nurses arrived with the innocuous-looking bag of liquid that could save Samuel's life.

Please work, I said to myself, as they hooked the bag to the pump and then attached the end to Samuel's Hickman line.

It seemed such a small thing, yet it could change the course of our future. Without it we would be going downhill fast, until Samuel's end, but with this new bag of chemotherapy came hope, and I felt restored by it.

Linda performed reiki on Samuel as the chemotherapy began to drip through. She also performed reiki on the chemotherapy bag itself, and around Samuel's cot. Then she chanted as she put protections around his room. I looked at Stuart's parents and wanted to laugh. I'd always called Stuart's dad "Captain Mainwaring". He had the same manner about him and I could just imagine what he was thinking about Linda and her reiki. I half expected him to say, "What a lot of nonsense, Amanda!"

Later that evening, Samuel demonstrated something his nanny had been teaching him. He tipped up the packet of chocolate buttons and watched as they all landed on my bed.

He then looked inside the empty packet, shrugged his little shoulders, and in a beautifully clear, singsong voice said, "All gone!"

I looked at him in amazement.

"Samuel, you spoke!"

He smiled and put the buttons back in the packet. I felt like I was with a little genius. It was as if he'd known how to do that all along and yet had just chosen not to. Sometimes it seemed as if I wasn't sitting with a baby but with someone very knowing. Perhaps Linda was right and Samuel had been in this world many times before.

"Well done, poppet!" I said, cuddling him. But he took no notice of my enthusiasm and instead pushed a chocolate button into my mouth.

Samuel's chemotherapy lasted for seven hours each day, but this was broken up into two sessions, which meant we were able to go out in between. Each morning the doctors would visit for the ward round. On the first few days I sensed trepidation at what they might find, but after that I got the impression they had relaxed slightly.

"Samuel, I'm just going to look in your mouth," Mike said, pulling on his dummy.

Samuel frowned at him and clamped his mouth shut round his dummy. Mike kept hold of the other end, and a tug of war began.

"You don't need to do that," Archana said. "You just need to ask him." She knelt in front of Samuel. "May I look in your mouth, please?"

Samuel took out his dummy and opened his mouth, whilst giving Mike a very pointed look.

"Oh, I see. You'll do it for Archana but you won't do it for me!"

"You just didn't ask him properly," Archana said. "Thank you, Samuel."

He smiled as if to say, "You're welcome," then looked at Mike and firmly placed his dummy back in his mouth.

We all laughed. Where did he get that determined character?

"Let's have lunch at Acorn House," I said to Stuart after Samuel was taken off his pump. "How about beans on toast?"

"Great!" Stuart said, and he really meant it.

We were genuinely pleased to be doing little things together, away from the ward. It made life seem relatively normal – in fact, better than normal because we were all together.

Going to Acorn House for lunch and chatting with the other families could sometimes seem a bit like being at a holiday camp. When we got there, with our tin of baked beans and a loaf of bread bought from the concourse, I sat Samuel down at the children's table next to another little boy from our ward. The boy, about a year older than Samuel, also had a nose tube in, which was why I'd sat Samuel there. I wanted him to see other children who looked like him so he would feel normal. There wasn't always as much opportunity on the ward for mixing as I would have liked, as Samuel had frequently been barrier nursed. So whenever I spotted a chance, I took it. Plus, I knew Samuel enjoyed being sociable. The children sat together and enjoyed playing with their toys until it was time for Samuel to have his dinner.

"Come on, son," Stuart said. "Let's get you up to the table."

Samuel turned to his little playmate and held up his hand to give him a high five, but the boy went shy and turned away.

His mum came over and said, "Come on, you know how to high five," but the little boy just hid his face.

I worried that Samuel would feel rejected, but he just smiled at the boy then turned to his daddy and held up his arms. I went to the oven to take out the toast from under the grill.

"Ot, ot, ot!" Samuel called across the room to me.

Again, I was amazed. Samuel often watched a programme called *Big Cook, Little Cook* on CBeebies, where the chef reminds the children to get a grown-up to help as the oven is "hot, hot, hot!" I'd never shown him the oven at Acorn House, so he'd pieced all the information together himself. Not bad for a nineteen-month-old!

I gave him a little plate of beans on toast but didn't expect him to eat. However, he ate almost half of it. We didn't make a big thing about it in front of him, but we both felt really pleased. Mike had predicted multiple organ failure and yet here was Samuel eating lunch. We tried as much as possible to enjoy each day with him and not think about the future, but every moment like that gave us hope.

The chemotherapy ended after five days. The doctors and nurses were always cautious, but even they admitted Samuel seemed better than before. He was, however, spending far longer than normal sleeping and would be drowsy for most of the morning, and some of the afternoon as well. Mike thought this was probably due to the morphine, so it was agreed they would cut down on the amount going into him via the pump to see if he still seemed pain-free without it.

Hoping to give Samuel as many happy experiences as possible, I decided I wanted to take him to the zoo. He'd really enjoyed his last trip eight months earlier, so I was excited to see what he'd make of the experience now he was a bit older. It was hard to believe that it was only last July we'd taken him to Colchester Zoo. We felt like different people from the innocent family that had enjoyed that day out together. I spoke to the nurses and play staff about my desire to take him to the zoo and, to their credit, all of them hid their anxieties and acted like it was a perfectly lovely idea. We were cautioned that Mike would have to approve, but I never doubted that he would.

Mike did look serious as he came in that morning to examine Samuel. He spent longer than normal checking him over and Stuart and I sat quietly, hoping for a positive response. Eventually, he declared him fit enough to go, but warned us to bring him straight back if he seemed at all unwell or if his temperature rose.

So, on 5th March, just seven days after he started the experimental chemo, Samuel went to the zoo. Angela, one of the play ladies, had found out about one nearby – Linton Zoo – and Mick came out of the kitchen to give us directions. The nurses waved goodbye and everyone called out to have a good time.

It's strange how you can put aside the terrible fear that your child might be dying, and instead concentrate on what you have at that moment. And at that moment what we had was a small boy who was desperately ill but who wanted to have a nice time. We were determined to give him the best time possible.

Samuel was wrapped up warmly, but it was so cold there were snowflakes falling as we drove up to Linton Zoo. There were only two other cars in the car park. I expect most families were waiting for better weather, but we didn't know if we had that luxury, so had to make the most of it now.

We entered the zoo and followed the grass track round, past the birds and giant tortoises, until we came to the monkeys. Samuel watched them swing from one tree to another and giggled when they came right up to the fence to look at him.

Before long we were all frozen, and sought sanctuary in the café. It wasn't the plushest of places, but it had row upon row of cuddly toy lions, tigers, bears and monkeys in all different sizes, which amused Samuel. I resisted buying him any as he already had two cuddly lions, a tiger, a monkey and countless bears back at hospital – and who knows how many more back at home! Instead, I steered him towards the food. I ordered soup and a roll for each of us, and then I began filming him. I was still filming him when our order arrived, and we were amazed when he picked up a piece of roll, dunked it into his soup and began to eat it. He then picked up the large spoon and just about fed himself.

"Daddy, help Samuel," I said.

Stuart picked up the spoon and tried to give him some soup, but he didn't make a very good job of it and some of it went down Samuel's top. Samuel immediately held the top away from his body and examined it.

"Uh-oh!" he said.

"Daddy! You didn't do that very well," I said.

"Sorry, son," Stuart said, then proceeded to spill more soup down Samuel as he tried again to feed him.

I don't think Samuel was very impressed but he carried on eating, helping himself to the roll and dipping it in the soup. As I watched him then (and even as I watch this scene on DVD now) I couldn't believe how ill he was. He looked so healthy and alert. His hair had begun to grow back in his five weeks off in January and, even though he'd had two further courses of chemotherapy, it hadn't fallen out again. I could also see a change in him, now that he was nineteen months old, from baby to little boy. His face had slimmed down and his body had lengthened. The look in his eyes was knowledgeable and grown-up. I don't know whether this was a result of all he'd been through, or just the way he would have been anyway, but he no longer seemed like a baby. Not only did I feel incredibly proud of him, but I was very pleased to see him out of hospital and happy, doing what a little boy should be doing.

After his soup, he helped his daddy eat a chocolate muffin. He liked the chocolate chips best and wasn't particularly interested in the sponge, so Stuart picked out all the chocolate and fed it to him.

"Mmm!" Samuel said in between mouthfuls, giving a little wiggle to show his appreciation.

He looked as if he was having the loveliest time it was possible to have, and it made my heart melt to watch him.

After we'd eaten lunch the sun came out, so we spent more time walking around, looking at the animals. Stuart and I couldn't get over how well Samuel seemed. We wondered if this was solely down to the chemotherapy, or if the reiki and prayers had anything to do with it. It was whilst we were walking around that Samuel pointed up at the moon, even though it was daytime. We told the nurses about it when we got back and they were all very impressed.

The next day was a Friday; the day all the doctors visited together for the ward round. So seven doctors heard all about our trip to the zoo. Samuel listened to me talking and smiled when I mentioned the monkeys. As I talked, he munched on a chocolate chip biscuit. He looked strong and alert, sitting on my lap with his back straight, listening to my story. As usual, they wanted to look inside his mouth to see if the chemotherapy had done any damage.

"Samuel, can I look in your mouth?" one of the doctors asked. However, he made the mistake of switching on his pencil torch before waiting for Samuel to open his mouth, so he became absorbed in watching the light waving around in front of him instead of showing the doctor the inside of his mouth. He did, however, carry on taking bites out of his biscuit. "Can I look in your mouth, please?" Samuel reached out to take hold of the torch. "Samuel," the doctor said, struggling to keep possession of his torch, "Samuel, can I look in your mouth?"

Boo said, "I think his mouth is okay. He's eating a biscuit."

"Oh, yes…"

Mike put his head round the door. He looked serious.

"All okay?" he asked.

"He's been to the zoo!"

"He's eating a biscuit."

"He loved the monkeys."

Mike gave a broad smile and said, "Very good."

I hadn't realised just how much they were anticipating organ failure. Samuel's good health defied their expectations, and they couldn't believe the difference between what they were seeing and what they'd been expecting. Every day Samuel had been given a little less morphine, and on that day they decided to wean him off it completely. I was so relieved. Not only did it mean he would have one tube fewer to contend with, but it felt like a sign that he was getting better and this chemotherapy might just have worked.

We decided to push our luck and ask if we could take Samuel to the pub for lunch with Stuart's parents. After the success of the zoo, the doctors decided to let us go. Unfortunately, later that morning the nurses reported a small rise in temperature, so they clamped back down again. It was a great shame, as Stuart's parents hadn't spent much time with him out of hospital since his admission in September, and had never been to the pub with him. However, I understood the doctor's caution.

After a couple of hours Samuel's temperature dropped back down to normal, so Stuart pushed for a rethink. Two doctors came to our room to tell us why they didn't want us to go, but Stuart kept pushing them. Eventually, Mike said his job would be on the line if he let Samuel out and something happened to him. Stuart suddenly realised how difficult it was for the consultants to make decisions about how much freedom to allow us when Samuel was so seriously ill.

Once they'd gone, Stuart said, "I can't believe I just argued with two of the most senior paediatric haematology consultants in the country about taking my son to the pub!"

I laughed.

"Yes, I think they might have better things to do than have that conversation with you!"

"I just got carried away with the idea of taking Samuel out. In the back of my mind I was thinking my parents might never get another chance to be out with him."

"Yes, they will. We have to keep thinking positively. Look how well he's doing. The doctors are amazed. He's going to get there."

"You're right," Stuart said. "There will be other times."

For the next week life felt a bit easier. There seemed a real chance, now that Samuel had had all the harsh experimental chemotherapy and had not experienced organ failure, that it might have worked and he might be back in remission.

Linda and Damien had been frequent visitors to the ward, doing regular reiki sessions with Samuel. We'd also discovered that the grandmother of another patient was a reiki master and she, too, had given Samuel reiki whilst he slept at night.

X-rays confirmed that his heart and other major organs were all working correctly and had not been damaged by the chemotherapy. Stuart began saying to anyone who would listen, "I said he was a strong little boy and wouldn't get organ failure."

Samuel seemed to be developing in the way a nineteen-month-old should. He was now quite proficient in humming the theme tune to *In the Night Garden* and would hum and do the actions to "Twinkle, Twinkle, Little Star". I remember him sitting on my bed with me, demonstrating this new skill. His big eyes shone with happiness at his achievement, and I felt so much love for him I thought my heart would break.

We made the most of this time when Samuel was well and took him out regularly. Spring was on its way and the days felt warmer, so we went for long walks in the countryside around the hospital, pushing Samuel in the pushchair. Unlike when he was well, he often slept during these trips out, and I wondered if this was because he felt safe at these times, knowing there wouldn't be a nurse approaching him at any moment to perform some horrible procedure. As he struggled to have his naps on the ward, I was glad to see him sleep, as I thought it would be restorative. We often ended our trips out at Acorn House, giving Samuel his lunch or tea there.

It was whilst we were there early one evening that Stuart gave Samuel his Bible to hold. We weren't religious and hadn't even had Samuel christened, but on a whim Stuart had brought in his own christening Bible as a sort of good luck token for this last lot of chemotherapy. Samuel took hold of the Bible and, ever so gently, turned the thin pages. Strangely, or coincidentally – we don't know which – he stopped turning the pages when he got to the chapters on Samuel. I am sure at nineteen months old there was no way he knew that was his name spelt out in front of me. I'd never made a big thing of showing him his name written down and I just don't think he would have recognised the word, so it did seem weird to us when he did that. Then he handed the Bible back to his daddy.

At the end of that week, Samuel had an unsettled day. That evening I couldn't get him to fall asleep, so we decided to stay in Samuel's room with him instead of going to the parents' room or Acorn House. After we'd eaten dinner, Stuart felt in need of a beer. Although things appeared to be looking up, we were never able to forget how seriously ill Samuel was, and were constantly aware that things could go the wrong way at any moment. I think Stuart was feeling slightly anxious when he decided to go to Acorn House to bring back a bottle of beer. Drinking alcohol on the ward wasn't really allowed, but Stuart's need to relax was greater than his desire to follow rules. Actually, Stuart has never been one to blindly accept rules, so perhaps he didn't even give them much consideration! He returned to our room with a bottle of beer and a bottle opener tucked in his trouser pocket. Samuel was sitting on my lap, as usual, and Stuart had one eye on the telly as he pulled the bottle opener from his pocket.

"Hmmm," Samuel said, grinning round his dummy.

"Are you laughing at my bottle opener, little man?" Stuart said. He flicked the top off the bottle. Samuel whipped out his dummy so fast you barely saw him do it and opened his mouth wide. Stuart cracked up. "How does he know what beer is?" he said. "Shall I give him some?"

"Well, let me see... He's nineteen months old and he's just had high doses of chemotherapy and morphine. I don't think it's the best of combinations!"

Stuart laughed.

"Shall I ask Mike?"

I shook my head in despair at him. Samuel was still looking longingly at the bottle of beer.

"Have some milk, poppet," I said, offering Samuel his bottle.

Samuel usually loved his milk, but right now he frowned at it. Stuart gulped back his beer and Samuel watched like he was being denied the thing he most wanted in the world.

It seems a strange thing to say, but right from birth Stuart's family had joked that Samuel was the reincarnation of Stuart's grandad, who had died over twenty years before. He had the same smile, which was completely different from mine and Stuart's, and the same lightning-fast mannerisms. When we told Stuart's mother about Samuel's antics that day, she said that her dad had been buried with a bottle of beer and a bottle opener, as he was such a lover of it.

Samuel had never seen Stuart drink from a bottle before, although he had seen him have a beer in a glass, so it does seem strange that he even knew it was something he could drink, let alone something he might really like.

That Sunday, 15ᵗʰ March, my mum visited us. It was now a day short of three weeks since we'd heard that the last lot of chemotherapy hadn't worked. Mike had said if this new chemo didn't work then Samuel only had two to three weeks left to live. I took comfort in the fact that we'd now had that time and he still seemed well.

We took Samuel for a walk and then went back to Acorn House. Whilst we were there he played with some toys and my mum took lots of pictures of him. He looks better in them than he had done in ages. After she left, we took advantage of the fact that Samuel was no longer on the morphine pump and gave him his first bath since January. I thought he would be okay as he was in a normal bath, not a baby one, but he got quite upset, and I wonder if he felt vulnerable in it or if he'd just got out of the habit of having them.

After we bathed him, we received a phone call from the ward to inform us we were changing rooms. The room we were to go into – D Bay – had a large window, which must have been south-facing as it let light in for most of the day. This room received the air conditioning first, so it was the purest, and was used for patients who'd just had, or were about to have, transplants. I think it may have been coincidence that we were given that room or, perhaps it was on the doctors' minds that we could be heading in that direction. I looked on it as a step closer to the bone marrow transplant and Samuel getting better.

We began to think about the transplant more now, especially when Mike came to our room to talk about it and to tell us what to expect. He went into details about the hospital in Bristol that we would be going to and the consultant there who would be looking after Samuel. We asked a lot of questions and later even met a family who'd been through the transplant procedure with their little girl, and were able to talk to them and hear about their experience first-hand.

Mike told us white blood cells would need to be collected to be put on standby for Samuel, in case he needed them after he'd had the transplant. Six family members were needed to provide the blood cells, including Stuart and me. So my sister and Stuart's brother, sister-in-law and sister all had blood samples taken at their doctors' surgeries to check compatibility. I remember we both felt anxious about what was to come, as a bone marrow transplant is a risky procedure and it would mean that Samuel would be completely isolated for much of that time. It also meant we would be spending the next three months in Bristol, but after that, if all went well, Samuel would be home and that would be the end of treatment.

We were already exhausted by what we'd been through: six months of treatment, and two months prior to that of Samuel being unwell and trying to find out what was wrong with him. It only seemed five minutes ago that I was pregnant and excitedly anticipating his arrival. Samuel, of course, must have been more than exhausted by what he'd been through: everything we had, all whilst feeling extremely ill and undergoing upsetting tests and treatments.

We rationalised that we had to just push through the next three months, and then Samuel would have the rest of his life to live. Life was beginning to feel more positive. Hearing the doctors and nurses talking about a transplant, rather than about taking Samuel home to die, was an extremely encouraging sign. But just as we, the doctors and the rest of our family were concentrating on the bone marrow transplant, Stuart's mother had a very strange dream. In it, Samuel came to her, although she wasn't able to see his face because it was obscured by an opaque mist. He said, in a childlike voice, "I've done what I came here to do." The dream then ended. She shot up in bed, convinced Samuel had died.

It was eight o'clock in the morning and she'd overslept. She immediately phoned the ward to find out if Samuel was all right. She found out he was but, still shaken, she asked to speak to Stuart. She asked him what was going on with Samuel. Stuart told her he was fine and the consultants were pushing ahead with the bone marrow transplant. He did think it strange that his mum was calling him so early in the morning but, still half asleep himself, he didn't think to ask why she had rung so early. She told Stuart's dad about her dream, but didn't mention it to us at that time for fear of upsetting us.

Towards the end of the week, Samuel got a temperature. It wasn't unexpected, so I didn't feel unduly worried about it. He'd been well for three and a half weeks. He'd been lucky not to have an infection, but the doctors decided they wanted him to have a CT scan so they could detect exactly where the infection was located. As Samuel had coped well with the scan back in October and hadn't needed sedation, we decided to take him down again whilst he was awake. However, whether it was because he was older or just not as exhausted as last time, he wouldn't stay still for the scan. He cried and held his arms out for me. I hated seeing him distressed, so we decided not to prolong his anxiety. We took him back to the ward to try again later with sedation.

That afternoon Cheryl, from Baby Bounce, came to see us with her partner and their son, Rowan. Samuel was unwell and not up to interacting with them. My mum and sister were also in the room with us and had been there for several hours, so I think Samuel was already tired out by the company. Cheryl tried to play with him, but he just lay in my arms, dressed in his Babygro and looking like a much younger baby than he was. Rowan struggled in Cheryl's grip and clearly wanted to get down and play. Although Cheryl kept a tight rein on him, it was not difficult to see the contrast between Samuel and Rowan's behaviour and energy. I wished they could be friends under normal circumstances.

About fifteen minutes before they were planning to leave, one of the nurses came in to give Samuel his sedation.

"He'll go a bit sleepy and might even fall asleep," she said.

Instead, he acted like he was drunk. It was the sweetest thing I'd ever seen and had us in stitches. Cheryl was just saying goodbye to us all and waving at Samuel when he suddenly sat himself up and began to blow kisses at her. I'd never seen him do that before, but Upsy Daisy did it all the time on *In the Night Garden*, and Boo would also sometimes blow him kisses.

He'd never done it back, though. Instead, he used to give her a look as if to say, "If you think I'm doing that then you've another thing coming!"

But now, smiling away like he'd just drunk a bottle of whisky, he blew kisses and tried to chat with everyone in his own little language.

"You're going to have so much trouble with him when he's fifteen and discovers beer," Nancy said.

Samuel fell asleep shortly afterwards and he had the CT scan. We were all feeling optimistic. Nancy had talked about the future and Samuel being a teenager, and it was beginning to feel like we would get there. However, the scan showed up a fungal infection in Samuel's lungs. I knew this could be very serious. I thought it may even put a stop to treatment, but Mike said they had antibiotics to treat it so we tried to remain calm.

But he went downhill over the weekend. He struggled to sleep at night, so an adult bed was put in our room instead of his cot, so he could sleep with me and feel comforted. At first this seemed to help, but gradually his sleeping worsened to the extent that he was awake, and seemingly in pain, for hours at a time. I was at a loss what to do. I would press the call button throughout the night and ask for more painkillers, but he was on the maximum dosage and couldn't have more.

Up until then we'd been given quite a lot of freedom and had been allowed to take Samuel out whenever he wasn't attached to the pump. Now, however, Mike said he wanted Samuel to stay in his room so he could keep a close eye on him. I didn't argue with him. Samuel wasn't up to doing anything else, anyway.

Sunday 22nd March was Mother's Day. I opened Samuel's card.

"Dear Mummy," it read. "Thank you for looking after me. I can't wait to be better and playing with you and Daddy in the sun very soon. Love, Samuel xxx"

I looked at Stuart and my face crumpled. Suddenly I didn't feel quite so confident that Samuel would ever be playing with us in the sun. Stuart hugged me.

"He'll be okay. It's just this infection that's bringing him down."

"But he doesn't seem right, does he?"

"He's had an infection with every course of chemotherapy he's had. It's normal. They've just got to get him through this and then we can go to Bristol. His blood test results have all been okay, haven't they?"

"That's true, although the neutrophils haven't gone up much."

"That's because of the infection. But his white blood cells have remained stable. They haven't shot up like last time. And his platelet count is normal."

I cuddled Samuel and kissed the top of his head.

"You're right. He just needs to get over this infection and then we can move forward again."

"Yes. Bristol for the summer. Just think – when Samuel's in re-covery we can take him to the beach. Weston-super-Mare is nearby. We'll go there."

The next day, however, Mike came to see us.

"I think we'll do the lumbar puncture tomorrow to see what's go-ing on in Samuel's bone marrow."

"Really?" Stuart said. "I thought you would have waited for the neutrophils to go up a bit first."

"They should have started to go up by now. I think it would be wise to see what's going on."

He didn't say he thought there was a problem, but maybe if we'd pressed him he would have done. I felt my heart race. Over the past few weeks I'd sensed the doctors and nurses becoming more hopeful, but now I detected caution again. Despite the sense of doom we'd both felt when Mike mentioned the lumbar puncture, Stuart and I immediately set about making each other feel more positive.

By the next morning, we were both so convinced Mike was go-ing to tell us Samuel was in remission that Stuart charged the video camera up to record us all once we'd heard the good news. We took Samuel into the small theatre in the day unit. We battled with our nerves but were both absolutely determined to stay strong. We con-centrated on Samuel. We cuddled and comforted him. We smiled, we praised him, and we gave him all our love. We talked cheerfully to the doctors, nurses and anaesthetists who were performing the procedure, and then we kissed Samuel whilst he had the anaesthetic.

I honestly don't remember what happened next. My next memory is of a couple of hours later, taking Samuel out for a walk around the park. With hindsight, I'm amazed we were allowed, but somebody must have given us the go-ahead. Samuel was now awake from his procedure but feeling tired, so I had him reclining in the pushchair as we wheeled him around the path that ringed the park. It was a beautiful sunny day and the pink and white blossoms were in full flower on the trees. A businessman was lying down on a bench. He had his jacket off and his sleeves rolled up with his hands behind his head. He looked relaxed and happy.

"Lovely day," he said as we walked past.

"Yes," I agreed.

I remember thinking about young celebrity Jade Goody, who'd died the day before. For weeks I'd been avoiding the newspaper stand on the concourse, as it seemed to be reporting more bad news about the spread of her cancer every day. I didn't want to think of her dying, and to end up wondering if that would be Samuel's fate. When I thought about it, it didn't seem right that she should have died when the weather was so beautiful and signs of life were appearing all around us. I couldn't believe that Samuel would die as well. Surely one death was enough. Samuel didn't need to be taken, too.

"It's going to be good news, isn't it?" I said to Stuart.

He smiled. He looked totally convinced.

"Of course it is," he said.

We returned to our room on the ward. As usual, we put on the TV. Samuel felt very cold. I wrapped him in his dressing gown and put socks on his feet over the top of his Babygro. He drank some milk, but he didn't seem right. I noticed the skin on his hands had gone very blotchy. This had happened a couple of days before and we'd been told this was all the blood going to the vital organs. Samuel had been given some hydration then and had been all right. I wondered if this was a result of the infection. We spoke to a nurse about it and she said she would mention it to the doctors.

Mike and Boo came in. It was only just past lunchtime. We were expecting to get the results of Samuel's lumbar puncture in the afternoon, and as they proceeded to examine Samuel I presumed they didn't have the results yet. They said to keep him wrapped up warmly. Then Mike stood up.

"Shall we go to my room," he said.

It wasn't a question. I felt the strength go out of me. I looked at Stuart. We were overwhelmed by dread. I passed Samuel to Boo. There was no one else in the room and I couldn't leave him in his cot on his own. He gave a little cry and Boo looked momentarily shocked to be left doing the caring.

We followed Mike down the long corridor. He walked briskly in front of us. I knew he didn't want to speak until we were alone. I returned the smiles of the other parents we passed on the way, but my body pulsated with fear and I felt a whooshing in my head as if I was about to faint. Somehow, I got to Mike's room. Stuart looked how I felt. We all took a seat. Mike had asked a nurse to join us, but I remember thinking I didn't like that one and I wished Sophie, or someone else I trusted, was with us instead.

"We've looked at Samuel's bone marrow under the microscope. I'm afraid the leukaemia has returned."

"No!" I wanted to scream. "No, no, no, no!"

But I didn't. I didn't say anything and neither did Stuart.

"I'm sorry," Mike said. "I know it's not what you wanted to hear."

"Of course it's not what we wanted to hear," I said. "You're telling us our son's going to die."

I buried my head under Stuart's arm. I wanted to disappear. No one spoke for a long time.

Eventually, Stuart said, "Are you sure? Are you sure it was Samuel's cells you were looking at? Could you have made a mistake?"

Mike shook his head. "There's no mistake. They were Samuel's cells, and 100 per cent of them have grown back as leukaemia cells."

"But he was doing so well," Stuart said.

"Yes, he was," Mike agreed.

"Did you think he was getting better?" Stuart asked.

"I did. I did think there was a chance for him when he survived the chemotherapy."

"I knew he was strong enough to cope with it," Stuart said.

Mike nodded and we all fell silent.

"What happens now?" I asked eventually, still clutching hold of Stuart.

"That's up to you. You can stay in hospital, if you want to, or you can go home or to a hospice. Whatever you choose, we will support you."

"Isn't there anything else we can try?" Stuart asked.

"I'll ask for you, but bearing in mind his fungal infection and how ill he is, trying more chemotherapy might not be in Samuel's best interests."

"I'd like you to find out," Stuart said.

Neither of us cried. I think, like me, Stuart couldn't take it in. We couldn't comprehend that it was all over; that Samuel would definitely die.

"I'll leave you now," Mike said. "You can stay here as long as you want."

Stuart and I didn't know what to say to each other. We'd been convincing ourselves for six months that Samuel would get better and we didn't know how to be anything other than positive. We walked back to our room. Samuel was sitting with Angela, the play lady. She must have been told, but she acted normal as she passed Samuel to me.

"Hello, poppet," I said.

I cuddled him tightly. I didn't ever want to let him go.

Mike asked to see us again later. Stuart went to his room and I stayed with Samuel. He'd had email correspondence with a top consultant from Great Ormond Street Hospital. The email said Mike could try using the very first lot of chemotherapy that he'd used on Samuel, but in a much higher dosage. However, in light of the fungal infection and the symptoms Samuel was now showing, he didn't think it would be successful.

"What chance do you think he has if we try this chemotherapy?" Stuart asked.

Mike shook his head. "I think zero per cent."

Stuart was deflated. There was nothing we or anyone could do. We'd all tried; no one more so than Samuel, who had bravely coped with five rounds of chemotherapy, two major operations and several smaller ones, nine nose tube fittings, and countless X-rays. For the past six months he'd lived mainly in a hospital. He'd not been on this earth long, and for a third of it he'd been unwell and undergoing intensive treatment. This was no life for him. We wanted to give him better. It was time to take him home.

CHAPTER 18
And Now It's Goodbye

OUR LITTLE BOY WAS GOING to die. We'd been told; it was official. But there was still a big part of us that didn't believe it. How could we when he was sitting with us interacting, trying to talk? Perhaps there'd be a miracle, we thought. We heard a story from another parent of a woman who had cancer, whose own antibodies kicked in and destroyed the cancer cells after she stopped the chemotherapy. I don't know whether it was true, but at the time we believed it and a seed was sown in our minds that this might happen to Samuel.

We had to ring our families to let them know. I don't remember the conversations, but I know I found it hard to deliver the bad news with no positives to soften the blow. I wanted to make it better for everyone.

I wanted to say, "It's all right. We'll be fine; he'll be fine." But I couldn't, so I was at a loss.

We decided we would go home the next day. We had so much to pack; we knew we'd never get everything done in an evening. The doctors, too, had things to sort out. If we were to go home, a support network would need to be in place to make sure Samuel continued to get treatment. This treatment would no longer be life-saving, but it would keep him comfortable.

My body felt jittery. It was a strange sensation for me as, even in difficult times, I am used to feeling calm. Despite our exhaustion, our brains went into overdrive, desperately trying to find the answer to keep Samuel alive.

"Perhaps we shouldn't rule out more chemotherapy," Stuart said.

"Good idea. We won't rule it out, but we'll take him home and see if he picks up first," I said.

Although the evidence was mounting, we just couldn't believe he would die. He seemed so special. Perhaps every parent thinks that, but we felt it was true – not just about Samuel, but many of the children who were undergoing treatment. They seemed to have a maturity and wisdom about them that I don't think stemmed solely from their time spent in hospital.

Samuel slept terribly that night. I initially attempted to sleep in the fold-down bed whilst Stuart went in the big bed with Samuel, but as the night wore on and Stuart got no sleep, I took over. The nurses gave Samuel painkillers, but nothing made a difference and the three of us barely slept all night.

It's difficult enough to keep functioning with that level of sleep deprivation, but to look after a seriously ill child and make sure they're getting all the medicines and care they need on no sleep is almost impossible. But there was no choice. We had to carry on; especially as we wanted to give Samuel the best life possible and take in every moment with him.

Mike came to see us the next morning. As usual, I felt as if I was functioning on two levels. On one level I was having horrible conversations with Mike about the practicalities of Samuel dying, but on another level I still couldn't believe it was true. Mike wanted us to be sure about our decision to take Samuel home.

"If he stays in hospital he can continue to have intravenous antibiotics to slow down the spread of infection," he said.

"But then he would be tethered to the pump for much of the day," I countered.

"That's right. Whereas if you go home, you will have more freedom but he may not live as long."

"What would the difference be in how long he lives?" Stuart asked.

"Two or maybe three days longer if you stay in hospital. But that doesn't necessarily mean he'll have a better quality of life. It's likely he'll be very medicated at the end, anyway, to keep the pain away."

"Whereas if he goes home, he may die from the infection, which would be quicker, and maybe less painful, than dying from leukaemia," I said.

I couldn't believe what I was saying. Samuel was sitting on my lap and I was talking about him dying. My voice shook and the tears ran down my face. Mike nodded sadly.

"I want to go home."

"We'll get everything sorted out for you," he said.

Stuart went over to Acorn House to pack and I took Samuel for a walk around the ward. We stopped to say goodbye to Rosie's mother. She'd heard the news – I don't know how, but everyone seemed to know. I was grateful that she came straight over to us and didn't turn away, as some people did. She started to cry as soon as she tried to speak, and then I did too.

"I'm so sorry," she said. "He's such a lovely boy and you're such a lovely family. You don't deserve this." The tears fell down her cheeks. "It's so damned unfair."

A consultant called Pat joined us. I'd not spoken to her much since we'd been in hospital, and now I knew why: she was the consultant who dealt with palliative care.

"You've given Samuel the best life," she said. "You've been there for him continuously. You were there at the start and you'll be there at the end. What better way is there to die than in your parents' arms?"

I hugged Samuel closer. I was desperate for him not to die.

I knew her words were meant to be a comfort – and in the future they would be – but at that point all I wanted was for someone to say, "It's okay. He's going to be all right; he's not going to die."

Stuart's parents arrived that afternoon. Cynthia sat with me and helped to pack away our belongings in our room whilst Derek went to Acorn House with Stuart.

Whilst there, Derek said to Stuart, "Let's hope Samuel's going to a better place than this."

He had accepted Samuel was going to die; but Cynthia hadn't.

"Samuel has an eye appointment in June," I said to her. "I mustn't forget to cancel it."

"I wouldn't cancel that yet," she said.

"Really?"

"I think he might surprise you."

Of course, I wanted to hear that. I wanted to believe more than anything that Samuel would defy everyone's expectations and live, but I couldn't ignore the doctors' prognosis. Mike had said he would have a week at most, but in a letter he'd written to our GP – which I'd opened and then resealed – he said he thought Samuel would die over the weekend. It was already Wednesday, so that gave us just three or four days with him. I felt as if we should be spending all our time with our son. It didn't feel right to be getting on with the practicalities of living, but in order to get home we had to pack bags, buy more nappies, and make sure we had food in. I suppose if we'd chosen to stay in hospital those jobs would have been taken away from us, but I knew Samuel would be more relaxed, and ultimately happier, in his own home.

Mike said that morning he wanted Samuel to go back on the morphine pump. I was prepared for it this time and didn't object. I didn't want him to be in pain and I knew the pump would make all the difference. But when the nurses arrived to attach the pump to his leg, he squirmed and wiggled in my arms, clearly recognising it from last time and not wanting it. I cuddled him close and reassured him it would be all right, and eventually he allowed them to put it in. It was incredible how quickly it made a difference. One minute he was cuddled into me, unable to interact and whimpering in pain, and the next he was eating the chocolate buttons his nanny was offering him. Deep down I knew this turnabout was just the effect of the morphine, but I was so desperate for the doctors to be wrong that I allowed myself to be deceived.

Cynthia got Samuel to put all his cards in the carrier bag she held open for him.

I watched him enjoy this game and thought, *How can he be about to die?*

We'd been told how ill he was, but all I could think was that we'd seen him like this before and watched him bounce back.

It was getting late now, almost five o'clock, and we still weren't ready to go home. Mike must have been nearing the end of his shift when he came to see us. He crouched down next to Samuel and asked if we knew what to expect when we got home. We talked for a while and the whole time he looked at Samuel and stroked his arm. He had tears in his eyes. Eventually, he got up and hugged me.

"Thank you," I said. I wanted to add, "Thank you for everything; thank you for all you've done and all you've tried to do; thank you for looking after Samuel; thank you for the hug; and thank you for caring so much when you didn't have to." But I couldn't speak, and neither could he.

He wanted to save Samuel, and although he must have saved many, many children, I expect he still felt the loss of this one child who he'd come to know so well over the past six months. Eventually, Stuart and his dad returned and we were ready to leave. Just as we were about to go, Boo came in. She, too, had tears in her eyes.

"You can have another baby," she said. "You're still young."

I understand now that she just wanted to make it better. So many people have said that to me since Samuel died, without realising just what an inappropriate thing it is to say to a grieving parent. I think in our Western world we are so unused to death, particularly the death of a child, that people just don't know how to handle it.

"But I don't want another baby," I wanted to say. "I want *Samuel.*"

Instead, I said, "Is that why you've had so many children – in case something like this happens?"

She laughed awkwardly. It must have seemed like a horrible thing to say, but Boo was pregnant with her third child and, at that moment, it felt terribly unfair that she should have that happy event to look forward to whilst I had to watch my only child die. She would then be the mother of three children; I would be the mother of none.

She made a fuss of Samuel and said, "I'm sorry we couldn't do more."

Stuart hugged her and so did I. It felt very emotional, leaving the ward for the last time. But a bigger part of me just wanted to get out – to run away; to escape.

Eventually, at about eight o'clock on Wednesday 25th March, we drove home. Cynthia and Derek followed in their own car and Samuel slept in his seat. Even though we knew we were going home because they could do no more to help Samuel, we both still felt relieved to be leaving the hospital. Six months of living there had drained us physically and emotionally, and I couldn't wait to sleep in my own bed without nurses walking in every couple of hours. That may not sound very grateful, but the truth is we'll always be grateful for the efforts that everyone made to help Samuel, and to the NHS that funded his care, and for the drugs that prolonged his life and eased his pain. But we needed to be home now, and we quickly realised this was what Samuel needed as well.

We had one small hiccup when we arrived back: our front door had seized up in the time we'd been away, so we had to call our next-door neighbours for help.

"Do you have room for some refugees?" I said to Nancy as she opened the door.

"Come in," she said, ushering us through the hall into the living room.

Stuart explained what had happened, then he and Jonathan went round to our house armed with some WD-40 and a bent wire coat hanger.

Whilst we were still in hospital, I'd sent Nancy a text to explain we were coming home and why. It seemed such a terrible thing to put in a text, almost like I was dismissing what we were going through, but I just couldn't ring all our friends.

Samuel sat on my lap and Nancy sat next to us on the sofa. Consumed by my own thoughts, it took a moment for me to realise she was crying.

"We're hoping for a miracle now," I said, as a way of comforting her.

A big part of me really thought there would be one. I just could not accept any other reality than one that had Samuel in it. Nancy nodded. She told me later they didn't feel worthy of seeing us on that day, so close to Samuel dying, but I was just grateful we were friends with our neighbours and felt comfortable enough to turn to them.

Stuart's parents arrived later, and where he and Jonathan had failed with the coat hanger and WD-40, Derek succeeded with a huge shove of the shoulder! And then we were back in the house. Back home and wondering what we should be doing in these unusual circumstances.

I sat with Samuel whilst Cynthia made everyone drinks and something to eat. Derek removed the lock from the door and fixed it and Stuart called Audrey, the community nurse, to let her know we were home.

We still had all the unpacking to do, but Stuart decided to just bring in the essentials and do the rest later. The whole car was stuffed full with our belongings, and it would take us weeks to sort through it all. What we did have to bring in was the palliative care box – a suitcase containing every possible medication that Samuel could need to keep him comfortable until he died. It felt like his death sentence.

Half an hour later, after ten at night, Audrey arrived. She should have finished her shift at five o'clock, but had been hanging on for us to come home. I felt terrible about keeping her waiting but, as usual, she was understanding and wouldn't hear our apologies.

"Now, Amanda, our job is to make sure Samuel's comfortable, so we need to think about how much morphine and anti-sickness medicine we want to go through his pump. I can increase it now if you think that would be a good idea."

Samuel had been whimpering as she examined him, so we all agreed she should do this so he would be pain-free and able to sleep. She rang the hospital to get their agreement and asked them to fax across a signed consent form.

"Now you have some extra morphine to give him through his NG tube if you need it, or you can use Calpol, but he's no longer on the antibiotics as we're not trying to cure him but just keep him comfortable."

Comfortable. It was a word I kept hearing. Never before had it had such ominous connotations.

"We're still hoping for a miracle," I said.

"Well, it's good to have faith, and I know it's a difficult thing to come to terms with, but most parents do eventually accept it and just try to make these last few days with their child as special as possible."

But I just couldn't accept it, and neither could Stuart. In our minds, a miracle would happen and Samuel would be saved. He just couldn't die; he was far too special.

Everyone eventually left, and then Samuel and I went to bed. I decided to put him in the double bed with me instead of his cot, so he'd sense me close by and feel safe. Stuart was to take the spare room in the hope that he would get some sleep. We didn't attach Samuel's night feed; it often made him sick so I saw little point. I also took up an empty syringe and some of the anti-sickness medicine that I was to give him at three o'clock in the morning. I cuddled him in bed whilst I gave him his bottle of milk and he quickly fell asleep in my arms. Ever so gently, I laid him down next to me and put Woof Woof and his dummy on the pillow beside him. He looked so peaceful.

I could hear Stuart moving around downstairs. Stuart remembers thinking how lovely it was to have his family back home and Samuel sleeping soundly. In contrast to the last few nights in hospital, Samuel only woke once in the night when I gave him his anti-sickness medicine, then he went back to sleep until ten o'clock the next morning when Vicky, the community nurse, knocked on our door.

I was awake, although still in bed, but luckily Stuart was up and dressed and feeling a bit better after a full night's sleep. Audrey was on holiday for a few days, so Vicky would be seeing us. She was a young lady, probably only in her early or mid-twenties, but she seemed capable, sensible and sensitive to our situation. I brought Samuel downstairs for her to check on him. Whilst she was there our GP, Dr Masters, turned up. As he examined Samuel, Stuart asked him about the possibility of Samuel having some oral antibiotics to keep his infection under control. We were surprised when he reacted angrily to the request. I think, with hindsight, he found the situation stressful, but at the time his attitude was upsetting and seemed, to us, lacking in understanding.

Dr Masters went into our garden and phoned Mike. Before he went out, he said he felt he'd been misled. I believe he thought we would've accepted our situation and come to terms with it by now. But as I told him when he came back in, up until two days before we'd been looking towards a cure. The conversation became quite heated and was distressing for all of us. It was left to Vicky to bring about some peace and understanding. She calmly explained to Dr Masters what a terrible situation Stuart and I were faced with, and it was to be expected that we would want to do everything we could for our son.

It was also our right to have faith in a miracle, however unlikely that might seem to a medical professional. Vicky explained to us that it wasn't usual for a GP to give this level of home care, and that it was only thanks to Dr Masters agreeing to see us and be on call twenty-four hours a day that we had been allowed to bring Samuel home. Calmness was gradually restored, but I was worried that Samuel had witnessed such a heated discussion – and felt our anxiety – at a time when he was so ill and just needed peace and quiet.

Mike had said oral antibiotics would make no difference to Samuel's condition; his infection was so advanced that only intravenous antibiotics would have an effect. He phoned Stuart later and told him we could take Samuel to the West Suffolk Hospital for intravenous antibiotics if we wanted, but that would mean he would be tethered to a pump for much of the day, just as he would have been if he'd stayed in Addenbrooke's. Stuart and I had a long discussion about this. Our instinct was to do everything we could to save Samuel. By now we'd started to convince ourselves that his own antibodies would kick in and cure the leukaemia and, therefore, the thing that was more likely to kill him would be the infection. It wasn't rational, but we were so confused by what we were going through. From our point of view, we were desperate not to lose our son, and we also wanted to make sure we'd given him every chance to live.

We thought long and hard about this. Our minds constantly flipped between thinking sensibly, taking into account everything we'd been told by medical professionals, and believing Samuel could be cured by the power of our positive thinking. Ultimately we decided we didn't want Samuel to spend what could be his last few days in hospital, so we decided to keep him at home. But this now meant Samuel was fighting his infection – and the leukaemia – on his own without help from any drugs.

We were glad to be home, but the peaceful days we'd envisioned were disrupted by visitors. Of necessity, Dr Masters and either Vicky or Audrey came round at least once a day, and Linda and Damien also came to give Samuel reiki healing. Of course, all our family needed to see Samuel as well. If these were to be his last few days, then we couldn't deny them the opportunity to spend time with him and, ultimately, say goodbye. We soon realised, however, that Samuel needed time to relax as well, and we also wanted to spend time with him on our own.

On our first day back, my mum, sister and dad arrived just after Vicky and Dr Masters left. We decided to take Samuel to the Abbey Gardens in his pushchair. He whimpered a bit as we put him in, but was fine when we got going. We tried to show him the ducks, but he wasn't up to much other than watching us feed them. Although it was difficult, we all tried to act as normal as possible in front of him so he didn't feel our fear or sadness, and I remember talking frequently about the possibility of a miracle happening. That evening, after everyone had gone home, we watched Samuel's DVDs with him and then put him in our double bed again. This time Stuart slept with him, and again he slept well.

Dr Masters came round on Friday morning. He sat on the footstool opposite Samuel and studied him. After a while, he looked over the top of his glasses and grimaced.

"I think he's looking a bit worse than yesterday."

Stuart and I looked at Samuel; he looked no different to us.

"Do you?"

"I do." He grimaced again. "Did you think about going into a hos—"

"Don't even say it!" I interrupted. "We don't want to go anywhere. We want Samuel to be in his own home, where he's comfortable."

In fact, the hospice supported us by sending their nurses to us when neither Audrey nor Vicky was able to come round. They also offered music and play sessions at home and, had he felt better, I would have been grateful for this.

Dr Masters nodded and said, "I won't mention it again."

Debbie and her daughters visited that afternoon. We took Samuel to the Abbey Gardens again, and this time we gave him some bread to feed the ducks. I so wanted him to be well, and for it to be like old times, that I got quite a shock when I saw him struggle to throw his bread. Watching him putting all his effort into such a small action upset me terribly and, much to my shame, I let my feelings take over and cried. I wish I hadn't; he saw me and I wondered what he made of me crying at him throwing bread for the ducks. If I could go back and do it again, I would have praised him for his efforts and made him feel good about himself, rather than giving in to my own feelings.

I think part of being a good parent is the ability to put yourself aside and to think about your child's needs. I couldn't go back and change my behaviour, but I did make sure I never made the same mistake again; for every achievement of Samuel's after that I praised him to the hilt.

Linda and Damien came round that evening to perform reiki on Samuel for the first time since we'd come home. It was past Samuel's bedtime, but he seemed very relaxed lying on his daddy, so we decided to keep him downstairs with us rather than putting him to bed.

"Wow, look at that aura!" Linda said as she came through the front door.

"What's it like?" I asked.

"Deep purple. He's existing on a higher plane. And he's got an angel with him."

"Has he?"

Stuart looked around him as if expecting to see one, seven feet tall with wings. I smiled.

"Yes. The angel is here to guide him to the next dimension."

I wasn't quite so happy to hear that. Linda looked at my face and could probably tell I hadn't accepted that possibility yet. "*If* that's his journey," she added.

I lit candles and dimmed the lighting. I put on one of Samuel's *Baby Einstein* DVDs that showed different colours and paintings set against classical music. Samuel focused on it whilst Linda sat in front of him and Damien sat by his side. They both held out their hands and began to perform reiki. After a while, Samuel closed his eyes.

"I'm getting an image in my head from Samuel," Linda said. "It's a street of Victorian houses. They have front gardens and little gates."

Stuart and I looked at each other. Although our house was Victorian, it didn't have a front garden and, therefore, had no gate.

"I've no idea what that could be," I said.

"There's a lot of green in the picture. It's a very strong image." Stuart and I shook our heads. "Now I'm getting another one," she said. "It looks like a lot of coloured balls on sticks – a bit like lollipops – and they're going round and round."

"I know what that is!" Stuart said. "That's the beginning of his *Brainy Baby* DVD!"

"Oh yes!" I said.

Linda had described it perfectly.

"And I've just realised what the other image is: it's the beginning of *Mr Benn*. We were watching it just before you came round," Stuart said.

"Of course!" I said.

Mr Benn began with a row of Victorian houses, and Mr Benn himself going up to his front gate. Samuel had images in his mind of the DVDs he'd been watching and Linda was picking up on them. How wonderful that he just had nice things on his mind after all he'd been through, and how amazing that Linda had picked up on them.

Samuel was settled on Stuart's lap. Sometimes he had his eyes open and would watch a bit of his DVD and, at other times, he let them close. He was calm and relaxed and didn't seem to have a problem at all with having Linda and Damien so close. As I watched them in the soft light, with the classical music playing in the background, I became lost in my own world. I'd been thinking my own thoughts for some time when I wondered what would happen if Samuel died. Suddenly Samuel sat up, held out his arm, and shook his hand at me.

"Mmm, Mmm," he said round his dummy. His face was creased in a frown and he looked upset.

"What were you just thinking?" Linda asked.

I was startled.

Unable to say the exact words I was thinking, I said instead, "I was having a negative thought."

"Well, Samuel's picked up on it."

I couldn't believe it. I looked at him. He still seemed upset with me. Was it possible he could pick up on my thoughts, like Linda picked up on his? I went over to him and gave him a kiss.

"I'm sorry, darling," I said.

Linda turned to give me some reiki to help me feel positive whilst Damien continued with Samuel. I felt the heat coming from Linda's hands. I couldn't take in what was happening – Samuel dying and he and Linda picking up on other people's thoughts. The world suddenly felt like a very strange place and not at all like the one I'd grown up in. I relaxed eventually and Linda went back to Samuel. It was almost nine o'clock and Samuel was due his anti-sickness medicine. I thought we should try to put him to bed, but before I said anything, Linda spoke again.

"Why does Samuel still have that nose tube in?"

"So I can give him his medicines down it."

"So you're not feeding him through it, then?"

"No. But if I take it out he'll have to take his medicines in his mouth and he won't like that. Why do you ask?"

"Because he's telling me, telepathically, 'Get this out of me; get this out!' He really, really wants it out."

"Really?" I looked at Samuel, who was looking directly at me. "I don't know what to say. I know it can't be very nice but I'm sure he wouldn't like to take his medicines in his mouth either."

"Okay," Linda said.

I carried Samuel upstairs shortly afterwards. He'd had two hours of reiki, which I hoped had done him some good, but now he needed his medicines, his milk and some sleep. I cuddled him into me whilst I gave him his bottle in the dark bedroom. He began to drink, but after just a few seconds he gagged. I held the cardboard bowl to his chin but he pushed it away. As he gagged again, his nose tube partially came up from his nose, leaving a small loop. He grabbed hold of it and pulled with all his strength. The nose tube came almost all of the way out, but there was still a small part of it left down and it was partially taped to his cheek. I had two choices: either push it back down and hope it went into the right place, or pull it out. I hesitated and Samuel began to cry. I grabbed hold of the tube and pulled the remainder of it out. I then quickly took the tape from his cheek.

"It's out! It's out!" I said, holding the tube up for Samuel to see.

He let out a relieved sigh and sank back into my arms. When he'd gone into hospital initially, he'd pulled his first two nose tubes out. However, having learnt that another one would just be fitted in its place he'd stopped doing this, which makes it all the more strange that he took this one out. If past experience had shown him anything, he would have expected another one, so it almost made me wonder if he knew there would be no more tubes. I also wondered if he knew this was the end. I cuddled him.

"I'm going to have to give you your medicine in your mouth now, darling," I said, holding up the syringe. Without making any fuss at all, he simply opened his mouth and let me give him his medicine. "Well done!" I said, cuddling and kissing him.

I gave him his milk shortly afterwards and then he fell asleep. As I walked downstairs, I thought about what Linda had said about Samuel not wanting his nose tube in. Was it just because the tube began to come up that Samuel so determinedly pulled it out, or was it because he really didn't want it in any more, like Linda had said? When I got back to the living room, I told them what had happened.

Linda just smiled and said, "He told me he didn't want that tube in any more."

That night, Stuart kindly said he would sleep with Samuel as he knew how exhausted I was.

"It's going to be difficult to give him his anti-sickness medicine at three o'clock without his tube in," he said as we walked upstairs.

"It is. Why don't you wait until he wakes up rather than waking him?"

"That might mean he's sick, though, as he won't have had his medicine."

It was one of many difficult decisions we made on a daily basis as we looked after Samuel. Parenting – and especially parenting a baby – is often about trial and error. This is particularly true when it's your first child, and when that child is extremely sick then the decisions and challenges you face are extreme.

Amazingly, the decision was taken away from us as Samuel didn't wake up all night. He wasn't sick either, so we couldn't help feeling a sense of optimism that morning; a feeling that was heightened by Dr Masters' visit. He didn't examine Samuel physically but just watched him.

He'd been doing this for quite some time without saying a word when I asked, "How do you think he is?"

Dr Masters gave his familiar grimace and looked over the top of his glasses at me.

"Well, I was actually just thinking he looks a bit better." Stuart and I were unable to hide our smiles. "I don't know if it's just that I'm getting used to the way he looks but…" He shook his head. "No, he definitely looks better."

"Have you noticed he hasn't got his nose tube in any more?" Stuart asked.

"No, I hadn't noticed. Does he mind taking his medicines by mouth?"

"He's been really good about it," I said. "Actually, he pulled his nose tube out himself."

Dr Masters laughed.

"He's a determined little fellow, isn't he? Well, I'll leave you to get on with your day. You've got my number if you need me."

We had a lot of visitors that day. Stuart's brother, sister-in-law and their oldest two boys, Jonathan and Joseph, had arrived just before Dr Masters' visit. After he'd gone we all went for a long walk at Nowton Park. The daffodils were in full bloom and the park looked beautiful. Samuel took the opportunity to have a sleep; he seemed relaxed and pain-free as we wheeled him in his pushchair. When we got back home we put on one of his DVDs for him to watch whilst we talked. At one point, Graham stood in front of the television.

"Errrh!" Samuel said, waving Graham out of the way like a grumpy old man.

"Sorry, Samuel," Graham said, moving aside swiftly.

I loved how Samuel had the confidence – even when he was so ill – to make sure things were done his way.

They had to say goodbye to Samuel. Living a couple of hours' drive away, we knew they wouldn't be back and, if the doctors were right, this would be the last time they saw him alive. It was painful to watch as they kissed him.

"Bye-bye! See you soon," Stuart said, speaking for Samuel.

It made us realise all the more that they wouldn't see him soon, but Stuart hadn't given up hope of a miracle, even though the medical professionals' assurance that Samuel would die was gradually wearing me down.

My mum, Nancy and Richie arrived just as they were leaving, and then Linda and Damien turned up just as my family were going. It was a constant relay of people, but despite our exhaustion we were glad of the visits; it felt like everyone was there to support Samuel.

A relaxing feeling came over the house with Linda and Damien's arrival. Just like the previous night, I lit candles and put on the same DVD with the classical music. It seemed that Samuel needed to know he could have the distraction of the television, even when it appeared that he wasn't watching it. Every time the DVD reached the end and I thought I wouldn't put it on again, Samuel would open his eyes and point at the telly, so I would have to replay it. None of us minded, though; we weren't watching it and it provided background music.

Samuel seemed to know what was coming with Linda and Damien, and it felt very much like he was in charge. As they sat in their familiar seats, Samuel settled back in his daddy's lap and closed his eyes. At one point, Damien quietly left the room to visit the bathroom. Samuel opened one eye to watch him go, then closed it again. As Damien came back, Samuel held up his hand to give him a high five. It amazed me that he had the strength in body and spirit to do that. As Damien sat down again, Samuel held out his hand to touch Damien's outstretched hand. He then rested his little palm in Damien's adult one. After a while, he leaned forward and did something very peculiar to Linda's palm: he made a turning motion, as if screwing a bottle top. Linda said that he was fine-tuning the reiki, and that it was the most powerful reiki experience she'd ever had with anyone. It certainly seemed like Samuel could feel, and perhaps even see, something coming from their hands. It was the strangest thing to watch, and again made me wonder at the world we live in.

Mike's letter to Dr Masters had predicted that Samuel wouldn't last the weekend. Conscious of this, and now that all our family had had the chance to spend time with him, I made the decision that Sunday should be just the three of us. Of course, the nurses had to come round to add more morphine and anti-sickness medicine to Samuel's pump, just as they did every day, but we told Dr Masters he didn't need to come; we would ring him if we needed him. We asked our families if they could give us the day to ourselves.

First thing that morning we got out some of Samuel's toys and played with him. He had a toy VW Beetle that was a shape sorter and now, as he sat on his daddy's lap, I passed him the shapes for him to put through the holes.

"Well done!" I said, as he put the cube through the square hole.

I was so impressed with him. He was supposed to be at death's door and yet he was still able not just to play with his toys, but to work out complicated things.

Despite what Mike's letter had said to Dr Masters, I didn't think Samuel was about to leave us, so we made the most of another sunny day and carried him to the Abbey Gardens. I'd noticed that although he was fine once he was in his pushchair, getting in and out of it seemed to give him some pain, so Stuart carried him and he put his little arms around his daddy's neck as we walked up the road, through the old cemetery, and into the Abbey Gardens.

"Look, a squirrel!" Stuart said, pointing at it leaping playfully around the base of a tree.

Samuel lifted his head to have a look, smiled, and then rested his head back on his daddy's shoulder. He was clearly weak, but I didn't feel this was the end, as had been predicted. However, I knew things could turn around at any moment, so we had to be vigilant.

Stuart and I hadn't had any breakfast that morning. Our time was so completely consumed with Samuel that we'd stopped thinking about ourselves. Now, however, we realised we were hungry. We decided to sit at the little outside café in the Abbey Gardens and have some tea and toasted teacakes. There were many other families around us, sitting at the little picnic tables. Children were being boisterous and parents were disciplining them. I realised we'd never had that with Samuel. He'd been too young, and then too ill, to behave inappropriately. My mother tells me I would have never thought Samuel was naughty whatever he did, and I think perhaps she's right, but I also think all the family felt the same way!

After we'd eaten, Samuel lay back in his daddy's arms. He looked pale and exhausted, but when I looked at Stuart I thought he looked the same. I expect I didn't look much better. I wondered if the other families noticed us and wondered what was wrong. But without his nose tube in and with a hat on, Samuel didn't look like he had cancer. He could just have been run down, and I suppose nobody would have guessed anything as terrible as our son being about to die from leukaemia.

I wandered off to the public toilets near the main entrance, and bumped into Stuart's parents as I walked up the path. They actually lived twelve miles away, so it wasn't coincidence that brought them to the Abbey Gardens that morning. They knew we spent much of our time there and, being desperate to see Samuel again, they'd decided to go for a walk around the gardens to see if they could bump into us. They knew we'd wanted the day to ourselves so hadn't wanted to come to our house, but they just couldn't bear the possibility that they might never see Samuel again. I didn't mind. Sitting with us in the gardens for half an hour was fine with me, and I was pleased for them that they were able to enjoy some time with Samuel away from hospital. However, Stuart, being completely exhausted, was confused when he saw them.

"Where's Amanda?" he asked as they walked over to him.

"She's just gone to the toilets," Cynthia replied.

"Oh, yes, she did say."

We were trying so hard to act normal and happy in front of Samuel, but the effort, stress and extreme tiredness were all taking their toll.

"Hello, little darling," Cynthia said, reaching out and stroking Samuel's hand.

She told me weeks later that that was the first time she actually thought he might die. Up until then, and despite the dream she'd had to the contrary, she'd been convinced a miracle would occur and he would get better. But now Samuel was beginning to look more ill. He'd been given a blood transfusion just before we left hospital, but Stuart suspected his body had now used up all the goodness in his blood and that his blood counts must be getting low. If there was going to be a miracle, it needed to happen now so Samuel could start making healthy blood cells.

Back home we spent a couple of hours together, resting on our bed, cuddling Samuel whilst he slept. Stuart and I tried to perform reiki on him. We imagined the bad blood cells disappearing and healthy cells growing in their place. We were so tired and could have fallen asleep ourselves, but we knew Samuel's need was greater so we tried to combat our tiredness in order to help him.

We took Samuel out again in the early evening. He'd picked up slightly after his sleep, so what had initially begun as a trip into our back garden became another walk in the Abbey Gardens. Our garden is typical of many belonging to Victorian houses: long and thin but well stocked with trees and plants. We had begun by showing Samuel everything that was coming into flower, and had ended up going out the back of the garden and then on a little walk. Samuel seemed to enjoy it, and I was pleased we'd made the decision to come home and were able to do this. If we'd stayed in hospital, we would have been tied to one room. At least the walks provided him, and us, with a distraction from his illness, as well as some time in the sunshine and fresh air.

We put Samuel to bed at seven that evening. We'd asked Linda and Damien not to visit that night, and Stuart and I were able to eat and then relax for a few hours. I didn't believe Samuel was about to die at that point, but my belief that a miracle would occur was gradually diminishing. Stuart, however, still had complete faith and was determined we should continue to think positively. I would have always given Samuel my very best, even if I'd been a single mother, but having Stuart there with me, being such a dedicated father and a courageous, optimistic person, helped me stay strong. It wouldn't have done Samuel any good if we'd been negative or sad around him. So, even if we were deluding ourselves, it meant we kept going and kept trying to give Samuel the best life possible.

Monday and Tuesday followed the same pattern as the previous week. We hadn't told our families what Mike's letter said about how long he thought Samuel had, so they didn't really know what to expect. My mum and sister visited on Monday, and on Tuesday Stuart's parents came round. As usual, Dr Masters, Audrey and Vicky made regular visits, as did Linda.

Samuel's health seemed stable, so early on Monday evening we carried him around the town and showed him the new shopping area, the Arc, which had just been built. We'd joked when he was first born that he would be hanging around the Arc when he was older, as teenagers do, but now we realised this might not be the case. We tried not to dwell on our negative feelings, though, and instead concentrated on living in the moment and keeping Samuel happy.

As Tuesday rolled on, I noticed Samuel's lip was swelling up and a bruise had appeared under his eye. We suspected he must be extremely low in platelets and we wondered what to do about this. In hospital Samuel would have had a platelet transfusion, but what was supposed to happen now we were at home?

At around six o'clock, Linda arrived to give Samuel reiki and also to set up a pyramid frame in our garden. She told us the pyramid shape had healing qualities and that by sitting in the middle of it, underneath the crystal that hung from the centre, it would slow down the rate at which Samuel's cells declined. Stuart had watched a *Horizon* programme about something similar so, although utterly exhausted, we helped her set it up.

Samuel and I took a seat in the middle, but whilst he was there he began to gag. What he brought up wasn't sick, but blood. I was terrified. We'd been warned that one of the ways Samuel could die was from bleeding from every orifice. I was not ready for Samuel to die and I would never be ready for him to die in such a slow, horrible way.

"We have to go to hospital," I said to Stuart.

He agreed immediately.

"I'll ring Dr Masters first so he can let them know why we're coming in."

Linda sat with Samuel and me in the living room whilst Stuart made the phone call. Samuel continued to bring up blood.

"It's okay, darling," I said. "Don't worry, it will be all right." I have never been more scared or more upset in my life, but I concentrated on keeping my voice gentle and even for Samuel. "I don't want him to die," I said at one point to Linda.

"Whatever is meant to be, will be," she said. "But I think you are doing the right thing getting him to hospital."

She offered to come with us but we declined, so she left before Dr Masters arrived.

"We want him to have platelets," Stuart said as he examined Samuel.

Dr Masters shook his head and sighed.

"Just let him go."

"No." I said. "I'm not having him bleed to death. We're going to hospital and he's having platelets. You said Samuel wouldn't suffer. Well, he *is* suffering and I'm not going to let that happen."

I think Dr Masters could see he was fighting a losing battle, so he phoned the hospital to let them know we were coming in. Had he known us better, he would have realised, as I'm sure he does now, that we only wanted the very best for our son. We weren't trying to prolong his life for our own sakes; we were just trying to ensure he didn't suffer.

Samuel clearly *was* suffering; not just by bringing up blood, but by the swelling. It was slowly disfiguring his face, causing his lip to stand out at almost a ninety-degree angle, and his eye to close like he'd been involved in a fight. Platelets, I knew, would counter all these symptoms, and whilst I knew they wouldn't save him, I knew they would make him feel an awful lot better. There was no way on earth that Stuart and I were prepared to let him have a horrible end, like bleeding to death, and if that meant arguing with everybody, then so be it. We would have fought to our own deaths to provide the best for him, and if the doctors and nurses thought they could stop us, then they didn't realise how deep a parent's love goes.

We drove Samuel to hospital with him sitting on my lap. We couldn't strap him into his car seat; he was far too ill for that. We went to Rainbow ward and were shown into one of the side rooms. We were prepared for battle and a battle is what we got. Some young, less experienced nurses tried to tell us what was best for our son, but we dismissed them and asked to speak to a consultant. Eventually, a consultant came in to see us. She'd been at home but was on call, so she'd had to drive in to see us. She tried to persuade us it would be wrong to give Samuel platelets and far better to let him die, even if that meant him bleeding to death.

"And what do we do to make him feel better whilst he bleeds to death?" I asked.

"Use coloured towels so he doesn't become too distressed."

I couldn't believe what I was hearing. This woman was a consultant; she'd trained for years to give us this nugget of information. She'd already told us she had children of her own. Would she have calmly got coloured towels out of the airing cupboard whilst her child bled to death?

Stuart was furious. He demanded she phone Addenbrooke's Hospital and speak to one of the consultants there. She hesitated, and I could see she was going to procrastinate further, but I'd had enough. Samuel was not going to be put through any more and his death was not going to be left in the hands of some stranger who didn't care. I burst into tears.

"If Samuel's not given platelets, he will die the most horrible death, and I will live with the knowledge for the rest of my life that I wasn't a good enough mother to him."

It did the trick; she looked suitably startled.

"Well, I don't want you to think that. I'll ring Addenbrooke's."

She walked out of the room and Stuart put his arm around me.

"Are you all right?"

"I'm fine, but I'm not letting her dictate how our son dies."

I'm not usually manipulative, but you resort to whatever you need to when it's your child's life at risk.

The consultant spoke to Amos, and he said if we wanted Samuel to have platelets he should be given them. Mike also phoned first thing the next morning to tell us we'd done exactly the right thing. It just goes to show that the so-called professionals don't always know what they're talking about and you should always trust your own instincts. Within half an hour, platelets were set up. At one point, Stuart walked past the young nurses we'd spoken to earlier, and overheard them talking.

"Yes, we thought he should have platelets," one of them said to the other.

Stuart took a deep breath and said nothing.

After a while, Samuel pointed up at the television set in the corner of the room. Stuart and I smiled at each other. Samuel had stopped coughing up blood and now looked calm and settled.

"Do you want the telly on, darling?" I asked, switching it on.

"We did the right thing," Stuart said.

Once the platelets had gone through, an older nurse came in to take Samuel off the pump.

"Well done," she said. "You did the right thing. That consultant has children of her own and she wouldn't let one of them bleed to death. If you want him to have platelets again, don't hesitate to come in. He's your child and it's not up to her to dictate what happens to him."

We knew we were in the right, but we were grateful to have her support.

When Samuel woke up the next morning, the swelling on his face had gone down significantly. He didn't look like his old self, and he was clearly very ill, but the bruising had almost gone from around his eye and he was able to suck his dummy again. As his dummy gave him such comfort, I think it would have been horribly cruel if he'd been denied it in the last days of his life.

It was Wednesday 1st April. Samuel watched as I turned the page over on our calendar. Throughout April, I was able to think Samuel had seen me turn the page to that month; I later found it very hard to turn the page to May, knowing that Samuel was no longer here.

Audrey and Vicky arrived at ten o'clock. During the night, Samuel's morphine pump had come loose from his leg. I'd tried to reattach it several times, but it was impossible without a needle. I'd had to give him morphine in a syringe instead, so I was glad when Audrey and Vicky arrived so they could refit it.

"These tubes are only designed to last a week," Audrey said, "so we would have needed to change it today anyway."

We told them what had happened at the West Suffolk Hospital the previous night and they sympathised with us. "To be honest with you, I don't think anyone thought Samuel would make it this far, so they didn't have a plan in place for what to do in the event of his platelets being low." She gently inserted a fresh tube into Samuel's leg. "I think what I will do is give Addenbrooke's a call and ask Pat to come here tomorrow to see you, and us, and perhaps Dr Masters as well, to come up with a plan for where we go from here."

"So didn't they think there was even a chance Samuel would live this long?"

"No, they didn't. He's been home a week – he's exceeded all expectations."

Stuart and I looked at each other and smiled.

"He constantly exceeds expectations. Don't you, little man?" Stuart said.

"You've certainly got a very special little boy there," Audrey said.

We didn't know then that it was to be our last day with him.

I feel now, remembering that last week, that Samuel's efforts were remarkable – not only in exceeding the expectations on the length of his life, but also in how he lived it.

When a person is dying of cancer, you imagine them stuck in a hospital bed for days, highly medicated and slowly slipping away. You certainly don't imagine them playing with toys and going out. And yet, even on his last day, Samuel came out with us, again to the Abbey Gardens. Looking back, I wonder at our nerve taking him out when he was about to die, but at that point we still didn't believe he was about to go. I also think that if it was my last day, I would want to spend it in a beautiful garden looking at the blossom and the birds.

When he'd coughed up blood the previous evening, I'd been terrified; not just of losing him but of what the end would be like. Like most people, I'd never seen anyone die before, and it felt wrong that the first person I should witness dying would be my own son. But I was increasingly aware this was coming, even though Stuart still hadn't accepted it. In fact, the thought of the consultants from Addenbrooke's coming the next day kept Stuart's belief alive that somehow Samuel would prove everyone wrong and get better. By the doctors' and nurses' own admission, Samuel had already proved them wrong so, in Stuart's mind, it didn't take much of a leap to imagine a miracle and complete cure.

I changed Samuel out of his Babygro and into a white top and navy trousers in order to take him out. As I took his little legs from his Babygro, I noticed how thin they were. He looked so different from the sturdy little boy he'd been, and I wished more than anything that I'd been able to make him better. I shouldn't have changed his clothes; it obviously caused him some pain and, really, what did it matter what he looked like?

The day was warm and sunny and it felt good to get out. Stuart carried Samuel up our road and he rested his head on his daddy's shoulder. As we walked up to the gardens, a man was digging up part of the path with a pneumatic drill. Samuel lifted his head to see what was going on. It amazed me that even at the end he had this strength. We found a sunny spot on the grass, by the blossom-covered trees, and sat down. Stuart lay back on his elbows with Samuel lying on top of him. Samuel put one arm under his head and closed his eyes. His face looked slightly disfigured, but still better than it had before he'd had the platelets. Stuart shaded Samuel's face, but the sun warmed his little body.

We stayed there for about an hour and then walked home. On the way back, Samuel began to gag. He wasn't sick, but he seemed unable to stop. He must have been so used to feeling sick, but we never got used to it and always wanted to make him better. We gave him lots of water when we got indoors and he drank it quickly. In the past he'd always loved his milk, but we'd noticed over the last couple of days he requested water more and more often. (We kept a bottle of water and a bottle of milk in front of him and Samuel would point at whichever one he wanted.) Mike told us later this was probably a sign that the leukaemia had infected his kidneys, but we'd heard that when the body wants to repair itself it stops eating and just drinks water. It was easy for us, and particularly Stuart, to become convinced this was what was happening.

Eventually, I called Audrey. I knew she was due to finish her shift at five and although I'm sure she would have come out to us later if we'd wanted, I didn't want to put her out. When she arrived, I asked her to increase the anti-sickness medicine that was going into Samuel via his pump and, at the same time, I suggested she increase the morphine dosage. I didn't give a reason for this, but in the back of my mind I was conscious that I didn't want Samuel to suffer if his condition worsened.

He looked exhausted. His breathing rate had increased and he was now panting as if he'd just run a race. His heartbeat had been double that of a healthy adult's for well over a week, and watching him now I felt like his little body was on overdrive, trying to keep going. I cuddled him into me and tried to calm him, but nothing I did or said made any difference. Eventually, I took him upstairs to our room and laid him back on me. I thought he would feel calmer there, but his heart still raced and he kept retching, even though the dosage of the anti-sickness medicine had been increased.

It was getting towards seven o'clock and, again, Stuart and I had barely eaten all day. After Samuel died, I noticed how thin Stuart had become. He'd always been slim, but in that last week or so he'd lost a stone in weight. Stuart decided to walk to the fish and chip shop, and I mistakenly thought I would be able to get Samuel to sleep so we could eat once Stuart got home. But Samuel's condition remained the same, so I brought him back downstairs and we took turns holding him whilst the other ate.

Afterwards, I carried him back up to our room and again tried to get him to sleep. I could feel his heart racing through his Babygro and he was still panting. He was clearly exhausted, and although his body wouldn't allow sleep, he kept closing his eyes. Every now and then he would gag, but he brought nothing up. From time to time he indicated that he wanted to lie down, but when I leant him back it made it more difficult for him to breathe, so I sat with him on the bed, my back resting on pillows so he could lie sideways on me and try to rest. It was impossible for him; his little body couldn't relax enough to allow sleep. I now know he had pneumonia as well, which must have been the reason why he couldn't lie down. It must have felt like he was drowning every time and yet he was desperate for rest.

At just after half past ten, Stuart came upstairs and said he would take over. I went to the spare room and lay down on the bed. I must have fallen straight to sleep, because at just after one I was woken by a terrible noise. It was Samuel trying to be sick, but it was far worse than before. I remember it took me a couple of seconds to get out of bed. I felt heavy with exhaustion, and even though I wanted to get to him I felt like my body was holding me back. Once out of bed, I rushed to our bedroom. Samuel was sat on Stuart's lap and he was gagging but bringing nothing up.

"He's not stopped doing this," Stuart said, clearly distressed. "I don't know what to do. He's so frustrated. He just threw his dummy across the room." (We left that dummy there for seven months; we couldn't bear to move it.) "I've just told God to either cure him or take him now, but don't leave him like this!"

"I'll ring someone," I said.

I went downstairs and looked in his notes. I didn't know who to call. Was it too late to call Audrey or Dr Masters, I wondered. I decided to ring the Children's Hospice for advice, but I soon realised I needed more than advice, so I hung up and called Dr Masters instead.

I'd just started to explain how Samuel was when he said, "I'm coming round."

I went back upstairs to Samuel and Stuart. Within minutes there was a knock on the door. I went down and let Dr Masters in.

"He's upstairs," I said, and Dr Master followed me to our room.

He crouched on the floor and touched Samuel's face. He got out his stethoscope and listened to his racing heart. Stuart and I didn't speak. Samuel was still breathing heavily but he was no longer gagging.

"I'll see what I've got in my case to give him," Dr Masters said.

I followed him downstairs. More than anything at that moment I wanted Samuel's suffering to end and, for the first time, I wanted it to end even if the only way this could happen was for him to die. Dr Masters opened the palliative care case and looked through the drugs it contained. Eventually, he looked up at me.

"He's very sick," he said.

"I know."

"His skin is cold and his lips are purple."

I nodded. In my heart of hearts, I knew Samuel was dying. And I knew nothing we did would change that. We'd tried everything. For six months Samuel had battled with this terrible disease. He'd suffered all the side effects of chemotherapy, living so much of his young life in hospital. And, in between feeling ill, he'd fought to live a normal life. But this was it now. Everything known to medical science had failed. The reiki might have helped him, but it hadn't cured him. And now I knew we were about to lose him.

The love that Stuart and I had for Samuel was beyond anything we'd ever felt before. It had grown bigger and bigger in the time since we'd had him and now, at twenty months to the day, and after eight months of ill health, we loved him more than ever. But I knew our love was not enough to save him. And I knew we loved him too much to let him suffer any longer.

"Is there anything you can give him to calm him?" I asked Dr Masters. "So he can sleep."

Dr Masters nodded. I went back upstairs. Samuel was still panting heavily and his eyes kept rolling back in his head from tiredness. Dr Masters came in with some medicine in a syringe.

"This is what we give to children who are having fits. It calms them and helps them sleep. I've got a very small dose here but, I have to warn you, he's very ill and he might not wake up from it."

I nodded. Stuart says now that he didn't take it in. He still didn't think Samuel would die and he wasn't prepared for it. But what he did know was that Samuel's suffering had to come to an end. He was sitting on his daddy's lap. It must have felt like a safe place to be despite his illness. Dr Masters showed him the syringe and Samuel opened his little mouth.

"This should take about six minutes to work," he said, and then went back downstairs.

"We love you, darling," I said to Samuel through my tears. "We all love you."

"What are you saying?" Stuart said, pulling Samuel closer to him. "You're making it sound like he's going to die!"

I looked at Samuel, who looked more ill than I could bear to see.

"Mummy and Daddy love you so much; so do Grandma and Grandad, Aunty Nancy and Uncle Richie, Nanny and Grandad, all your cousins, Aunty Debbie, Uncle Graham and Aunty Wendy. Everyone loves you, darling," I said. "We all love you."

I held his little hand and watched his breathing slow down. Dr Masters said it would take six minutes to work, but I don't think Samuel wanted to wait that long. I think all he actually wanted was his mummy and daddy with him. He'd fought hard; for us as well as for himself. He'd heard me make the promise many times that I would get him better and maybe he had felt like he couldn't go before. But I knew now that I mustn't hold him back any longer.

"Go to sleep now, my darling," I said.

We watched as he closed his beautiful blue eyes for the last time. And then, at last, he found some peace.

> Twinkle, twinkle, little star,
> How I wonder what you are.
> Up above the world so high,
> Like a diamond in the sky.
> Twinkle, twinkle, little star,
> How I wonder what you are.

'How to be Human' by Stuart Murray is a commercial philosophy book inspired by Sam's Story.

ABOUT THE AUTHOR

⁓

AMANDA MURRAY WAS INSPIRED BY her son, Samuel, to work with children. In addition to writing, she is studying for a bachelor's degree in education studies. She lives with husband Stuart and daughter Sophie in England.

28487324R00213

Printed in Poland
by Amazon Fulfillment
Poland Sp. z o.o., Wrocław